STEVE DEVEREUX

BLAKE

Published by Blake Publishing Ltd,
3 Bramber Court, 2 Bramber Road, London W14 9PB, England

ISBN 185782 355 9

British Library Cataloguing-in-Publication Data:
A catalogue record for this book is available from
the British Library.

Typeset by BCP

Printed in Great Britain by CPD, Wales

1 3 5 7 9 10 8 6 4 2

Every effort has been made to contact the original
copyright holders. In the case of any problems
we would be grateful if those concerned would contact us.

**Names have been changed to protect the identities
of individuals and companies concerned.**

TO ALISON
MY LOVE MY LIFE

ACKNOWLEDGEMENTS

Thanks must go to all those guys who have supported me during the writing of this book. Some are still serving, some are due to finish their 22 years service, some are out, and some have never been in.

I would also like to thank my good friend Billy Budd, who has been an enduring source of endless banter whilst writing this book and also during those BG jobs we have done together; TG, whose simplistic approach to life always amazes me; Smiler, with reference to Africa; Steve B and Mike P, who lent me their bashas for all those weeks whilst in the Middle East — Cheers, guys! — and my editor, Mr Civilian, who really knows the score.

Lastly, I would like to thank the most incredible lady I have ever loved, Alison. You have had to put up with a lot from me over the years. No other woman could or should have, but you did, and I thank you from the 'heart of my bottom'.

CONTENTS

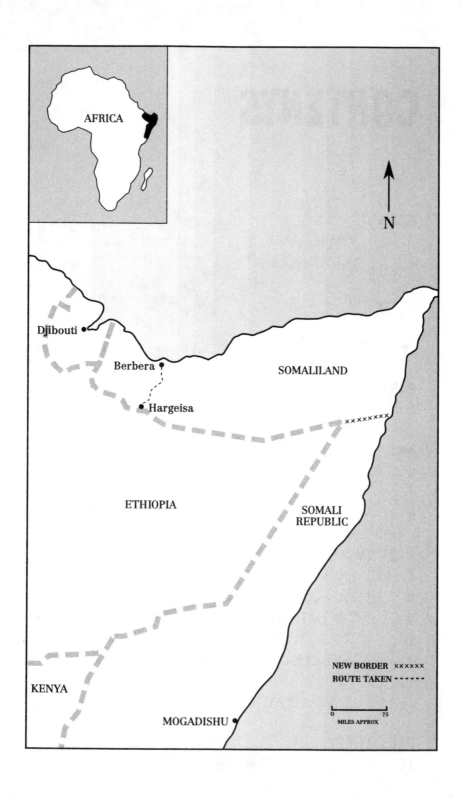

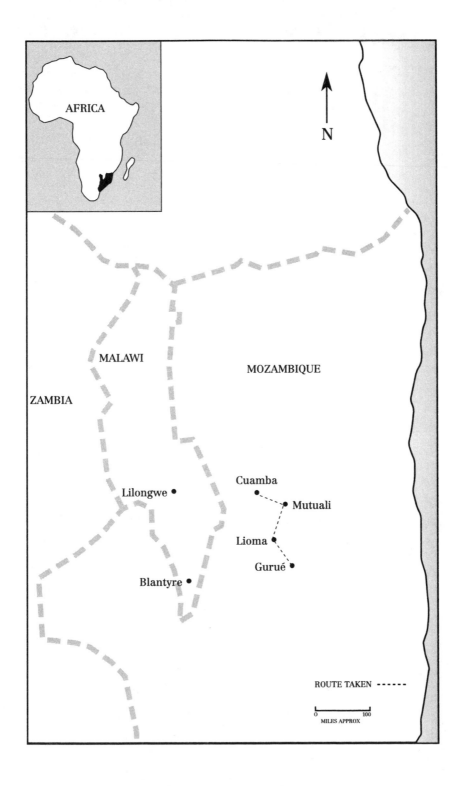

AFRICA

N

ZAMBIA

MALAWI

MOZAMBIQUE

Cuamba

Lilongwe ●

Mutuali

Lioma

Gurué

Blantyre ●

ROUTE TAKEN ------

0   100
MILES APPROX

GLOSSARY

ASAP	As Soon As Possible
APC	Armoured Personnel Carriers
AWOL	Absent Without Leave
Basha	A place to sleep
BG	Body Guard
Bone	Incredibly stupid
Bootneck	Royal Marine
BTR 60	A Russian-built armoured personnel carrier (wheeled)
Casevac	Casualty evacuation
CO	Commanding Officer
CV	Curriculum Vitae
Dick Dastardlies	Would-be pretend spies
DPMs	Disruptive Pattern Material
E and E	Escape and Evasion
EOD	Explosive Ordnance Disposal
Frelimo	Mozambique troops
IA	Immediate Action drill
ic	in command
IHA	International Humanitarian Agency
HALO	High Altitude Low Opening
high port	A weapon drill order where the rifle is held in a high position. Looks comical.

ks	kilometres
LO	Liaison Officer
MID	Mentioned in Dispatches
MSF	Médecins Sans Frontières, an aid organisation
NI	Northern Ireland
NGOs	Non-Governmental Organisations
ops	operations
OPs	Observation Posts
PE	Plastic Explosive
prayers	formal or informal debrief (SAS jargon)
REs	Royal Engineers
REMF	Rear Echelon Mother Fucker
Renamo	right-wing Mozambique terrorists backed by South Africa
RM	Royal Marine
RTU	Returned to Unit
Rupert	slang term for an officer
sit rep	situation report
SBS	Special Boat Squadron
SOPs	Standard Operational Procedures
SF	Special Forces
Walter Mitties	Persons portraying someone they are not — bullshitters, in other words

Weapons

AKM	folding stock version of the AK47
AK47	semi and fully automatic 7.62mm rifle
AP	Anti-personnel Mine
20mm cannon	Russian-made ground-to-air weapon
Makarov	standard Russian issued pistol
SA80	5.56mm standard British Army-issue rifle

PREFACE

This book is not about the SAS. It's about the work I specialise in, 'out of the SAS'.

You'd think that when I left such an élite body of soldiers the world would be my oyster. Multinational companies would be queuing up to employ me to run worldwide security operations. Foreign governments would somehow trace me through covert channels of communication and entice me to come and work for them. I wish I could say that was true. Unfortunately, the SAS's fierce reputation as portrayed by the media (and rightly so) since the Iranian Embassy siege of 1980 scared off these potential employers.

Ironically, the SAS almost put themselves out of a job when they assaulted that embassy. They did such a good job that potential terrorists no longer dared hold hostages in the UK for fear of being wasted before getting their chance to act out their cause on the media's world stage. In some ways I, too, was lucky in that I was involved in the last 'embassy' operation. That was at the Libyan Embassy in 1986, and the result was a negotiated settlement, however you look at it, even though a policewoman — WPC Yvonne Fletcher —

was shot and killed in the line of duty.*

That's not to say that ex-SAS men don't keep their hand in with the security industry; they *do*. One such friend runs one of the biggest personal security operations, for one of the wealthiest men in the world; another handles the security for a premier football club. Many more look after film stars and wealthy Arab families who own entire countries, while still others work for foreign governments, but only on short-term contracts which are either overseen by the British Government or openly sanctioned by it, without first-hand involvement.

On the other hand, there are none of those 'cloak and dagger' MI5 or MI6 jobs on offer that many novelists seem to write about. They would have you believe that such activities are the normal next stage for someone from my professional background. How wrong could they be! The reality is that MI5 and MI6 are far less glamorous than such authors imagine. Sorry about this, guys, but the majority of these people spend their days writing papers and pushing paperclips around, and very rarely leave the secure confines of their offices. I don't know of any ex-members of the SAS who have joined MI5 or MI6. To be honest, if they had, I think they would be bored shitless.

'You're in the big wide world now. No mothering and being told what to do, and more importantly, no regular salary. Just you and your wits to do battle with the commercial world. Good luck.'

That's what the officer, my old boss, had said to me when finally I left the SAS.

He said it with a calmness of someone who'd done his

---

* As I described in my first book, *Terminal Velocity*.

22 years, with a reasonable gratuity and a tidy pension. And good luck to him. This country had had more than its fair share of his life. He in turn had a sackful of war stories — and two dodgy knees to give him something to think about in a couple of years time, when the war stories were spent.

The commercial world, what the hell was that? I wondered. Having spent the best part of my youth and early years fighting around the world for Queen and Country, I had no idea what the 'real world' was all about, and if most people from my background were truthful, they didn't know either. Why should we? For most of us in the Armed Forces, the challenge of doing the job had been exactly that — doing the job. Being part of the best fighting force in the world and having a good laugh as we did it. Basically, enjoying what we were good at. No need to worry about PEPs or the interest rate; everything in that department was taken care of by the system.

There was an interesting phrase always bandied about when one of us had just accidentally broken a really expensive piece of high-tec equipment, or just 'expended' a £6,000 anti-tank round at a target and missed: 'It's a big firm, they can afford it.'

Someone would say it casually without knowing, or wanting to understand, that 'they' were, in fact, everyone, including ourselves! The tax payers, in other words. But somehow, that truth was never real to us.

We really had no worries. As long as we kept out of trouble and didn't screw up, our pay was there at the end of each month. Why should I worry about the commercial world? That was my attitude. I'm in for life. It was a very short-sighted view.

Towards the end of the 1980s when it seemed that everyone outside the services was getting themselves mortgaged up to the hilt and getting into all sorts of financial worries, my brother said to me, 'You know, Steve, most of us, if we lose our jobs tomorrow, then we only have about three months' savings at the most, if we're lucky, to carry us through while looking for another job. Then the shit really starts to hit the fan. You know what I mean. Money rows at home with the wife. Getting pissed because you're worrying and coming home later and later. Spending more time down the pub with your head in a pint of beer with the Johnny Walker optic winking at you every time you lift your head, wasting what little money you have left. Upsetting your mates for no reason because of your own self-pity. Then, nothing. One day you wake up to find your wife has left you. The mortgage hasn't been paid for three months. The phone's cut off and then you look at yourself properly in the mirror for the first time in weeks. You look like shit and now you smell like shit. It don't take long.'

He said all this jokingly, and I knew this wasn't based on a previous experience of his, but I sensed that this was his own way of getting me used to civvy street and to the fact that now that my honeymoon period after leaving the SAS was over, I had to work for a living. He was, of course, right.

Unfortunately, I'd never had much to do with the intricacies of assessing people's personalities in order to get what I wanted. I'd always been 'black-and-white' in my approach to life, not one to suck up to someone just for personal gain. I took as I found, and generally gave an opinion if warranted. Stroking people's egos to get something or somewhere was not my style. (My approach is still generally the straightforward approach, but I'm working on it!)

Whanging off CVs to prospective employers in the vain hope that I would be called for a real interview for a job — as opposed to having lunch with them only to relate my soldiering experiences over a pie and pint, just so they could see what a man from my background was really like — soon became a pain in the arse. I got nowhere fast.

I spent my own time and money thinking I could learn the ropes of selling or wheeling and dealing in the money markets on the London Stock Exchange, when really all the skills I had been taught in the Paras and the SAS were as useful as a pair of tits on a nun.

I reckoned I could turn my hand to something different from what I had been doing for the past 12 years or so, but this wasn't the case. Soon it was looking a certainty that I was to be doomed to work in the security industry for the rest of my life, a thought that didn't appeal to me one little bit. I'd had enough of roughing it in piss-poor places all over the world, and the dangers of my past way of life held no attractions for me anymore. I'd become bored with being scared and desperately wanted a change. But like most of us in this life, I had to go with what I knew best and where the money was, so at this particular time (the summer of 1990) I had to wrestle with my conscience whether or not to take a particular job which was on offer to me.

There was this vicious guerrilla war raging in Mozambique, East Africa, and had been for many years. I went down to WH Smith's in Hereford and flicked through a copy of a tourists' guide to East Africa. It wasn't much cop, there was no section on Mozambique, only a lightly shaded area on the map, outlining its slug-shaped borders: Tanzania to its north, South Africa to its south and Malawi and Zimbabwe bordering on its west. On the east, Mozambique ran for over 1,000 miles down the Indian Ocean. Shit -- one of those countries that you certainly couldn't get a package deal to.

A visit to the reference section of Hereford's library squared me away. It was the first time in 25 or so years that I'd actually been in a library. (The previous time was occasioned by a school archaeological trip.) Libraries are like time capsules, they just don't change. The people, their dress, their attitude are all still the same. The only other time I had been close to a lot of people not speaking but communicating through their expressions and body language was in the jungle; there, too, you might get away with the odd whisper to attract someone's attention. Weirdly I felt quite at home perusing the literature on Mozambique, and the atmosphere left me feeling mentally relaxed.

Two hours later I left with a headful of theme tunes and statistics. Once a Portuguese possession, Mozambique was a post-colonial mess. Still I wasn't too concerned about the country's entire history, only its recent past. I just needed to know those bare facts which would be relevant to me and my safety. So such statistics as it had a population of over 15 million with 600,000 killed in the past ten years, half of them now faced severe food shortages, and two million had been driven from their homes, were all I required to realise that this could be one helluva trip. Maputo was the capital, but that was way down south, in a pretty safe area. The bulk of the fighting was taking place in the central part of the country (around an area named the Beira Corridor) and to the north. The population had been drastically displaced by war, and many inhabitants had travelled south to the relative security of the capital. Looking at it cynically (which, I find, helps a lot in these situations), I guessed one of the good points about this job was if I got any R and R, there would be vast tracts of human-free golden beaches to explore.

Only things turned out rather differently ...

PART ONE

War is a continuation of policy by other means.
It is not merely a political act,
but a real political instrument.

Karl von Clausewitz,
Vom Krieg 1832-34

1

MOZAMBIQUE — A NON-REACTIVE CONTRACT

It was almost silent now. The convoy had stopped abruptly. The crack and thump of a quick burst of incoming small arms fire was over. I waited in the Land Rover's cab, my weapon sighted in the probable direction of the threat. It was impossible to see exactly where the shots came from, but I knew they'd come from the left.

The sun was up at 12 o'clock and burning through the left-hand sleeve of my DPMs as I held a steady aim. Men, women and children were screaming but I didn't know if any of our soldiers had returned fire. Engines were still revving but no movement could be seen. Motionless, I watched and waited in silence.

Almost immediately, another burst of gunfire spat out from my left and rear.

Fine red dust from the bush track, recently kicked up by 17 assorted trucks had all but settled, leaving just enough in the air to screw up my vision. Luckily I caught sight of the bullet strike markets — they fell well short of my position, but on line. Worse, the dust had filled the Land Rover's cab and I could now feel sweat trickling down the back of my neck, around my ears and down the side of my nose, forming a pastelike crud. I didn't dare risk moving either hand to wipe it off. The slow wet movement was infuriating, but experience had taught me to keep both hands firmly on my weapon and to keep it well sighted. The strange enjoyment of picking the congealed bogies from one's nose was a pleasure that would have to wait.

Suddenly Jimmy — a short pugnacious-looking Glaswegian with more NI contacts under his belt than you could wish for — screamed at me from the driver's seat to get out. I reacted immediately without thinking. We were out of the wagon like a flash, me almost knocking him flying as we both disembarked from his side. Common sense dictated that I did not get out of *my* side of the Land Rover — the side facing the threat. The whole incident, from the sound of the first shots to de-bussing, took less than five seconds.

We'd just run into a typical 'suck-it-and-see' ambush by Renamo, the faction opposing us. It was the first time that we, 'The Specialists', had made contact with this particular guerrilla organisation. None of us returned fire, it was pointless. We couldn't see anything and if it was a big ambush, they would be still firing at us. Maybe they wanted to test our reaction. Maybe they would test our reaction a bit further up the track, with a much larger ambush. It was a game of chance. Probably it was just a small group wanting to try their luck — shoot-and-scoot tactics, more than likely.

In this sort of situation, driving straight through the ambush, along a track that was unfamiliar to us and which had not been driven on for over a year, would have been the wrong option. A split in our convoy of slow-moving trucks would mean halving our firepower, and since all of our 80-strong force was riding on them, it would have meant a split with them, too. The SOP was that if we got hit really badly, we would all take our chances on foot in the bush — but, of course, as in every contact with the enemy, the ground and the amount of incoming fire would dictate what evasive or aggressive action we took, and if the enemy had sited their ambush tactically, then our escape options would be limited, if not impossible.

I'd learnt a vital lesson in the Falklands War, several years earlier. You can plan, plan and plan, but when the shit hits the fan and all your well-intentioned planning suddenly disappears, you have to improvise. So in this situation, although we were sitting ducks to some extent, a few bursts of 7.26mm small arms fire was no cause to abandon the trucks and make haste into the bush — even though some of our civvy travellers did just that.

Without warning, the 20mm anti-aircraft cannon wedged into the rear of my Land Rover let off a few rounds before it jammed. That was the signal for the rest of the troops to fire; at what wasn't quite clear. I couldn't see any likely targets. It was their nerves, more than likely.

'What the fuck's going on?' I shouted to Jhundo, ic (in command) of the gun.

'Dunno, Mr Steve. We thought we saw something over there on the ridge.' He was pointing to an area about 100 metres over to the left.

We'd been caught in the narrowest part of the track so far. It could prove an ideal ambush site if the enemy had kept on firing. *Not* a place to hang around in.

'Tell them to stop firing, for frig's sake,' screamed Jimmy. 'If "they" ain't firing and you can't see fuck all, then don't shoot. Save your ammo.' He zigzagged down the line of the convoy, still shouting his orders. For a brief second I felt very alone and very scared.

Some of our troops had seen us get out of our wagon so they decided to do the same, thinking they might be sitting targets otherwise. It was all getting chaotic. There was no more incoming as I could make out, but there was a hell of a lot of our boys letting off a bit of nervous tension. Empty bullet cases began flying all around the place. A combined smell of spent cartridges and diesel fumes filled the air.

I ran up to the lead vehicle, which was an old BRT 60 (a Russian-built armoured personnel carrier, wheeled), and told the commander to get ready to move. Although we were in radio contact with each other, it was impossible to get any coherent transmission between our troops once something like this started. I looked back down the line of trucks and could just see Jimmy through the dust as he headed towards the rear of the convoy. He was sorting out those soldiers who had disembarked, trying to encourage them back on to their vehicles. The rest of the convoy I couldn't see because the track dipped and turned sharply to the right, but I guessed it was strung out about 300 metres. Brad and Josh, the two other Specialists, were bringing up the rear. They would be sorting out their group — I hoped.

Seconds later the radio crackled. 'Alpha One, Alpha One, this is Bravo One, send sit-rep. Over.'

It was Brad trying to find out what was happening.

'Yeah. Roger Bravo One, this is Alpha One. Two bursts of gun fire from our left. No casualties. No damage, but our boys are letting off a bit of steam. How you? Over,' I said.

'No casualties and no damage. I can see Jimmy coming down the line. I'll get a quick sit-rep off him and send him back up. Let's get the fuck out of here ASAP. Over.'

'Alpha One, Roger. We're ready to move as soon as Jimmy gets back. Over,' I replied.

The radio crackled and his voice disappeared for a second, then, 'Roger out,' Brad puffed. I reckoned he had two cigarettes on the go. He sounded really nervous.

Brad, a grey-haired, wiry six-footer pushing 50, had been working in and around Mozambique for years, ever since he had left the Regiment, yet as he once told me he still couldn't get used to being shot at. An obvious statement you might think, but he had more experiences in firefights than you could have shaken a stick at, and you would have thought he'd be used to it by now. But I guess you never do get used to it.

He was the most experienced bloke amongst the four of us and had got into all sorts of shitty little conflicts in this part of the world. I could never understand why he always put himself in the firing line. At his age I would want to be tucked up back in England with my pipe and slippers, but no, Brad wasn't having any of that. 'You're a real hardcore bastard with an age complex,' I used to joke to him. 'Always thinking you're still 21.'

Anyway, right now, there was no need to have a cosy chat exchanging war stories. Brad was right. It was best we left the area soonest.

Meanwhile, our 100 or so freewheeling hitchhikers had run off into the bush at the first sign of trouble. Most of them were making the trip up to Gurué to see relatives they'd been separated from for the past year because of guerrilla activity there, but it was looking likely that they wouldn't see them this trip — not unless they could get to the next major village, Mutuali, 20 ks south. Mutuali was to be one of our watering stops and we had planned to rest up there for an hour or so before heading further south and on to another village, Lioma, the halfway stage, then finally on to Gurué.

The hitchhikers had all been in full voice since leaving Cuamba, our main base. It was like travelling with the Mozambique equivalent of a Welsh Male Voice Choir — nice for ten minutes but a real pain in the arse for ten hours. The harmony turned into mayhem as soon as the first shots rang out, then their screams of anguish got fewer and fewer as they put more distance between the ambush site and themselves. Hell, these people could run barefoot through fields of six-inch nails if they had to! I thought. Where the frig were they off to? We were in the middle of nowhere!

As far as I could see, the ground around had been baked dry by the sun and was rock hard. Water was not a common element in these parts, in fact it hadn't rained properly for years. Apart from an earthy type of sand with a few football-sized rocks scattered around, the landscape was filled with bizarre brown shrubs: a cross between the most vicious of cacti with two-inch, needle-sharp spikes sticking out all over the place and bonsai trees. No higher than five feet, they were almost impenetrable at pace. The entire area for miles around was covered with these 'bastard' bushes, so named because, every time you had to walk through a clump of them you invariably got spiked and ended up cursing: *'Bastard!'*

As I was skirmishing back to the Land Rover, my radio crackled into life again. I could see Jimmy running back up to join me, ducking and darting, keeping his head down low. Most of our soldiers had stopped firing now, but there were sporadic bursts, seemingly from both sides. One or two of the enemy would fire a short burst during what we presumed was their retreat. This was enough for both Jimmy and I to keep moving down as low as we could.

Jimmy was also listening into the transmission.

'Alpha One, Alpha One. Let's get moving and put your foot down!' I replied to Brad's most obvious of requests. He really did sound nervous by now, I guess he had every right to be, stuck back at 'tail end Charlie'. A cigar-shaped barren strip of greyish rocks ran for about 100 metres parallel to the track we had been caught on. Brad and half the convoy still had to drive through what we all knew was the middle of the ambush, the so-called 'killing ground', and there was no real way of knowing what lay behind the high ridge on the left. Not a lot, I would have thought, having seen our men pour half the world's lead resources into it over the past few minutes. If anything, it had kept the Renamo heads down, those who had been firing at us, and if we were to believe past 'enemy contact reports' they would be miles away by now.

Not in this case though. As soon as Jimmy and I were in the Land Rover, a very familiar sound came from our left. At the same time Jimmy gave the horn three long honks and the vehicle in front started to move. We turned to face each other.

'Was that a fucking mortar or what?' Jimmy growled, not really sure.

'No, it was fucking TWO of the bastards! Shit!' I screamed.

I would know that noise anywhere. It was like a muffled version of the sound you get when you blow the top off an empty Smarties tube; that build-up of pressure as you blow into the tube and then 'pop' as the top comes off. Only with mortars, the result was totally different.

There were at least two rounds in the air as we roared off. I checked to see if the trucks behind were following. They were. I radioed Brad and gave him the good news about our leaving present. He was too far back to hear or see what had just gone on, but replied with a muted grunt as if to say, 'What's fuckin' new?' It didn't require any response from me.

The point about not getting too worked up in a situation like this is that you have to know 'your enemy'. It's not a case of having a cocksure attitude or anything like that. Many soldiers who've experienced war and who understand about weapons would know that mortars — in particular the type Renamo used — are small, lightweight, two-inch jobs. A good piece of kit, but only in the right hands. It would have had to be effectively aligned to have made any impact.

Only two rounds were in flight and I hadn't heard any more, and I knew that these bastards had to carry everything on foot and their training was pretty poor, so the chances of one or both rounds hitting us were pretty remote. They would have had to fire off at least two rounds just to get their trajectory and their point of impact right — presumably the track we were travelling on. In this instance, it was a waste of their ammunition.

Suddenly two bangs, like the sound of an aerosol tin

exploding in a fire, came from an area some distance to our right. The mortars had landed well off target. We were safe for the time being. Those two mortars signified the end of the ambush, since no more incoming was expended in our direction.

Once through the ambush site, the going became easy. The track straightened, and for the first time since leaving Cuamba I could see at least a couple of miles ahead. The ground around us was flat well into the distance, and the covering of the bastard bushes wasn't so dense now. Jimmy reckoned this was a good place to have a check of the convoy. He drove up along side the BTR and shouted to the commander to stop. In turn everyone got the message and the convoy came to a halt.

Without prompting from us every vehicle commander ordered sentries to get down and stand guard in all-round defence, some five metres off the track into the bush. (This is a basic tactic adopted by all well-trained armies where, for example, troops disembarking from vehicles or helicopters move into circular formations a few metres from their mode of transport, facing outwards, to get into a good fire position with cover from view and cover from enemy fire, so all their arcs of fire are linked, covering all the ground around them.) Quite amazing, I thought. All of them were facing away from the vehicles, weapons to hand and the ones I saw had adopted good fire positions. They were taking this operation very, very seriously.

Back at Cuamba training camp it had been a nightmare task to get the troops to understand the tactical importance of this de-bussing drill. Maybe this morning's brush with the enemy had encouraged them to 'switch on'. Secretly I felt quite proud of these guys. They had survived three months hard training and had adapted really well, considering the shit-poor conditions they had had to endure.

Jimmy and I went down the line of vehicles checking that all was well. The guys were in good spirits and we had a laugh with them, shaking hands as we went. Some were kidding themselves that they had a higher body count than their mates. They were exchanging war stories, using their weapons to re-enact what they imagined they'd done in the first battle! Jimmy reckoned they were head cases.

'Jesus Christ, look at these poor bastards! You'd have thought they'd just shot half the Renamo in Mozambique, fucking arseholes,' he joked as we met up with Brad and Josh.

Josh was another from the school of the 'Old and Bold', of the same era as Brad. A short muscular man with greyish hair like Brad's, he gave the impression that if you got into a fight with him, you either had to put him down with one punch or smack him around the head with something thick and hard, because if you didn't, he would come at you like a pitbull. He had very little dialogue and from what I could make out over the months I worked with him, had no real aims apart from that of soldiering on until he met his Maker. He and Brad were longterm buddies but, strangely, Josh was teetotal, whereas Brad, on a good session on the ale, could quite easily drink for Britain.

'Come on, Jimmy. They did a lot better than we expected, didn't they? We thought most of them would fuck off into the bush at the first sign of trouble,' I argued.

'Yeah, you're right. They did well, but what's gonna happen when they actually see the enemy face to face, and not just hear them from behind a million tons of rock?'

This type of ambush happened every day all over Mozambique. In the bigger picture of things, this was nothing out of the ordinary, nothing to get excited about. The only difference was that it was personal to us. Probably its only lasting effect would be getting logged as another Renamo contact by those in Intelligence who considered it necessary to collate such things.

Brad and Josh were in good spirits. We had a quick debrief; no great problems were forthcoming. All the vehicles were still going, water and fuel were not a problem. Our collection of mixed flatbed trucks, mainly Mercedes *circa* 1960, should have been laid to rest in that great big scrapyard in the sky years ago, but they hadn't. It was remarkable how their 'owners' had kept them going. One of the twin-wheelers had a puncture but was still driveable, and apart from that we'd come out of the contact untouched. Still, we didn't want to hang around for too long. Brad suggested we go for the relatively safe haven of Mutuali at full speed. Full speed was ten miles an hour, max.

As I looked around I saw that some of our hitchhikers had returned to their places on top of the tarpaulin-covered vehicles.

Just before we got under way, I sorted my weapon out. I checked the safety catch to see that it was still on. Cocked it, caught the round as it ejected from the chamber. Locked the working parts back, unclipped the magazine, checked that no dirt had got inside. Gave it a good hard blow. Put the ejected round back into the magazine. Had a quick look down the barrel and inside the weapon itself. All clear. Put the magazine back on, released the working parts. Felt the familiar movement of the working parts picking up a round and delivering it back into the chamber. The weapon was now made ready again.

Constant rechecking of the safety catch was second nature to me, but I looked at it again just to make sure that it was on 'safe' and also did a cursory check over the rest of the weapon to see that no bits had dropped off. This is not really a problem with most weapons, but it has been known for the sights to be knocked off accidentally, so if you weren't switched on to this, you could get into a contact, go to take aim and find you'd got frig all to look through or line up on. Pretty embarrassing, I should think!

After that I released my webbing belt and adjusted it all so it hung more easily off the shoulders. Checked to see that everything was where it should be and all the pouches were done up. Squirted a load of delousing powder down my crotch to soak up the sweat that had run down my body during the past 30 minutes or so. Took a couple of swigs of water with a handful of crushed dried biscuits. That was my late 'elevenses'. I was all done and dusted.

This was the regular routine all of us went through, the basics any good soldier adheres to when he gets the chance. Who knows what devilish iron-eating insect might have crawled inside your weapon and devoured the firing pin?

I could see Jimmy doing the same as I got back into the Land Rover, but just after he finished he dropped his trousers, bent over and let out an almighty long staccato fart, followed by a cry of 'Renamo! I've shit 'em.'

Jhundo and his gang roared with laughter as they all pointed to Jimmy's white backside sticking up in the air. Then he ceremoniously pulled up his trousers, turned and walked towards the Land Rover, his left arm and clenched fist held high, victoriously punching into the air to the chant of 'Jimmy white arse'. Here I was, thousands of miles from home in probably the most dangerous and without doubt the most isolated environment I had ever experienced, and my mate Jimmy was mooning in the middle of it!

Then it occurred to me that this was the first time I'd had such a good laugh since arriving in Mozambique.

Christ! Was that only a few weeks ago? I thought. So much had happened since then ...

2

COVERT
INFILTRATION

L ife can really suck sometimes. I was standing on a
platform of Reading Station waiting for a connection to
go to Heathrow Airport. Very soon I'd be flying out to
Mozambique to make up a five-man team of ex-Regiment guys
on a six-month contract to train up the Mozambique Special
Forces, a part of the Mozambique Army — called Frelimo —
to assist in its war against the South African-backed Renamo
terrorists, and I was debating whether to give Lynn, my wife at
the time, a quick call. Things had been a bit strained before I
left. In some sense she didn't want me to go on this job but
didn't go out of her way to try and stop me. For my part, I
wanted to go. Now I'd got my head around saying in this

'business', I was keen to get back in the field of fire and get operational again. I had five minutes before my train arrived. I made the call, and I knew immediately there was something wrong. The strained pauses in our conversation made me think the worst. Finally as my train pulled into the station, she said that she was leaving me. I didn't have time to ask the obvious questions: Why? What? When? All I asked was what any man would have asked. 'Who is it?'

Lynn had always been an honest girl and if she'd said there was no other man, I would have caught the next train back to Hereford. But she didn't. She came straight out with it — she was seeing someone. I was stunned. There I was, going off to one of the most dangerous countries in the world with a good possibility of getting my balls blown off, with no time to chat away. I told her that I would call her later. How much later I didn't know. Then I put the phone down with only one thing in mind, to make sure that I caught that flight out to Mozambique. I didn't need a headful of theme tunes during the flight, so mentally I shelved the problem. The last thing I wanted was to carry a load of emotional baggage into a war. That could easily get me killed.

At Heathrow I had over two hours before take-off, so like most travellers I had a couple of beers in the terminal lounge to kill time. A couple went on to a few, so by the time the 'boarding' sign came up for my flight I was well on the way to getting drunk.

I've always found airport bars unreal places. You end up chatting to a total stranger about where you come from and where you're going to. Normally you're both on business. Invariably you cannot speak their language but they always seem to speak English or at least pidgin English, even people from countries you'd have trouble finding on a map.

You always end up telling them even more about yourself than you would someone you might meet on holiday, since in that instance you know that you will at least see them the next day. Sometimes you subconsciously try to cram in as much about your personal life as possible, as if it was a competition between you, before your or their plane leaves and you never see them again. Most times when they've gone you think, Christ! I hope I don't *ever* see them again! I wonder if they understood what I was talking about, because I sure as hell didn't understand *them*.

Then, some months later, you pull out a piece of crumpled old card from an inside pocket. A business card from a plastics company with an address in Montevideo, Uruguay and a handwritten telephone number scribbled on the back. It all comes flooding back; the next time you're in Uruguay you're to get in touch. Then you think hard to remember if you offered your hospitality cards in return. That's God's way of reminding you — don't network with strangers in this business. This time, I didn't.

The flight was good so I slept most of the way till the 747's descent woke me up. Unexpected pain was coming from the inside of my mouth. The change in pressure had popped a filling out of a lower molar. As well as nursing a severe hangover (which hadn't gone away, not even after I'd forced down a litre of water later into the flight) I now had to contend with toothache and the acidic bile building up in my mouth. I was thankful that the seat next to me was empty, so I could suffer the descent in silence without some gawking passenger leaning across me trying to look out of the window as we landed.

The aircraft touched down. I was now in Malawi, a country neighbouring Mozambique. No international or local civilian flights would fly into my ultimate destination, so Malawi was to be my first port of call. I was to spend three days there before being driven south to the Malawi Airforce base at a place called Zomba. This was where the team I was joining got regular resupplies and sometimes the occasional mail drop, or so I was briefed.

I hadn't read up on the political climate of Malawi. There hadn't seemed much point. All I knew was that it was a fairly stable place with strong ties with the Brits (whom they liked) and was ruled by some old guy, a Dr Banda, who had been in power for years. That's all I really needed to know — my business was in Mozambique, not here in luxurious Malawi.

There was no arrangement for anyone to meet me at the airport just outside Malawi's capital, Lilongwe. Instructions I'd been given back in London told me to make my way south by whatever means and book into the Bounty Hotel in Blantyre, the next biggest city in Malawi. If I could make contact with the LO, a Mr John Ball, then all the better.

Once through passport control I made my way across to the baggage claim. The airport looked quiet tidy, basic but fairly well organised; not at all what I expected. Passport control was easy, no queues and no questions. If I'd been asked the purpose of my visit, my cover story was that I was working for a giant multinational company, which to be fair was not far from the truth. Their head office in Blantyre was to assist the team with whatever administrative support we required, from sorting out cross-border flights with the Malawi Airforce to booking hotels on R and R, dealing with any medical problems and aiding our resupply of fresh rations. In fact, all sorts of things were expected of them.

At the time it didn't seem in any way sinister, and made quite good sense. As far as I understood from my brief back in London, this was essentially a quasi-sanctioned operation, but on a 'need-to-know' basis. I guessed that these long-term ex-pats were only too happy to help us. They would certainly be the people I would befriend when I got to Blantyre. Their local knowledge of the dos and don'ts, the safe places to drink and areas best left alone would be invaluable, probably even life-saving.

Baggage was now coming through on the makeshift carousel. There was only one in operation so I reckoned every flight's baggage would be chucked onto it. Still, I didn't expect to have trouble identifying my kit. All I had by way of luggage was a small bergen (carried by hand) and my old para bag, which I'd liberated from the Regiment, as hold luggage. Ten minutes later I spotted it. I always got everything in it I needed for trips. Once full and tied together with para cord and two or three bungees it looked more like a giant pumpkin, and one containing nothing of value. Anyway, if someone wanted to get into it for whatever reason, it would take them ages to unstrap it all. Any switched-on baggage thief would have gone for a more upmarket designer case, not my dark green, raglike affair.

There was no trouble locating a trolley usually found at airports, because there weren't any. So with luggage in my possession I proceeded through swing doors into the next part of the terminal. Here it was full of noise, human and mechanical. Most people I saw didn't appear to have any reason to be here. They all looked like locals who'd come in off the street for a chat with their mates. Most were sitting down on the floor in groups of three or four surrounded by primitive cooking stoves, brewing up. One saw me, said a quick one-liner to his mates, got up and came over.

'Hey man, what do you want?' he said.

A strange thing to say, I thought. I want naff-all from you, pal.

'Fuck all, mate. Now do yourself a favour and fuck off, will ya?'

I couldn't think of anything else to say. My answer had put him on his back foot and he turned and sat back down with his mates. They roared with laughter as he relayed his brief encounter. Had I missed something or was it just the Malawi sense of humour?

The terminal itself was little more than a single-storey brick building with the odd ceiling fan slowly jerking round to disperse the smell of those arrivals whose sweat seemed to hang in the air. The decor was 1930s, I guessed, sparsely furnished with a sort of red-oxide paint peeling from the walls. No 'paradise' pictures conveying what a lovely place I'd arrived at. The floor was covered with dog-ends and assorted rubbish, and what litter bins I could see were brimming to the top with days-old crap. I noticed the exit doors had been left open, which let the outside aroma waft in. Not pleasant. It reminded me of the smell of corpses, stagnant sewers and spent aircraft fuel all at once. When mixed with body odours and those of the bins, it made me retch. I made my way through the gathering crowd of African businessmen dressed in wrinkled safari suits holding on to cheap briefcases, and one or two African women sombrely standing behind their man, then I headed off in the direction of the Customs signs. Being a pretty basic airport it wasn't far to walk, I just had to follow my nose and head for the exit. I got in line and waited patiently.

Only one Customs desk was open, and they seemed to be stopping everyone and having a real good sniff inside most cases. This was going to take ages. As I approached I tried to recall if I had any 'naughties' with me. No, couldn't remember. Anyway, it was too late — I was next. I held out my British Passport so the officer could inspect it if he wanted, and to let him know that I wasn't a South African*. He looked me up and down as I approached. 'Hello,' I said. I couldn't ignore him because he was looking straight at me. He nodded. I wasn't stopped but felt his glare bearing down on my back as he waved me through. The only white man in the airport and he lets me go, I thought. Was this part of a bigger plot which I hadn't been briefed about? Any stranger in town carrying an army-style para bag and bergen surely stood out like a bulldog's bollocks.

As I moved towards the outside of the terminal, through hordes of traders offering me their wares — from what looked like barbecued snake on a stick to kiddies' toys made out of old tin cans — I got the feeling that I was being watched from every angle. I wasn't, though; it was paranoia creeping in. This was the first time I'd been out in what was deemed as the 'badlands' as a civilian, without the full force of the British Government behind me, so I guess I was feeling a little vulnerable: the new boy in town. It had crossed my mind that maybe the Customs man had a hunch that I was a mercenary or something, which, of course, I was not.

---

* This was before the final collapse of apartheid in South Africa, when its government was very different.

The word mercenary certainly, in my time, had connotations that derived from the Angola days, when the famous but deceased 'Colonel' Callan commanded a band of white (mainly British) 'crazed, bloodthirsty killers' — as they were described at the time. To some extent it is a misplaced word in my business, but the media always like to use it to describe the sort of people *they* think are working on any mission like the one I was about to embark on. Any job overseas, and in particular in Africa, that warranted an ex-pat to carry a gun, would be the trigger for them to use the word mercenary. In my business, the only people who get tarnished as mercenaries are those who wish to be called that, and make a point of telling people so, through some misconception that it makes them look 'hard'. I certainly don't class myself as a mercenary and I object to the word strongly when it is used to describe what I do; nor do I class myself as 'hard'. I'm a professional security adviser, with a very limited knowledge of putting in house alarms — if you see what I mean!

I had no idea where I was going in the short term, but in these situations, if you ask someone, 'Where can I get a taxi?' or 'How far to the nearest hotel?' as soon as you come out of the terminal, then you're in big trouble. Putty in their hands. They'll see that you are a newcomer and that means fair game. This could cause trouble if you didn't want to part with lots of your hard-earned currency for, say, a five-minute taxi ride, or even a ten-metre porterage with your luggage to a taxi.

In the past I have made problems for myself by telling these rip-off merchants to 'Fuck off,' or asking sarcastically, 'Where's the airport, mate?' That comment tends to throw them off balance because they're not expecting such a bone question, but it can create a menacing situation. In the relative safety of the airport you can get away with it, but outside is a very different ball game. Most of these types have diddly-squat, so having a go at you is no big deal to them if you drop your guard. They see that as a weakness, then they're in. Actually, it's all a big con. Most of them are of a cowardly nature, so if you understand that, you will only be ripped off a little bit. That doesn't cause me much anxiety; it's all part of travelling. Someone — I think it was a Yank businessman — once said to me, 'Every time you land in a foreign country be prepared to lose 50 bucks because that's the minimum you're going to be ripped off for during your trip. It's an inescapable aspect of the fun of travelling.'

So I found a place to sit, dropped my bag, sat on it and pretended to get something out of my bergen, all the time keeping a wary eye on who and what was closing in. I was quite lucky, most of 'Fagin's' men were hovering around a crowd of well-dressed Moroccan-looking gentlemen who seemed like the Mafia from Marrakech. It was still early morning. The sun wasn't too bad but the humidity was up in the 80s, and I was sweating like crazy. What I really had to do was find a half-decent hotel with a phone, get myself cleaned up, and try and sort out this toothache, which was becoming a real bitch. My hangover was no problem in comparison.

I decided the best plan of action was to jump into one of the official-looking taxis, lined up alongside the terminal building. As I made my way to the front one, two lads aged about nine or ten came up to me, hands out-stretched, begging to be given something. They looked like street children, pretty grubby but not short of the odd bacon butty. I explained I had no money, no local currency.

'Hey Mister, give me something, you give me something,' they chanted undeterred. I looked down at them just about to tell them to scarper, then had second thoughts. I wanted to give them something but I didn't want to delay walking to the taxi. This may seem cynical, but it was only my travelling experience which had taught me to be so careful. I remember one time in Jamaica when the same situation occurred. I stopped to give a child a couple of pence when an older boy came from nowhere and tried to grab my bag. So today I was well switched-on to the old decoy method and kept on moving. At the same time I reached into the top of my bergen and pulled out a T shirt which I always kept handy for that very purpose. As I handed it over they both grabbed it, inspecting it as though they were about to buy it, probably to check if they'd seen the design on it before. As I left them behind they seemed happy enough. Well, it was clean!

Now I reached the taxi, a beat-up, sun-bleached mustard Datsun. The driver, a well overweight man in his 60s with fat forearms as thick as Humpty Dumpty's neck, and wearing the remains of a straw trilby, came round to help me with my bag.

'Sir, sir, please let me, let me take that, sir!' he sung with a big grimace.

Not a chance! I thought. 'I'm alright. I'll hang on to that, thank you very much,' I said quickly. I was still very wary, trying to stay on top.

As we pulled off I saw the two lads continuing to examine the T shirt. They looked up, saw me and waved excitedly.

Ten minutes out of the airport and all it had cost me was that T shirt. Looking at some of the sorts that were hanging around there, I reckoned it might have cost me a lot more if I hadn't been wearing a head on me like the Grim Reaper.

Of course it was all an act, but it worked.

I told the driver to take me to *the* hotel, not knowing what hotel was what and not knowing if there was an Intercontinental or Meridian in Lilongwe. This prompted him to say, 'I take you to the *best*, sir.' The best, of course, nearly always means the most expensive. That was good enough for me because it meant a clean environment with, hopefully, a workable telephone and staff that could speak half-decent English — anyway, as long as it wasn't his brother's fleapit in some back alley, I didn't give a toss.

I didn't say much to the driver, just exchanged the usual niceties. He sensed that I was not in the talking mood. As the car bumped along, I was going through my options on getting down south. Usually I like to see a bit of the country so try either to hire a car and drive, or travel by coach, but this time I was still feeling like shit. I had to get some oil of cloves (or the Malawi equivalent) to deaden my tooth. I toyed with the idea about a trip to the local dentist, but dismissed the idea almost immediately: What was I thinking? I must have been suffering from a touch of sunstroke or something. A trip to the dentist was bad enough back in the UK — Christ knew what they'd be like over here. If I couldn't get any oil of cloves I would suffer big time. That was one of two command decisions I made on the spot. The other was that I opted to take the easy route down south — flying. So ten hours later I was back at the airport, waiting to catch an internal flight to Blantyre.

Whilst at the hotel I got cleaned up, actually managed to buy a small bottle of oil of cloves for the obvious, and touched base by phone with the team's LO, John Ball, an expat, who had spent almost 20 years in the country. He was going to meet me at Blantyre Airport and take me to my hotel.

Blantyre. 19.00hrs. There was something especially mystical about Malawi. I had felt it even more so when I arrived at this airport. The unspoken threat which I felt and guarded against in most Third World countries no longer seemed present. I put it down to the nature of the people. Everyone I'd met so far seemed to be content with their lives. They had a sense of humour and would laugh at anything. This feeling of being carefree was something I had to get a grip of fast if I was to enjoy my stay here. However, I had a pretty serious job to sort out, and that was in the back of my mind, *constantly*. To drop my guard before I started would not be professional. As the day unfolded I found the infrastructure of this country was, in fact, very good. For example, the taxi driver back in Lilongwe didn't try and rip me off or create a scene like a lot of them do. Also the telephone system seemed OK. A first-hit call to John Ball with no interference or getting cut off was a plus. From what I saw of the local markets they all seemed to have more than the basics on their stalls. The people were really friendly, not threatening as they can be in some parts of the world. The roads and buildings were all in a good state of repair and my internal flight took off and landed on time. What more could I ask for? I was starting to think I just might enjoy my time here.

John was a short, thick-set man in his 50s, black hair kept tidy, well-spoken and really hospitable, complete with the standard-issue safari suit. We chatted at length about the usual shite when one Brit meets another: what was happening back home; football; cricket; the weather. Just small talk really, but it was nice. He told me that I was to be here for two days and on the third I would be picked up by one of his drivers from outside the hotel and taken to a town called Zomba, a Malawi Airforce base to the north-east, then flown across the border into Mozambique. He didn't say anything about my job over there (which I thought he might have done since he was the LO) so I didn't ask. Going by his tone, I reckoned he hadn't been across the border, so I took it that he didn't really know what the team was up to. That's how I read it, a need-to-know basis. I needed to know, he didn't. He also said that what I did on these days off was up to me. He was a bit abrupt, but there was no offence in this, it was just his style.

He dropped me outside a hotel that was obviously used regularly by John's people. The staff knew John very well and expected my arrival. When my bag was lifted out of the car and taken into the hotel, I didn't worry; this was a safe area. John gave me his home telephone number; any problems, all I had to do was call. As he left he said he and a few of his friends were meeting later at Cloggies, a local bar, and I was welcome to join them.

'Just ask any taxi, they know where it is. As regards money to change, the hotel gives as good a rate as any,' were his parting shots.

That was that. A short and sweet introduction, just what I wanted. I don't think I could have handled a long drawn-out 'story of my life' saga, especially any past war stories. I was too knackered.

The room was tidy, with air conditioning, a big bed, hot and cold water, a clean-smelling towel and toilet paper. A bog that could handle toilet paper — another plus!

I needed to get my head down for a couple of hours if I was to be half sociable later, and went to sleep wondering what

Cloggies was. Was it a nightclub packed out with the local talent, a bottle shack for the 'Whites' that have 'gone bush', or even a high-class whorehouse? I was intrigued. I hoped John wasn't batting for the other side. Not that I have anything against gays, I say live and let live, but what I needed was some female company, even if it was just to talk to. Because where I was going to in the next couple of days would surely be devoid of the furry triangle.

I awoke 12 hours later, sweating like a bastard. The air conditioning had packed up. I had a mouth like an escaping Iraqi's flip-flop on the road to Basra. I'd missed the RV at Cloggies. Still, there were bound to be other times.

Two days later, I was on the road to Zomba, which was a good one. It had tarmac, lots of it. The time was 05.00hrs and I hadn't seen a single vehicle since leaving Blantyre. Once outside the city the countryside opened up into acres and acres of flat, well-cultivated fields of all sorts of vegetables and fruit — cabbages, corn, watermelons, every field had something planted in it. I didn't have too much of a conversation with the driver. He spoke to me mainly in his native language, Chichewa, with just occasional bursts of broken English, and anyway, riding in a Land Rover is the vehicle equivalent of flying in the back of C130 Hercules transport. With the engine sounding like it was on the back seat and the noise caused by the tyres on tarmac, I couldn't hear jack shit, so just stared out of the window enjoying the view.

Every so often we would pass through a village. There seemed to be a mass exodus from them. Hundreds and hundreds of men and women, brightly dressed with what looked like floral-patterned curtains wrapped round them, could be seen walking along the road on their way to work in the plantations. Every now and then the smells of wood-burning fires and their spicy breakfasts still cooking away would waft through into the Land Rover and tantalise me.

Avenues of trees bordered the village roads, types I had never seen before. The most striking were the jacarandas. These were like the old gnarled oaks which surround a lot of commons in England, but the difference was that they were covered in magnificent purple blossom and every so often, when the sun caught them right, the flowers looked blood red. This, mixed with the rich greens and yellows that made up the landscape, was a delight. I wondered if such a flamboyant tree could grow back home. Probably not, otherwise it would have been introduced into the UK years ago.

My journey through this apparent paradise took a couple of hours, then we eventually drove into the air base. The guard at the barrier was expecting me. A single-strip tarmac runway with a few buildings and two large newly-built, dark-green hangers off to the right was all there was.

We drove up to the neatest-looking of these buildings, which I could see was the Mess and Operations room for the pilots. It was a single-storey L-shaped building painted sky-blue, with a dark corrugated roof. In front was a well laid out garden and a car park containing a solitary vehicle. The whole complex was bordered by small boulders painted white, and I laughed as I saw these. Typical legacy of colonial Britain! The monotonous routine of painting rocks was something these Malawians took just as seriously as the British had done.

As I walked into the Mess, I saw it was definitely RAF vintage. Framed pictures of aircraft old and new covered the walls and small wooden plaques donated by previous visiting military units filled in the spaces between. Air conditioning, a cold water dispenser and a small wooden table laid out with aircraft magazines, and Henry my pilot, dressed in his pilot's khaki one-piece overalls waiting to greet me, completed the RAF-clone impression.

Henry was a short black Malawian around 30, about five feet four inches, thin and sinewy, and sported an almost-but-not-quite handle-bar moustache. He spoke excellent English, a great comfort to me. I'd had visions of being flown across the border by the seat of my pants in a 1940s Dakota DC 3, and not being able to communicate with the pilot should the shit hit the fan. Actually, it didn't really matter what the aircraft was like. I'd flown in a few rust-buckets before and hadn't banked on this flight being any different.

We had an hour or so to kill before flying so I made the most of the conversation and got a lot of information out of Henry. It transpired that he'd learnt most of his flying from the Brits, Americans and until recently the Germans, who had 'donated' three brand-new aircraft to the Malawi Government — for what reason I never found out. He had been flying for almost 12 years, mainly fixed-wing aircraft and choppers, but now he had been promoted to flying cross-border missions in one of the three military versions of the German-built Dornier DO 228, a small but robust 20-seater twin turbo-prop transport aircraft.

Things were looking better and better. A very articulate English-speaking pilot, with stacks of flying experience under his belt, and three state-of-the-art aircraft under his command. Was this too good to be true?

After about 30 minutes Henry's navigator came into the mess. He introduced himself as Sam but his real name was

Samalukatauka as far as I could gather; it certainly had a lot of tongue-twisting syllables. Sam said that there was to be a delay of about one hour. It transpired that although the pilots were up to scratch with these new aircraft, the ground crew was still in training and there was a problem with something or other. Henry and Sam went off to sort it out.

Henry had been able to give me what appeared to be an unbiased view on the war I was about to fly into. First-hand knowledge was invaluable in these circumstances, so I tried to take it all on board and add it to what I already knew about the two warring sides, the Renamo (the baddies) and the Frelimo (the side I was working for, the good guys).

Henry didn't know too much about the team's operation in this country, or if he did he didn't let on. All he said was that he and his team flew into Mozambique once a week, sometimes twice if it was a Priority One mission, Casevac or 'special delivery' — whatever that was! — to pick up and drop off supplies, mail and pax (an airforce term for passengers). It was really a high-class taxi service, but with the risk of getting blown out of the sky on every flight.

Our time of flight was to be just over an hour. The aircraft shook violently as Henry released the brakes and sped off down the runway. Soon there were heavy thumping sounds, and the aircraft bounced as the undercarriage hit the least-used part of the runway — the end. This was Henry's cue to pull back on the controls and get us airborne. The engines strained to capacity as we put height between us and the earth. We were now up and flying out north-east.

A river of sweat continually poured off my nose and onto the map I was holding, it then dripped off into one of the hessian sacks filled with cashew nuts, which were stacked two-high and covered the floor of the aircraft. I had no seat as such. I sat perched on a cool box, gazing out of a window.

Curiously I watched my body fluids drain away — nose to map, to hessian sack — and wondered when I would get the chance to replace them. Two bottles of fizzy orange back at the mess an hour earlier were obviously not enough for the old body. Already I had drunk half my canteen of water and needed to save the rest in case we had to put down unexpectedly. This was my survival supply and experience had taught me not to drink it, no matter how tempted I was. And now I was gagging. The dehydration was not helping my brain to register the dried-up river beds 1,500 feet below and compare them with those which I was trying to follow on my map. I was trying to orientate myself with the ground but the map I had was pretty useless, so I eventually gave up.

I couldn't hear much above the drone of the twin engines, which drowned out everything else. The sacks of nuts were not for resupply but to act as bullet stoppers should a horde of roving Renamo guerrillas spot us and decide to have a day out on the range to practise their anti-aircraft drills, knowing full well that we were not armed. These sacks would probably turn out to be the most expensive 'bullet stoppers' in the world, once their contents had been repackaged and stacked on the shelves of Tesco's.

Every now and then Henry would put in a steep turn, drop or pull the aircraft up severely to avoid the small arms fire which occasionally came our way. There was not much chance of being shot down at 1,500 feet but the odd stray 7.62 round could rip open one of our fuel tanks, or worse, a lucky shot could take out the pilot, which would *not* be good news.

Furthermore this was good tactics, to keep any baddies on the ground guessing where we were heading. Varying our insertion route into Mozambique was OK by me. Henry could fly upside down if it helped put the Renamo off our scent. Luckily for us they possessed no aircraft. Hitherto, all their atrocities had been carried out on foot, according to local intelligence — but this was no time to find out that this was wrong.

There was ample headroom and I could stretch out my legs, which was great. There's nothing like a bit of legroom when one flies. The aircraft was a bit of a Tardis, bigger inside than it looked from the outside. It could have carried about 20 seated passengers, but had been totally gutted to accommodate as much supplies and kit as possible. The only two seats left were those of the pilot and navigator.

The heat was unbearable and, to make matters worse, kit and equipment constantly shifted about as Henry banked sharply, changing course. A box of tinned tomatoes broke free and fell on a sack of potatoes, then the rest of the stock followed. I couldn't hear a thing, I only *saw* the stack tumble. I had tried to hold them back as much as I could, but since Henry had now put the aircraft into a Stuka dive I really wasn't achieving much. Then the aircraft levelled out.

'Jesus Christ,' I screamed, to no one in particular. I was now getting pissed off with this white-knuckle ride. A mixture of dehydration, fear and that nauseous feeling everyone gets when they fly was getting me really angry. I looked at my watch. Can't be long now, I remember thinking.

A couple of cardboard crates ripped open and sent their contents rolling all over the place. I turned to look up front and made eye contact with Sam. He'd been trying to catch my attention and was just about to come back and shake me. His head phones were half off his head and he was pointing downwards. I jumped across all the shite which had come loose and looked out of one of the windows. I could see a small airstrip and, off to one side, a small town. This I guessed was the town of Cuamba, and the Stuka dive was obviously our tactical descent.

When we took off from Zomba I remember looking down at the fields. I didn't need a map now to know when we crossed the border into Mozambique. The cultivation literally stopped. It was as if the Malawi farmers cultivated every field up to the border, yet on the Mozambique side there was nothing; no tracks, no hedgerows or defined barriers. A desolate land with no sign of habitation, the scene continuing for miles. We did fly over a lot of water but these lakes were covered in weed and looked pretty much stagnant. Then, as we came in lower, I could see there *were* fields of sorts, but not as cultivated as those in Malawi. Still, it was an obvious sign — man at work.

Cuamba looked a heavily populated place, so I could easily make out the town and its boundary, bisected by a single railway track leading to sidings beyond it. It seemed to be a couple of miles across, and contained low-level villa-type buildings, none over three storeys high. Outside the town I could make out hundreds and hundreds of small mud huts, dotted all around the place. People were everywhere and it looked like they were all heading towards the runway.

I felt that landing was a bit of a problem for Henry. As we hit the runway I had a mental image of the fuselage breaking in two. You know that feeling you get when something really unpleasant is about to happen, and the situation is totally out of your control? Well, that's how I felt!

I still remember a time when I was about 12. I had climbed a tree in my friend's garden, the aim being to see who could reach the highest point. Even before I started, I knew that something was going to go wrong. And, of course, it did. I lost my grip trying to stretch out and grasp the highest branch on the tree, and fell to earth. I was falling through the air, quite conscious, just waiting to hit the ground, knowing that it was going to hurt, that terrible pain was just a second away. The long and short of it was that I broke my left wrist. It was that feeling I now had in the aircraft.

But this time, the ending was different. The fuselage held together. We still had two engines and two wings. There was no problem, no catastrophe.

'Welcome to Mozambique, the arsehole of the world,' joked Henry. He turned round to me with a grin as wide as the Zambezi river. 'Sorry about the landing. That was Sam's first! I'm teaching him how to fly the baby. It's unofficial, but then again, so is *your* business here.'

There was nothing I could say. I was just grateful that I was in one piece. When I used to fly in the Paras or the SAS there was usually a heart-stopping episode at the end of each flight. Why should it be different now I'm a civilian? I was left wondering. Same shit, different day.

The port door of the aircraft was suddenly opened by someone outside. It was a small door and, like on any of these aircraft, very flimsy. Tins of tomatoes fell out on to the ground. A cool gush of wind rushed in, followed by a friendly face with an outstretched hand.

'Welcome to Mozambique. Brad Tasker, ic of the team. You

must be Steve,' said a Scouse voice.

Brad was from the 'old school'. I'd heard that he left the Regiment back in the late 1970s after a pretty distinguished career, mostly spent fighting in Oman against the LMD (the Liberation Movement of Dhofar, Dhofar being a vast stretch of desert between [at the time] South Yemen and Oman). The LMD was a communist organisation backed by the regime of South Yemen, who considered they had rights to this land as part of the six provinces of South Yemen. Oman thought otherwise, hence a long but little-known war, backed by the British Government and mostly carried out by the SAS. All the guys on this team had served at one time or another in Dhofar and were from the same mould: 40/50, very fit, very experienced in the art of warfare.

I was introduced to Kenny, another team member, in charge of our stores. He was organising the off-load of all administration and stores into the back of two Land Rovers. Stores for the local militia had come on the same flight, so it was important that our kit was identified and grabbed as quickly as possible, because there would be no exchanging of kit with the militia if 'by accident' they took something which was not theirs.

'Well Steve, what d'ya think of the show so far? Pretty shite eh, a load of bollocks or what?'

I detected a certain amount of sarcasm in his voice. After all, he was only doing what all soldiers ever do, loading and off-loading stores, in the event of 'closing' with the enemy.

'Fuck, I love it. I can't think of anywhere else I'd like to be.'

'Fuck aye. It's fucking great, this. Getting a sun tan and getting paid for it, it's just like being back in the

SAS,' Kenny replied.

I instantly liked Kenny, who looked a lot younger than his 53 years. A Jock and proud of it, he had come from the Parachute Regiment and then into one of the Air Troops of the SAS — the same background as mine, but a generation before. He, too, had seen a lot of action around the world, and had loved every bit of it.

Crates of beer and 'stims' — a slang word short for stimulants: cola, lemonade, etc. — were at a premium and only our team could afford them. That's what Kenny was telling me as I helped sort out our kit. Everything with red tape wrapped around it was ours, he added.

He had formed a line from the aircraft to the Land Rovers, and with the help of half a dozen of our Frelimo recruits, we shifted the lot in no time.

Cuamba Airport consisted of just a runway, because the main terminal and surrounding buildings had been bombed some years before. Their remains had then been systematically stolen, brick by brick by the locals. Perhaps 'stolen' is too strong a word; 'liberated' would be more correct.

From what I could see, there wasn't much of anything at the airport: no perimeter fence, no Customs and certainly no other aircraft. Nevertheless, that didn't really matter. Only one thing did — the guerrilla war being fought 20 ks north, east and south of us.

The ride to our camp took only a few minutes. The thick red dust which covered the area reminded me of Hereford during the ploughing season. Tractors would come off fields on to country lanes taking half the earth with them. When this dried it created exactly the same sort of coloured dust I was seeing now.

Soon we pulled up outside a small compound, about half the size of a football field, enclosed by a locally-made wooden lattice security fence, about eight feet high. There was no specific access for vehicles so we had to leave them outside, with a local guard on them. The entrance was just a part of one of the lattice sections propped open wide enough to get through.

'This is home. Get your kit and come and meet the others. I'll get a guard to watch this lot,' Brad said. Squeezing through the hole in the fence, I followed after the other two.

Inside the compound was a series of brick, wooden and metal-clad buildings, and in the centre of them all was a small jungle-type hut with no sides. The roof was made out of what looked like palm leaves, and beneath it were seats fashioned out of two Y-shaped pieces of wood driven into the ground, with a log resting in the Y. This was typical SAS-style furniture. I did not need any more clues to its function — it was the bar. Thirty feet to the left of the bar was a 15-foot long single-storey concrete building beyond which was the ablutions area. Around the rest of the compound were three 20-foot containers — obviously our accommodation; washing hanging out to dry around them proved the point.

Behind the concrete block I could see a small telegraph-type pole poking up above a small apex of a roof, supporting electrical wires which criss-crossed the compound. That had to be the generator hut. The only other building which stood immediately to the right of the entrance was the ops sitting room hut, a similar concrete building, about the same size. This is where I met with the rest of the team: Jimmy, a short Jock whom I was to work with and Josh, another old hand who had worked out in this part of Africa for many a year.

It all seemed quite genial. I got a rough in-country brief from Brad, then the other guys filled me in with their own views, not only of the war, but also of the nature of the job and all the hows, whats, whens, whys, dos and don'ts. They seemed a good bunch, with their priorities in the right order. Every evening, after 'prayers' (a formal debrief on the day's events and training) in the ops room, it was SOPs to meet in the newly constructed bar and thrash out, unofficially, any problems that might have occurred during that day's 'prayers', sort out any niggles that might be pissing someone off in the team, or assess any personality clashes with our fellow Frelimo unit.

This was a throwback to my Regiment days. Doing the job required in the harsh environment of Mozambique was hardly different from life in the SAS. The sobering contrast was that it was a lot more dangerous, because we couldn't call upon the rapid support at hand in a Regiment operation. If we got into any situation requiring an immediate extraction, such as Casevac, reinforcements or calling a chopper in, we would be in deep shit, because there were no such luxuries here. So it was even more important that all of us understood how each of us worked, and what made each of us tick. In any case, having a few beers at the end of play each day was always a good thing.

After all the intros I went with Kenny to draw my stores, since I'd travelled light, and hadn't brought as much as I would have liked. Fortunately Kenny's stores had everything. I signed for what I took: three sets of British lightweight combats; a doss bag; mozzy net; and an assortment of British webbing, pattern 58 — basically everything I needed for the job. Next I went to the armoury, a converted 20-foot trailer, and drew out my weapons. I had the option of two rifles: surprisingly, a new SA80 or a Czech-built 7.62mm AKM, the folding-stock version of the famous AK47 rifle (designed in 1947 by a Russian called Mikhail Timofeievich Kalashnikov). I chose the AKM plus ten magazines, a Makarov pistol and an old Luger as back up, plus four grenades. The SA80 I left in the same place I left it when I was in the Regiment, still wrapped up in its oiled bag.

I preferred the tried and tested system of the Kalashnikov — after all, there have been over 55 million manufactured and at that time I knew the rifle better than the SA80. The SA80 was an unreliable, shite-looking shoddily made piece of kit. I'm not into looking good or anything like that, I just wanted to have a rifle that would perform to its maximum without stoppages or bits falling off when I fired it.

I was then shown to my half of one of the three 20-foot containers, the other half of which was occupied by Brad. Within an hour, I had sorted all my kit out, had a shower and joined the guys in the bar. Earlier, Brad had given me a copy of the task's SOPs and other bits and pieces, including some intelligence reports of recent local Renamo activities to read, so I retired early and went to bed reading it all by candlelight. The compound generator had broken down soon after I had arrived, so there were no lights and no air conditioning that night. This is what I read:

INTRODUCTION
Brad's notes, all to read, in no particular order

Home for the next six months is to be half of a 20-foot transport container. We are situated one mile outside the old Portuguese town of Cuamba and about 100 miles east from the Malawi/Mozambique border. We have no rank as such, so we have no powers or authority over our 'hosts'. We are here purely as a training team. From the highest authority in London, no one — and I mean no one — is allowed to go on or carry out operations with this Special Forces unit once it has been trained and becomes operational.

The locals are very friendly and are happy that we are here. The buildings in Cuamba look like they have not had a brick relaid since the Portuguese left in 1975. The inhabitants who are lucky enough to live in the town, live there in relative safety, albeit in less than ideal conditions. The rest of the locals, plus a few thousand refugees, live dotted around in a five-square-mile area of the town, in mud huts. Those who are on the outer edge of the makeshift shanty town are at the most risk. They are easy prey for Renamo, who, at night, sometimes come into the outlying villages to attack, rape the women and capture the men and march them off back into the hills to use them as human camels, to transport their war machine to their next target. Those who resist are, in general, systematically hanged, drawn and quartered, Mozambique style: basically, hacked to death with machetes where they stand, their heads mounted on wooden stakes for the rest of the villagers to see.

We are located just outside the town, to the south, in an area I have named 'The Compound' just by the town's airstrip. It is a small, fenced-off camp about 20 metres by

40 metres. Everything we own or use — weapons, ammunition, food, and training aids and personal kit — is to be secured inside the compound. This is to be constantly guarded by one of the training team. It is Kenny's main responsibility when the training team is out on the ground. We don't own the Land Rovers or for that matter any of the vehicles, but it is recognised that they are for our use for the duration of this contract.

Everything from water through to petrol is at a premium. We are quite likely to be invaded at night by a few locals in search of anything they think might be of use to them. This is to be expected and we have to guard against it. I have arranged with Major Consista, the local Frelimo camp commander, for his men to carry out roving night stags (guard duty).

Everyone here including the army has limited food and water supplies. Most of the locals living out in the huts are seriously undernourished and most of them have nothing to look forward to, apart from an early death. If we catch them trying to steal, make light of it and let them go with a swift kick up the arse. That's all — nothing stronger. I cannot stress this enough, we have no command over the locals or the soldiers. All local problems; discipline (including the troop's discipline) and our proposed daily training programmes, must go through Major Consista or, if he is not about, then one of his officers.

On an operation like this, hearts and minds — it goes without saying — are paramount to the smooth running of the contract and also to our livelihoods. The last thing I want to be involved in is an uprising by the locals, or worse, the troops, because one of us has battered the shit out of a thief just because he had broken into the compound and stolen a tin of beans.

The camp has a limited water and electricity supply. Both are supplied via a petrol generator. The water comes from a recently sunk and tested borehole situated behind the ops room building inside the compound. When it breaks down (which it has, many times since I installed it three weeks ago) we really have to watch our personal and compound hygiene routine until it gets repaired. Sometimes this can take two or three days.

The two water tanks situated behind my basha should be kept full at all times, and are to be checked by any one of us who is passing them at the time to see that they are just that.

Hygiene is a big problem. The insects, the open sewers outside this compound, and basic lack of sanitation in Cuamba in general might land any one of us in the local hospital, a notion none of us even wants to contemplate. Although it is run by a couple of French Aid doctors from MSF, they still have very limited equipment and drugs to work with.

The only link we have with the outside world (apart from the radio) is the sometimes twice-weekly flight by the Malawi Airforce. It is hoped that we will get at least one flight a week of fresh rations and mail.

If the shit hits the fan, and we are attacked by the Renamo, we have no real means of escape apart from running in the opposite direction. SOPs in the event of an attack — to take them on head to head if the force is not too large — can be discussed when all team members arrive from UK. If it looks likely that it will be a big attack, then we might be lucky and get an early warning by the amount of refugees fleeing past the compound gates. In this case I have arranged with an old Russian pilot, Uri, based in the city of Nampula to our east, that I will call him up on the radio and get him to fly in with his Antanov cargo plane and get us out.

We are, in effect, very much on our own in a county which has absolutely nothing apart from millions and millions of rounds of ammunition and enough rifles to fire them through.

Mozambique is basically a weapons graveyard. The assortment of arms and ammunition is unbelievable. It equates to children back in the UK and McDonald's burgers — every kid has got to have one. I reckon if I looked hard enough, I would eventually find a nice, original 18th-century blunderbuss left over from the colonial days.

Our mission is to train two groups of 100 soldiers in SF (Special Forces) tactics in two three-month periods to an adequate standard so they can safely and professionally protect the tea convoys to and from the town of Gurué 100 miles to our north.

The tea is to be brought back to Cuamba and then loaded onto trains which will then take the tea across the border into Malawi, where it will be sold at Tea Auctions to create revenue for the Mozambique Government. This entire operation seems to me to be a little farfetched because the Mozambique Government is going to have to shift an awful lot of tea to sort out the effect that this war is having on its people. (Finally, just so we all know the score about Mozambique, this war was once described by the American State Department as 'one of the most brutal holocausts *against ordinary human beings since World War II'.)*

Vehicles are also at a premium. We are the only people in the whole of this part of the country to have them. Six Land Rovers, ten beat-up old Mercedes flat-bed lorries for the transportation of tea, and an old water bowser are at our disposal. We also have a selection of old Russian military APCs to act in support when the convoys are to start.

I will be issuing formal Standing Orders. However, we are not in the Army now but there are a few salient problems that need to be urgently addressed. I will endeavour to sort out a camp routine and to get everyone's agreement as to how that should best be done.

In the short term, the main point is for all of us to get to know and get on with each other and enjoy working together as a team.

Brad

Team ic

3

DAILY ROUTINE

I didn't sleep much during that first night. The mosquito net I'd hastily erected had somehow been pulled down, probably when I was tossing and turning, so the mozzies had had a great time biting shit out of my neck and arms and I was bitten to fuck. It also didn't help that the air conditioning had packed up during the night and, stupidly, I'd opted to sleep with the door to my container locked. In any case, the bastards still managed to find their way in through the wire mesh window.

That night my AKM was by my side, since after reading Brad's notes I had visions of Renamo entering our compound and attacking us all whilst we slept. This was a bit over the top; we would have been alerted to any movement by Renamo through the outlying villages, which acted like an early warning system. Just as in NI, where the dogs picked up the scent of the many security forces in their area, the local stray dogs which roamed outside the compound would do the same.

First light was around 05.00hrs. The sun was not yet up but, as in Malawi, the humidity certainly was. My room was as stuffy as a sauna. I arose from bed, a single cast-iron-framed affair with a mattress as rigid as a soggy Kit Kat, soaking in sweat and completely knackered. I opened the locked door to let fresh air in. There was no breeze blowing outside so the air around me was motionless. I stood there naked, looking out across the compound, still sweating like a bastard.

Brad and Kenny had worked well during their first three weeks sorting out the compound. Apart from setting up the electricity supply, sinking a fresh-water well and digging the bogs, they had rigged up a really good set of 'field' showers utilising three old 50-gallon barrels set on a wooden tower construction, constantly fed by water via a pipe from the well. The sun would heat the water to a half-decent temperature, so if you got there first you were guaranteed a warm shower. However, when the water in the barrels had been used once, you were guaranteed a heart-stopping one, because the water pumped from the well was icy cold. A later shower was always to be avoided, unless you were a masochist.

Breakfast was whatever you wanted. We had bacon, eggs, beans, etc., all the usual kit one would expect to find back home. Generally, though, we settled for just a cup of coffee or tea and a plate of watermelon. It was Kenny's responsibility to keep us all fed well and he did surprisingly well.

Every day we would be up between 05.30 and 06.00, then

usually off for a run around the airfield perimeter for four to seven miles. There were two decent well-defined runs which led through part of the village closest to the airfield. The locals must have thought us mad — in contrast, they spent all their time walking around, looking for food and firewood. Their routine was designed around basic survival, and they would think nothing of walking 15 ks for wood or food, and as the population grew by the week, these items became harder to find. Apart from wild tomatoes and watermelon, there was not much growing locally. Supplies would occasionally come in by train from Malawi, but only those who had money were able to buy them.

I've always found running good for calming the mind. Once I've made the effort to start, and get over the first few minutes, I've found I quickly settle in to a steady pace. The weather was cool enough that early in the morning not to be uncomfortable, and though the humidity used to make me sweat as soon as I started, I always believed it was doing me good. Of course, I had to drink a gallon of water every time I got back, just to stop myself from dehydrating. Nonetheless, after this I felt on top of the world and ready to face the day.

Because it was still early days in the contract, not all the soldiers to make up this new Special Forces unit had arrived. They were coming from all over the country, mostly by air, and the transport being what it was, I was surprised that any got here at all. It was to be at least another ten days before the full complement of well over 100 soldiers was assembled. This delay gave us a chance to formulate training programmes and designate who was going to teach what, and with whom.

In typical SAS style we threw on the table what each of us would like to teach and do, and what we were best at, and we assessed who had the most up-to-date training in certain skills. Then Brad decided who would do what. This procedure worked most of the time in the Regiment. It was a case of trying to find round pegs for round holes, talking about it all together, and then one man coming to a decision that was agreeable to the majority.

I was to pair up with Jimmy to write the Weapon Training Policy for all of us to teach, and because I had the most current knowledge of demolitions, I was ic of teaching the art of making bombs and booby traps. I was pleased. Demolitions was a subject I really enjoyed.

Over the next few days we really got to grips with the camp. Jimmy planted an assortment of salad vegetable seeds which we had brought over from the UK: lettuce, tomato, radish, etc. He dug the vegetable patch next to the stand pipe by the well, so the seeds were constantly watered through a series of small interlinked trenches. It looked the business, very professionally planned. He reckoned that in a couple of months that we would all be eating fresh produce. Jimmy's vegetable patch was a constant butt of jokes, but as the days went on and the seedlings started to show everyone used to visit it on a day-to-day basis, just to make sure the water supply was OK and that none of the locals had jumped over the fence at night and vandalised it.

The only thing missing from Jimmy's attire when he was tending his patch was a flat cap and a pipe. After work when the rest of us did a bit of weight training, Jimmy would be next to us, viewing the day's growth of his 'fresh'. In between reps on the weights, one of us might stroll over and chew the fat with him.

'Hey Jim, how're the toms doing today?'

'Fuckin' brill. Have you seen this shoot? It wasn't here yesterday. Fuck, things grow fast over here!'

Jimmy would be pointing to the new growth. This would have us all in bouts of laughter, but he never saw the funny side of it. Gardening, like soldiering, was a very serious business to Jimmy.

The Frelimo officers, who only ever wore the Frelimo khaki battle dress and were distinguishable from their men only by the red badges of rank they wore on their epaulettes, used to join us at night for a few beers and were amazed and baffled that we were actually growing our own vegetables. According to the Mozambique macho attitude, only women did that sort of thing. Indeed, the women did *all* the work; fetching firewood, cooking, cleaning, you name it they did it. The men were generally lazy bastards and did absolutely nothing by way of contributing to the family, apart from making babies.

'Where did you get the seeds from?' one of them asked. It was a pretty bone question but as Jimmy said, 'Well, some of these blokes have been at war since they were kids, and I guess they lack a bit upstairs.' In some ways Jimmy was right. About 90 per cent of the people were almost illiterate. All they knew about was the shit side of life: how to kill and be killed.

Little did the officers know but a few months later, when the Malawi resup aircraft didn't come in for over two weeks, we, 'the Specialists', were the only people in this province to eat fresh rations — from Jimmy's vegetable patch.

Sorting out the stores was another immediate job. There was loads of extra kit, and it all had to be unpacked, checked, counted, recorded and stored, before awaiting issue to the troops. The stuff included weapons, ammunition, dems kit, medical supplies, all sorts of brand-new equipment (mainly British Army stuff including our uniforms which were British Army light-weights).

For all of us, this phase was just like being back in the Regiment. Had any outsider looked in, they could have been forgiven for thinking that the official British Army was operating in Mozambique. If the uniforms were not enough to convince them, then why were the majority of the Frelimo troops carrying new British Army SA80 rifles? This was a question I asked myself, but wasn't able to suss it out for myself until much later on.

Then there was sorting out our camp security — who was to be allowed in and who wasn't. Without setting some kind of precedent, we could end up with every Tom, Dick and Harry coming over for a brew and a chat, or even worse, a beer. Beer, like the petrol and water, was at a premium, and very expensive, too, so the last thing we wanted was to share it.

However, all of us had learnt from our past military careers about the need to adopt a hearts and minds programme, especially in this type of war environment. It was essential never to forget that there were fundamental differences between us and the local people. Although they, and the local troops, knew we were here to help them in their plight against the Renamo attacks, we were still foreign. We looked and dressed differently, we ate differently, and we were well provided for. All our extras, luxuries in a way, which the majority of the people would probably never experience, could lead to dissent, jealousy on their part and possibly the death of any of us. Life in this part of the world is very cheap — an old cliché, but that was, and is the truth. People in desperate times with desperate needs could do anything, even kill to get what they want, and in most cases all they ever wanted was a fat belly full of decent scoff. That was worth killing for.

So we implemented a hearts and minds programme with the powers that be. Firstly, we invited the officers over to our beer shack every other night, just for one or two, and then, once every two weeks, the provincial commander and his civilian equivalent. Sometimes they would come over unannounced with half a dozen of their hangers-on and clean us out of beer, but in the long term, if we kept these people happy, then we kept our freedom and respect.

This may seem a simplistic view of the situation if you've never experienced being in a wartorn country and seen just exactly how desperate it can make people, but a few beers with the right people can make your job a hell of a lot easier. Especially if you're in a country where all the tribal chiefs, and the militia, rule their people with a ruthlessness that went out in the Middle Ages back in the UK.

Protocol and our ability to understand 'the Mozambique Way' made up another very important area we had to work on and adhere to during the first couple of weeks. We had to familiarise ourselves with, and get along with, the key players in the Frelimo command structure. Being a major did not necessarily give an officer a higher status within the camp if one of the subordinate officers was from a well-connected and/or respected family. We had to learn to juggle with each of the people who were introduced to us at any one given time. All these key players had something to contribute to our operation, which in turn could only make our lives more bearable as regards getting things done.

All in all, we were sure we made a good job of hosting these important people, from the main man who distributed the petrol, through to the Mr Fix It guy who eventually became Kenny's sidekick. He was able to get, basically, anything that was available 'in country', from spare parts for our vehicles through to local intelligence information from passing tribesmen.

As far as the big chief himself was concerned, we had him in our pocket the day Brad gave him one of the Land Rovers. This secured the rest of the vehicles' safety, a wise move. It gave the chief the equivalent rank of Lord Mayor and High Executioner, and a lot of street cred with his people. It also kept him off our backs, and if we had not given him one Land Rover then he might well have taken *all* of them. He had power, the power that came out of the end of an AK47, and we weren't about to argue with *that*.

Surprisingly, by the end of my second week, we had a full complement of soldiers to start the course. They were in a makeshift camp just across from the compound — not so far away that you had to drive there, but far enough so they wouldn't be bothering us every two minutes. We had just over 100 in all, but it was recognised that we might end up losing about 20 per cent due to injury or lack of interest. The 'Company' was to be made up of two 30-man platoons with two 'Specialists' in charge of each, plus an HQ element under their own command consisting of medics, admin and signallers (radio operators). Because of the lack of suitable terrain on which to carry out training, ranges work and (especially) patrolling, it was very rare that both platoons were ever out at the same time. To some extent this helped with admin problems, which occurred every day.

Because the soldiers came from all over the place, and were in effect volunteers, we did not know what level of soldiering skills they might have. All we knew was that they had about two years service behind them. But what did that consist of? We had to find out.

Unfortunately their past history had not been properly documented by their previous units and certainly we had no files on any of them. So our priority was to interview them, ascertain who was skilled in what, then try to put the obvious pegs in suitable holes. There was only one common denominator between the lot of them, and that was they had not been paid for nearly a year. This could pose severe discipline problems. Would they do what we told them? Would we have any soldiers left after the first night? Would these so-called bloodthirsty warriors stage a coup or string us all up and run off with our stores and supplies? For all we knew, any or all of these things could happen. Because of all this, the first day of introductions was of vital importance not only for the soldiers themselves but also for us and our well being.

To alleviate any anxieties the soldiers, or indeed, we ourselves, had, Brad decided to brief them all up at once, in their camp. His style wasn't particularly dictatorial, and he spoke to them through our two civilian interpreters (who had been given the 'field rank' of Captain for the duration) about our intentions for the next three to six months. He spoke very generally about the training programme and about the operational task they were to perform once their training stage was over. He also touched on the fact that we were here as friends of Mozambique and that once they had all passed the training, then they would be without doubt the best-trained Company in the Mozambique Armed Forces. This last part was not a line of bullshit out of the British Army 'book of man management'. It was going to be *fact*. All of us wanted it, and

I was sure we'd achieve it.

Another point about the troops' well being was that they would always be fed as well as the situation would allow, with fresh rations, meat, and so on. They had only ever been fed on meleme, or maize, for their entire army career, and this was obviously not good enough for the training we had in mind. A comprehensive signal was sent back to the capital Maputo, which both sorted out a special ration allowance for the troops, and addressed the issue of payment for them, including back pay.

By identifying the need for the right 'sweeteners' — that is food, back pay, and additional pay if and when they passed the course, and being awarded the coveted 'Red Beret' to wear (a symbol recognised all around the world as a Special Forces) — we believed we had started off on the right foot with the troops. Certainly they all cheered after Brad's speech. But I did wonder how long their enthusiasm would last!

For the first week all we did was run a basic fitness selection programme. This was our first problem, because although the soldiers were keen to play, most of them were very undernourished. Their long-term diet of a plate of maize for breakfast and a plate of maize and a piece of bread for dinner was just not enough. There was hardly sufficient calorific intake in their daily scoff to keep a child going, let alone a soldier. So until we got them the food which we had promised, we had to adjust the physical training to what they could realistically do: basically, a three-mile run in the morning and that was that. With one-on-one introductions with the team during the rest of the day, that was all we could do for the time being.

It was to be two weeks before the rations arrived. They

were flown in by air, and we met the aircraft and unloaded it under a heavy armed guard. This was absolutely necessary. At the time, it must have seemed to the locals that *we* were the bad guys. Here we were, guarding the unloading of a hell of a lot of food, right in front of all these hundreds of undernourished onlookers, who could only stop and stare at the heaps of rice, flour, tea, coffee, meat and fresh veg. If we gave a sack of rice to one then we would have had to give it to the rest, and there were far too many of them to do that. So, to prevent unrest, we had to put a hard front on during the unloading. Keeping an armed guard on the food stocks was going to be the officers' problem. We did not want the strife of internal politics that would more than likely come about through any unfair food distribution.

Even though the men were not used to running, two or three had impressed me with their athleticism. I reckoned that if these men were put on a proper diet and training programme, they might even be Olympic material. There was one lad in particular who was just 18. He came from the highlands region (we called him 'the Mountain Man') and was so fit that he kept up with us all the time. When I was struggling he would be chatting away, not even out of breath. One day Jimmy, a sub two-hour 30 minute marathon man himself, decided to see just what Mountain Man was all about. He took him out for a ten-miler up and down the airstrip. Mountain Man didn't falter once, keeping up with Jimmy all the way. Mountain Man was later given the responsibility of carrying the support machine gun plus 400 rounds on future tabs. This slowed him down considerably.

One of our aims during this first training course was to identify potential officers and soldiers who could form the training staff, the DS (Directing Staff), for the second three-month course. It was hoped that this one would run back-to-back with the first, keeping some continuity going. This would also allow two convoys to go on the ground at the same time and, in theory, double the units' capacity to shift tea.

Weapons training, tactics (mainly Convoy and Anti-Ambush Drills) and live firing were the core of our training programme. Although the soldiers were dead keen to learn, they were far from competent to go out on operations, even given their two years' previous experience.

The training was based around the basic British Army tactics and use of the SA80 rifles. These were first-generation and weren't up to much, so I felt sorry for the soldiers who had to use them. We had nothing but trouble with this batch: stoppages, magazines falling off, rifles breaking for no apparent reason. The whole SA80 saga was a complete nightmare. None of the team carried them — we all used the AKM, a tried and tested, no-nonsense combat weapon.

In the hands of a trained British soldier the SA80 is a pretty neat and very accurate rifle, and on the streets of NI or on the ranges at Bisley, 'It'll do very nicely, thank you'. But in the hands of eager but uneducated, poorly equipped and undernourished soldiers, it was totally the wrong rifle. For these soldiers, to strip clean such a fiddly weapon, in 'the field', with the minimum of cleaning kit, was a serious headache. Pieces would get lost or, because the working parts of the rifle are for design reasons much trickier to reassemble than the AK47, it would take them too long to complete, especially in an operational environment, where a soldier has to strip, clean and put back together his weapon in minutes. If I'd had my way, I would have reissued them their old AK47s, but there was a political and a commercial reason why we were not allowed to. One which was never explained to us, but I had my theories. I reckoned the government wanted to dump this batch of first-generation rifles in a war zone, just to prove the capability of the weapon in the field. But they didn't have to stitch up a Third World country to do that — any soldier could have told those in charge that the SA80, at that time, was not up to much. It was a liability and it was untested in a war zone. Also, the 'company' that employed us probably wanted to make a quick buck on the equipment side of the contract.

Much of the day's training was to be spent on the ranges, live firing. One problem, though — there *was* no range. So a week was spent clearing a stretch of land four miles north of camp. It was pretty hard to locate at first because outlying makeshift villages had already occupied much of the level ground. However, once sited we set about clearing the ground and building an eight-foot wall of earth at one end to act as a bullet stopper: the butts. All in all, the range turned out to be more than adequate. The only thing was, every time we used it, we had to physically 'area clear' the range of kids who would come and play in and around the area, looking for spent cases and any other useful pieces of kit which might have dropped off the soldiers' webbing. These kids — mainly lads, no more than ten years old — never got the hint, even when a couple of them were caught and severely punished for 'trespassing'. I guess they were just too stupid. Occasionally we had to stop firing because an old man would stray on to the range as we were firing. When dogs ran across, it was almost impossible to stop the soldiers from shooting at these moving targets. The usual British Army procedure of flying a red flag when the range was in use was considered and implemented early on, but no one took any notice of it. So we binned the idea.

Most evenings I'd spend about 40 minutes working out with Jimmy and Brad in a make-shift gym we had put together. The weights and bars were made out of lumps of old metal liberated from the railway yard. Anything small but heavy was used as free weights. Most of the lumps of iron were not exactly balanced or symmetrical, but it just about passed muster. After that, a quick shower, then 'prayers'.

Sometimes we would have a Chinese Parliament, normally instigated by Brad on how to run the following day's training. This may seem slightly unprofessional but most of what we needed for this — the vehicles and, more importantly, the men — was not really under our control. What we *could* plan was how the day should be run, and when the morning came, if we were devoid of, say, two vehicles when we planned for four, or missing ten of the soldiers because they had been tasked elsewhere by their officer to collect firewood or do some small favour for a local chief, then we would remain totally flexible. If it all went to rat shit early in the morning — which it quite frequently did — we would arrange for those soldiers we had to board any vehicles available, and take them off down the range. We worked on the principle that we had tons of ammunition and explosives to get rid of, and if we could teach these guys just *one* thing which would benefit them, and us, it was the art of shooting straight.

After 'prayers' we would sit down to a communal scoff. A TV and video machine had been flown in, but Mozambique TV stations were not broadcasting — their transmitters kept getting blown up. Other times we would go down town

Cuamba to drink warm beer and socialise with the locals. Considering what these people were going through, they were always cheery and well pleased to see us, probably because we were some of the few people with hard currency to spend. However, I like to think they were genuinely pleased to see us. After all, we were there to help them — at least indirectly.

The town did not show too many battle scars, but was filling up daily with refugees from the surrounding area, so its original population of a few thousand had grown dramatically. What it lacked were the materials to rebuild itself after 20 years of neglect. At one time it had been a beautiful colonial-style Portuguese town full of villas with faded pastel walls and overgrown vines running up their sides. The wooden and concrete buildings, one- and two-storey, still standing were inhabited by the lucky few. Roads, once tree-lined avenues, were now just dirt tracks, the tarmac having long since disappeared. I could see that if the rainy season ever returned, the roads would turn into quagmires, like something out of the Wild West.

There were no civilian vehicles, only military ones, and even they were scarce. In fact, all were under the control of the unit we were training. So the only interruption we would get whilst sitting out on the veranda of one of the town's three bars would be kids who came to see us out of curiosity. Perhaps if they stretched their hands out, they might just get a reward for chancing their luck.

Every one of our British Army ration packs contained a tube of boiled sweets, so when we went into town, we armed ourselves with handfuls to give away. Once these kids had had their ration they would be shooed away by the local proprietor, who would then concentrate on trying to sell us more of his lovely warm beer.

I enjoyed those nights out, even though it was pretty basic stuff: drinking under candle light in the warm heat of the evening, listening to the music (a cross between Latin and African, with heavy sexual undertones) and trying to dance with the local girls. All played on a music system which any one of us would have binned years ago. Still, it helped take away some of the feeling that a civil war was raging all around us. The only giveaway was on the road back to the compound — about half a dozen burnt-out Russian tanks and military vehicles, destroyed some time in the not-so-distant past.

It was about halfway through training that I was woken quite sharply by Kenny. 'Hey Steve! Get up. Get up.' His voice had an edge to it, which was unusual. Kenny was a laid-back guy. But this morning he was definitely worried.

'What the fuck's going on?' I was still groggy as I struggled to get out of my mozzy net.

'Take a look outside. You won't believe it! Masses of people heading our way.' He started to run off.

Automatically I got into my kit, threw my webbing over my shoulder and grabbed my weapon. All of us carried our weapons *everywhere*.

'Shit, Kenny! Calm down, will you?' I followed in hot pursuit. Outside the compound I could see what he was excited about.

'Jesus,' I said to no one in particular, though I was now standing with a group of our soldiers who had been on guard that night.

'All these people are coming from up north, they have walked about 30 miles during the night. Renamo put in a big attack, killed a lot of them, so they ran away,' one of our interpreters was saying.

'There must be hundreds of 'em. Where are they going? They can't come here. There isn't enough room for them,' I retorted.

As soon as that was out, I knew that it was the wrong thing to say. Not because of what the interpreter might have thought — he didn't care what happened to them. He was a pretty laid-back guy; after all in a few weeks he would be back with his family in Maputo. But I felt it was callous of me, a knee-jerk remark for which I was sorry as soon as I said it.

Not a sound came from the fleeing villagers — men, women and children — as they passed us. It was eerie. All they were carrying were any items to hand when the attack took place: water jugs, large bundles of rags containing some personal possessions. Some had nothing at all. Every one of them was absolutely silent, heads bowed low, deep in thought, following one after another. Even the children were quiet.

Every now and then our soldiers would call out in an attempt to get information on what exactly went on, and to find out if Renamo were on the offensive and heading this way. Then Brad appeared, fully dressed. He looked agitated. 'Right Steve, round up the rest of the team. "O" Group in the mess in ten minutes. Tell them to bring all their kit with 'em. Looks like some shit is coming our way.' He disappeared back into his basha.

There was no need to reply or to rally up the guys, because they were already all up, waiting to see what the next move would be.

This was going to be pretty serious. It would be the first time I had been in Africa as a civilian in uniform, not as a soldier of the Crown under the umbrella of the British Government.

We all gathered to listen to what Brad had to say. Earlier he had been to see Colonel Rameka, the CO of the SF. Now he was standing by the ops map, pointing with a pencil. 'Right. I'll get straight on with it. What happened last night was that a force of Renamo staged a night attack on this village some 30 ks to our north. The result can be seen outside, a few hundred fleeing villagers. Only one village was attacked, but as a result of its exodus, people from other surrounding villages decided not to hang about, so they did a runner as well.'

He paused while Colonel Rameka and three of his officers joined us.

'Any more news, Colonel?' Brad asked.

'No. Only we have made contact with the air base at Nampula and that they are aware of the attack,' the Colonel replied in broken English.

'Good. Did you request an aircraft to fly in and stand by?'

'Yes, of course, but all the aircraft that were available have now been detailed on other missions. It appears that Renamo are co-ordinating many attacks around the country. So we have to wait.'

At that moment things weren't too bad, although we didn't have an escape plan. No, what we *really* required was a Casevac plan should the shit truly hit the fan. The last thing any of us wanted was to get into a firefight, get seriously wounded and not be able to get out. The MSF people were very good, but they had their own set of patients and problems and weren't really geared up to treat battlefield injuries.

Brad continued his briefing. 'I've talked it over with the Colonel and we've come up with a plan. Let me run it by you all first, then I'll take any suggestions. Remember, let's not hang about here discussing the pros and cons. The important thing is that we get OPs on the ground as soon as possible to get established some kind of "trigger", an early warning system.'

Brad explained that we had no real intelligence of the attacking force and that we did not really know if they were heading this way. The usual form of past attacks was that Renamo would usually 'shoot and scoot'. However, since the previous night's attack appeared outside the norm, we had to assume the worst.

It was even more unusual that there were no available aircraft at Nampula to come to our aid. Rumour had it (the suspected source one of the interpreters, who always seemed to come up with 'A1' intelligence) that they had come under attack and that all aircraft had flown down south for safety. This might mean that Renamo was intending to mount a full-scale attack on Cuamba, to test our capabilities, at the least. They must have got wind by now that we were not there to build the town hall, but to train up a Special Force.

A few ideas were thrown about, but it was soon decided that Kenny and 20 men would stay back to man the radio and act as camp and compound guard. Kenny's main priority would be to try and establish communications with Uri (the roving Antanov pilot) and let him know of our possible plight. The rest of us would shoot off up north in the wagons, to a position just a couple of ks past the ranges, set up OPs in line with one another, and try and establish comms between each of the OPs and Kenny back at base.

The maps we had been using were not much use, so trying to plan or show our troops exactly what we were proposing was very difficult. Still, since all of us now knew this particular area well enough — we had carried out enough dry platoon attacks over it during the past weeks — setting up OPs and road-blocks was not going to be a problem. The only difficulty was that we had a limited amount of radios, which most of the time didn't work further than a few ks; and *that* was in line of sight. It was decided that we would drop off four men at a point halfway between the base and our proposed OPs, then test comms until they could talk to us as well as back to Kenny. In turn, these four would act as a relay station between the OPs and base.

The whole operation was planned 'on the hoof' and in situations like these you can't have an attitude of a 'classroom course' soldier. You can't expect things to go like clockwork. Life in battle had taught all of us on the team this fact many times. Basically, it's all down to the experience of the men who you work alongside with. Our deployment tactics were based on the acronym KISS: Keep It Simple — Stupid. If everyone is in tune with one another, switched on to what's going down, then things will tend to go your way. Which is exactly what happened.

While we roared off up north, another of Kenny's tasks was to get hold of the Province Mayor (or his deputy) to try and sort out the problem of all the refugees. It was suggested they be moved to an area on the other side of the town where there were some old railway sidings. This would keep them out of the way for the time being, and would also keep the tracks clear of people for the free movement of our vehicles should fighting start.

It was about 06.00hrs when I got into position with ten men. I had established a position high up on a rocky ridge. The lie of the land allowed me to see well into the distance to assess where the threat might come from. The land some ten ks ahead was bordered on both sides by mountains, giving what looked like a U-shaped valley, about four ks across. The valley floor was covered in small bushes, any trees having long been cut down for firewood. Along with these bushes, huge boulders made up the ground to my front. Down to my left, about 200 metres away, Jimmy had his men guarding the road and three vehicles — we were in both visual and radio contact. To his left was Josh, who had set up on another track, while to *his* left Brad, some 400 metres away, had set up high on a hillside.

Anything moving to our front would be spotted by any one of the OPs. We were initially concerned that Renamo might cross grain — i.e. move tactically over topographical features rather than use tracks, roads or obvious routes — over one of the ridge lines, miss us out and attack the town from the flank, but this was reckoned not to be an option Renamo would use, since it would have been hard going for them and not their usual style. But anyway, not wanting to take the easy route out, and to be doubly sure, Brad ordered two OPs up on either ridge line to view over the top.

These were to be our two most exposed positions, so we put our most trusted men out on them and told them to keep low and out of sight. Being compromised was *not* the order of the day. All we were trying to establish was how many Renamo were heading in our direction — if any; we were not to engage them, just observe. A battle plan would then be made for any subsequent action. If we were switched on, then we would always have the upper hand. We would have the element of surprise, and with that we could dictate the exact game plan — for at least the first 30 minutes or so, depending on the strength of the enemy!

As foreigners, our brief from London was not to get involved in any operations, certainly not in any head-to-head with the enemy. But what option did we have? How could we be expected to train a fighting force in a country with a war raging all around, and when the time came to protect ourselves and our fellow soldiers, just turn and run on to the earliest available aircraft? We all had been put into an impossible situation. London really had no idea what it was like to be on the ground. We were all soldiers, and there was no way we could sit back and not lead the men we were expected to train into battle, should the occasion arise. It was unthinkable. Apart from the huge loss of face on our part, the British Army's name would be shit in this part of the world from that day on.

For two days and nights we stagged on, waiting for some kind of movement from the north. Nothing happened. It was decided that we should pull off but still keep a state of alert and have regular roving mobile patrols out on the ground. In effect, this took our training programme even further into rat shit. In essence, the soldiers would now have to be ready to go operational at any time; nonetheless, we proceeded as best we could with the training. We kept out of the day-to-day operational command of the security patrols and concentrated on teaching those who were not on duty the skills of Vehicle Anti-Ambush Drills, for when they were out on the convoys.

As the days passed the threat of a Renamo attack faded, so the villagers eventually made their way back to their villages. Then the local militia came out from hiding, giving their usual story of how they chased the Renamo out of the area. They were full of shit, and everyone knew it; they had high-tailed it southwards at the first sign of trouble. However, to appease the militia, one of the local chiefs in his wisdom decided to honour their bravery. There was to be a parade just outside the town where locals gathered to see these 'heroes' honoured for their part in repelling Renamo. The whole thing was farcical, but I was to experience more of this 'special' kind of bravery later on.

I had been in the country for six weeks now. Once the excitement of the so-called mass attack by Renamo had died down, things got back to normal, if you could call it that. There was always something to talk about at the end of each day. On one occasion a couple of our soldiers were caught stealing from one of the town's warehouses where we stored uniforms and kit. I think all they'd taken was a couple of pairs of army boots each. For that, the punishment was short and swift, as I discovered, passing their camp as it was dished out.

The two soldiers were strung up, upside down, on what could only be described as a rack from the dungeons of Dracula. They were screaming in pain — for the rest of the camp to take as a warning — as the bare soles of their feet were thrashed down to the bone with canes. This went on for ten minutes. Then they were left strapped upside down for the rest of the day as a spectacle for the rest of the camp to take note of: 'This is what will happen to you if you fuck up.' To me, the punishment seemed extreme, but then, this was a desperate country going through desperate times. Apparently this was an old, traditional method of punishment, rarely used till recently revived. I never saw those two soldiers again.

The Malawi flight came in pretty regularly. If I was about, I used to go down and help with the unloading, partly in anticipation of getting hold of the mail sack and partly to have a chat with Henry and Sam. They were always ready to crack a joke or two. One time when they were taxi-ing up I could see Sam unstrapping himself and making his way, I guessed, to open the aircraft's forward door. I could see Henry through the cockpit, beckoning me in a frenzied way to go and see what Sam had to say, even before the plane had stopped. Kenny and I ran up to Sam. Through the noise of the engines and the shit still being thrown up by the props. Sam was shouting.

'Hey, Steve, Kenny, Steve, Kenny, we've just flown over a bunch of Renamo. I think we've been hit.'

He jumped out frantically, looking along the fuselage for any signs of this.

'What the fuck! How many and how far?' Kenny shouted back.

'Many Mr Kenny, many! More than what I've ever seen before — and they're heading this way, for sure.'

This sent me and Kenny into big-time switched-on mode and we started to look for a driver to send back and inform Brad and company. The aircraft's engines switched off and Henry appeared, also in a flap. A large shot of the old adrenalin and loose-bowel syndrome surged through my body. I felt scared but calm, both at the same time.

'Henry, what the *fuck* did you see? What did you see? Sam reckoned there were hundreds of 'em. How many?' I was inquisitive, to say the least.

Sam had now joined Henry and, without saying anything they walked off towards a shaded part of the runway, laughing like a pair of hyenas and slapping each other's palms.

'Hey, Mr Steve, we really had you that time, got your white arse going, shit!' Henry shouted.

'What was all that about? Stupid pair of bastards,' Kenny

muttered as he saw me burst out laughing.

This was a typical everyday wind-up that these pilots played on us all and each other; but I couldn't help recalling that old children's story about the boy who cried wolf. How would these guys react if the curtain *really* went up?

Sometimes the aircraft would bring in a sack of fruit, oranges, apples, bananas and the like, that Henry and Sam had personally bought for the team from Zomba market. Other times, a special delivery of their locally brewed whiskey, piss yellow in colour, smelling and tasting like shite. It would knock you out for the night after just one gentlemen's measure. In fact, it was generally put by the medical kit, but Jimmy loved it, so we let him drink it.

On one particular occasion there had been a lot of Malawi troop movement in and around Cuamba. Their job in Mozambique — they were here officially — was to sort out the train and the tracks, getting everything operational for when the tea started to arrive, which was not far off now that training was coming to an end. Their other task was to mount Clearing Patrols up and down the section of the railway which led over the border into Malawi.

I waved goodbye to Henry and Sam, then the aircraft taxied out on to the runway for take-off. It was full of Malawi soldiers returning home for one reason or another, so most of our kit that should have gone on this flight did not make it. Only the most important stuff was put on — the empty returnable beer bottles; without them we wouldn't have got our beer resup. One for one was the policy. The return of empty bottles in Malawi was a growing black market trade and they had a perceived value. Indeed, people made a living out of returnables.

Then, instead of the aircraft flying off, I heard Henry circling the airstrip, preparing to land again. Five minutes later the aircraft taxied back to where we were still standing. Maybe they'd forgotten something. Anyway, the props were still turning, and I could see that Sam was telling one of the Malawi soldiers to do something. He was pointing to the back and then to the nose of the aircraft. With that, the soldier, plus one other, got out and started to off-load four empty crates of beer bottles. My initial reaction was that they were overloaded and that Henry wanted to discharge some weight. When all four crates were on the ground, another soldier crossed the runway and opened up the nosecone of the aircraft so as to store the excess beer crates. Without thinking, one of the original pair of soldiers grabbed a crate and went forward. Instead of moving back and around the wing (thus avoiding the port propeller) for some reason he walked straight into the son-of-a-bitch.

Result, his head was cleanly severed from his body, along with half his left shoulder. The wind of the props, which, of course, were still turning, blew the head down the taxi-ing area towards us. It happened so quickly that most of us could not believe what we had just witnessed. It was pretty gory stuff, but the strange thing was the attitude of the dead man's colleagues. They didn't get at all worked up about it, being more concerned about how long they would have to wait until another aircraft came and picked them up. Henry was equally unaffected. He was more worried about the state of his aircraft and when was he going to get a replacement propeller. He said that if we could get the bent prop off he would fly the plane back, but I wasn't sure about that.

Another incident involving the Malawians, which was a

butt of jokes amongst us, was the story about an aircraft technician back at Zomba. He was checking the state of one of the newly donated German aircraft. Whistling could be heard coming from the hangar, so he was in good spirits, when all of a sudden it erupted into a ball of flames. The poor man was obviously a goner, since he had gone into the hangar to check the fuel state of the aircraft — with a lighted cigarette in his mouth. I could see the funny side of that to a point, but Henry and Sam considered it one of their best stories, and told it all the time. Of course, it got better with every telling!

I must have seemed a pretty sad bastard to the rest of the team when it came to receiving letters, because although I was quite a frequent writer, I never seemed to get many. In fact, all the guys on the team were married, which was a bit out of the norm. However, my romance with Lynn was well and truly over. She was seeing someone else and that was that. Sometimes I got angry about it, but there was jack shit I could do about it over here and I wasn't going to ask Brad if I could fly out to Malawi to call her, just to vent my anger in a stream of one-liners which would make me feel better. What's more, I wasn't going to give her the satisfaction of hearing me let rip. I'd learnt over a period of time that she was quite cutting and rude enough about me to her friends, even when in my company. Christ knows what she said about me when I wasn't around. Was I really such a jerk to warrant all this emotional upset, or was she just not the woman for me? I put it down to the latter.

I'd written letters to her a couple of times, but nothing too lovey-dovey. It was a release for me, more than anything. At that stage in our relationship, I don't suppose she even opened them. Thinking that hurt me a bit. I was convinced that our relationship was well and truly over, but no man likes female rejection, and I guess I was no different. When you're thousands of miles away in Shitsville, with no access to a phone, it's very hard not to think about relationships: past, present, and, in my case, future.

I also wrote to my brothers but it was a standing joke that I didn't expect them to reply. There was nothing in it, but a few times when they had replied I'd never ever got their letters, because I'd always moved off somewhere else before I received them. So their letters always seemed to be chasing me and would invariably reach me when I had been back home a couple of weeks, by which time the contents would be old hat.

We were three weeks away from the official passing-out parade when Brad asked me to go to Malawi to organise the pick-up of the red berets and a couple of other resup items. The trip meant spending a night, Saturday night, in Blantyre, so I jumped at the chance. An aircraft was due in that day so I made ready my overnight kit and disco shoes, and within four hours I landed back in Malawi. Obviously, there was no passport control to go through, and I was soon speeding off to meet John Ball at his office.

John had booked me into the same hotel as before and there was really nothing I needed to do, since he had organised the berets and everything else that had been required. It would be waiting for me to pick up the following afternoon to take back out with me, John said. The most important thing to do was actually to make it to the RV this time, again at Cloggies, he added.

My trip into Malawi was really just an excuse for a big piss-up, which was just as well because I needed one. I dumped my kit in the room, showered, got changed, and decided to have a wander around Blantyre. It was 19.00hrs now and I had arranged to meet John in a couple of hours at Cloggies.

Blantyre at night still had a magical feel about it. It was quite dark and the street lights were dimly lit. The air was hot but a cool breeze kept the sweat from rolling down my back. A white shirt was the order of the evening; any other colour would have shown sweaty patches. I had a drink in the hotel bar, then went across the road to another more upmarket hotel and had a couple more.

This other hotel was further back from the main drag than the rest. It had large lawned gardens surrounding all sides, a drive-in and drive-out reception area, and more lights on than the *Titanic*. It also had a large swimming pool which, surprisingly, was not at all busy. I sauntered up the drive and passed the concierge who was looking very dapper in a typical Dorchester concierge attire; long dark Crombie-style coat, ribbed in blue, tall velvet hat. He must have been roasting as it was still very warm outside. He tipped his hat as I approached, as one would have expected to see in colonial times. Out of courtesy I asked him where the swimming pool was, though I could make it out through the open reception. He walked with me to the pool, snapping his fingers at one of his colleagues to take his place outside while he escorted me.

The pool was clear and inviting. I could have quite easily taken a dip, but instead, I ordered some food and drank a few more 'brown' bottles of beer in anticipation of RVing with John. The beer was Carlsberg but I have never seen this lager sold in brown bottles anywhere else. I got a bit local 'int' from the bar man; the usual encouragement of the offer of a drink oiled his tonsils. He told me about the bars. Cloggies was apparently the in place to go. Now I was getting somewhere. I got him to sort me out a cab. Ten minutes later, after screeching around a few narrow and poorly lit backstreets with the driver constantly on the horn, tooting every living creature we passed, I arrived at a large detached wooden structure fronted by neon lights. A flashing sign spelling 'Cloggies' stuck out like the spaceship from *E.T.* The throbbing soul track blaring out and a crowd of about ten men surrounding a couple having a drunken brawl, all shouting and having a laugh just to the left of the entrance, gave me some idea of what I was about to walk into. Anxiously I made my way in. No doormen, no payment asked for; nobody gave me a second look. This was pretty strange considering the place appeared to be off the 'tourist track'.

At first sight, Cloggies looked an exclusive type of place (by local standards), not exactly a bar or a disco, a sort of in-between place, more of a clip joint for Blantyre's trendies. I suppose really it equated to the 'sticky carpets' pub-cum-club we have in every town back in the UK, nice and loud and ready for a refurbishment, but you wouldn't want to take your mother there.

Inside, the place looked like a huge log cabin with just one bar running down the centre. It was heaving, and everyone was dancing. I managed to find John tucked up in a corner down at the far end of the bar, drinking with a couple of expats and surrounded by a slack handful of the local talent.

'John, John, some place this is!' I screamed above the ceaseless Marvin Gaye.

'Hey Steve, glad you could make it this time. You like it? Good.'

As he was speaking I caught the eye of one of the girls. She was a small pretty little thing with a firm pair of breasts. She smiled. Instantly I got turned on.

'Let me introduce you to everybody,' John was saying.

Before I knew it I had a beer in one hand and a girl on the other. All the girls were locals. They weren't exactly on the game, John had said, but they used their attributes — good looks and all that — to get on in life. They generally long-term dated the ex-pats, since they were the ones with the American dollar. Most of them had day jobs. It was a brilliant night, John's mates were a good laugh and we all got totally slaughtered, including the girls. It was just what I needed, a good laugh and stacks of female company. Being out in the field for so long you can get pretty pissed off with the same old faces and no fanny. It made a change, it refreshed me, and it made me forget about Lynn back home. She, as far as I was concerned, was now history. I had my soul well and truly cleansed that night by an olive-skinned, firm-breasted beauty by the name of Maria.

Less than 24 hours later I was back in the compound. Nothing had changed, the only thing was that Brad had been told by the Colonel that the passing-out parade for the troops was to be brought forward by one week, so they would be issued their berets the Friday after next. Orders had come down from Maputo that they had to start ops on the following Saturday. There wasn't a lot any of us could say about it. The Colonel was in charge and that was that. The training programme was almost complete anyway, so it didn't really matter that much.

Another reason for all this was that intelligence had also come down from Gurué, the tea plantation region the convoys were heading for. Apparently Renamo had been seen in and around the hills and there was a ton of tea already picked and refined, waiting to be shifted. Reports hinted that Renamo might be planning an attack on Gurué to burn this tea. Well, that was the story we were given, but more than probably, the real issue was the fact that next Friday was Armed Forces Day, one of the biggest dates in the country's calendar. It would be good for the troops' morale to pass out on this day. It would also be good for us, because we could take a break from the training for a week or two until the next course arrived. That was our intention, anyway.

That night I went to bed earlier than usual, which I put down to the previous night's extra-curricular activity. But I couldn't sleep. I experienced extreme nausea and was sweating really badly. Every pore in my body seemed to be working overtime. I wasn't sick and I didn't even feel I wanted to chuck up, I felt just so drained. The morning was no different. I tried to get up and walk around, but I just didn't have the strength. The guys thought I was suffering from a humungous hangover, but the strange thing was that I hadn't felt hungover the morning after being on the beer.

Come the afternoon I was wasted, and started to hallucinate really badly. Meanwhile, my body was approaching boiling point, and I was still sweating like a bastard. The guys took their turns in coming over every so often, to check that I was still alive and to top me up with water. (I'd dehydrated a lot and had to replace these fluids that were draining out of my body at a rapid rate of knots. Without them, I would have been in an even worse state than I was at that moment.) Death felt pretty close.

The door to my half a container was open, but it made no difference to me if the air conditioning was on or not, as

The spoils of war. Two trainee SF soldiers posing on a Russian tank, Cuamba.

Top: My home and gym in Cuamba.

Bottom: On sentry duty with the new SA80 rifles.

Top: My small arsenal – which I carried with me 24 hours a day.
Bottom: SF soldiers out on a clearing patrol.

Scoff time at the ranges – maize twice a day.

Top: The point vehicle on our first major operation. I was one vehicle behind.
Bottom: A relic of an old Renamo attack.

The finished product – the SF after being awarded their red berets.

Top: Effective enemy fire on one of our tanks.

Bottom: The tea train into Malawi, complete with its own armoured guard.

I was past noticing. I kept drifting in and out of consciousness — at least, this is what I was told later; I couldn't remember anything!

One of the doctors from MSF was rushed up to see me. He took a blood sample and had a good poke about but couldn't really assess what the trouble was until he had analysed my blood. He and his team worked under pretty primitive conditions and because he was operating in the field he had this all-singing-all-dancing portable blood tester for every strain of nasty that lurked around this part of the world.

It took a day to get the blood test back, but nothing had showed up. All the guys could do was to keep force feeding me with solutions of Dehydralite. Sometimes I would come around and start to talk, then I would drift off again. I really believed I was going to die. It was five days before I came out of whatever condition I was in. I hadn't moved, not even to go to the toilet. I don't know if I ever passed anything — if I did, then the guys kept quiet about it. It can't have been nice, cleaning up after my incontinence spasms: a shit job, as they say!

I lost almost a stone in weight during those five days, but the really strange thing was that I recovered as quickly as I went down. Within a day, I was back eating and feeling OK, just a bit dizzy from lying down for so long, that was all. I never found out what it was that sent me into nightmare mode for those few days and, strangely, none of the others went down with anything similar during the trip. I was just thankful that I was going to be fighting fit again in time for the passing-out parade.

The final week was spent preparing the troops, their kit and their vehicles. There was now an urgent need for hardcore intelligence about recent movements of Renamo in the area the convoy would drive through. This was a problem, but the best we could do was ask the Command in Maputo to fly up their latest intelligence reports for the north and collate them the best we could. It was far from ideal, but we had been asked by Colonel Rameka if we would have a go: 'An int brief by Mr Brad would make the soldiers think that the threat is real. Of course, we all know it *is*, but it might just make them all switch on to make them talk through their anti-ambush drills as they have been taught,' Colonel Rameka had said.

Most of the troops had responded really well to our teaching methods, taking on board nearly everything we had taught. This was quite a feat on their part, considering the conditions, and the entire team was pleased with how the course had gone. We were all genuinely proud of them.

Another surprise. Brad had received a signal from London, notifying him that an independent TV company was flying into Mozambique to make a documentary on the newly formed Special Forces unit, and requesting that he and the rest of the team 'make them most welcome and give them all the support they require'. That was *all* we needed! Babysitting a Brit film crew in the middle of a warzone. This particular contract was not going to be as covert as we had been led to believe!

The film crew landed in our laps two days before the parade, four men and a woman. They were a jovial bunch of mixed ages, the director and cameraman mid-40s, the others late-20s. All were university types and it was pretty obvious from the amount of kit they had that they were expecting to rough it big style, with tents and all. There was a funny incident on the first night, with their portable Chinese camp beds — a canvas sheet which you lie on, pulled tight between four thin metal bars which act as the bed's legs — when they all broke as soon as each of them went to get their heads down. The canvas tore away from the legs as soon as any weight was applied, making them beyond repair. Because it was their first night, we'd all stayed up until midnight drinking and getting to know each other. We were laughing our heads off as we heard them swearing and tripping over all of their gear, trying to sort their bedding arrangements out under torchlight.

The following morning over breakfast, as the crew were walking in, just for a joke Jimmy and I openly discussed the 'six Ps' we had been taught back in recruit training: proper preparation prevents piss-poor performance.

'Steve, what *were* those six Ps we were taught back in the army, somethin' about prior, proper preparation ..?'

'Yeah, Jimmy, I know what you mean, proper preparation prevents piss-poor performance ...'

'Oh hello, guys, have a good nights sleep did we?' Brad interrupted.

There was a slight pause before everyone broke out laughing.

'What a right bunch of gentlemen our hosts are — and not one offered to give up their bed for me,' Sarah, the girl amongst them, chirped up.

Another slight pause.

'You know, *my* door's always open,' I said.

'Ah well, that can all change as from tonight, if you're luck's in,' Jimmy joked.

'Is that right? Choices and more choices. My, my, aren't I a lucky girl!'

'Now seriously, you should always check your kit before going out in the field, it's SOPs, isn't that right Brad?' said Jimmy.

'You're fuckin' spot on there, Jim boy, you master bullshitter you. Will the real Mr REMF please expose himself?'

Jimmy pushed back his chair and was just about to do his full-moon party trick. Sarah, who was obviously used to this sort of banter and messing around, was not perturbed at all, and soon realised what was about to happen.

'Please Jimmy, can't it wait until we have all eaten? I'm not sure I want to see your tackle before my tea and toast, thank you very much.'

This little episode broke the ice. We hadn't known how to take Sarah when she first arrived and, being gentlemen, had been on our best behaviour. But now we knew she was up for a laugh, and she was treated like one of the boys.

During their stay we gave them every possible assistance in escorting them around the local area so they would get their story and use up their film.

They interviewed a couple of us, asking us how we had got involved with this type of work, what we thought of the war, etc. None of the questions appeared to be loaded and the crew seemed genuinely interested in what we had achieved. They were also looking forward to filming a bit of live action. What their idea of live action was I didn't really know, but we tried to get them involved with a bit of live firing down on the ranges for a start. However, trying to entice a 'come on' with Renamo was not a good idea, if that's what they had in mind. Too many people have this Hollywood attitude about what happens in war, but believe me, when one human being sees another get his or her brains blown out, it ain't pretty.

Meanwhile, those troops who had made it through training were going to be presented with a 'Red Beret'. Even those we felt didn't quite make the grade were awarded one. To be honest, we knew this would happen, right from the start; all the troops on the course, good or bad, would pass. However, not all of them would take an operational role — as I've already mentioned, about 20 or so of them would form the HQ element of the force.

The issue of red berets was to make them feel they had achieved something special in the eyes of the rest of the Frelimo Army, and that they had been trained by the Brits; in other words, they would appear an élite unit. And in our eyes that's what they were. They were certainly the most disciplined, switched-on troops we had seen in the country. This was not because we were the best instructors in the world, but because of the methods and attitude we managed to put over to them.

It was the day of the Passing-Out Parade, held at the airport, the only relatively flat stretch of concrete for miles around. Hundreds of locals turned out, as well as many dignitaries, ranging from the Province Commander and the Mayor to other local VIPs and two characters who had flown up from Maputo. No one really knew who they were. They weren't in uniform, but looked the part, if you know what I mean. Unsmiling and a bit strandoffish, they seemed a bit too clean-cut, big and healthy to be men from Mozambique. Jimmy reckoned they were spies for the Americans, working for the CIA, or perhaps something much more sinister.

But really we didn't know, and to be quite frank I didn't care. At this stage I wasn't interested in politics and the games politicians played. I've always had a great mistrust of people who play cloak-and-dagger — most of them are Walter Mitties, anyway. On the other hand, the Colonel didn't hold my view and was constantly looking over at them to see what they might be up to.

The camera crew was in action, filming the entire parade, and the soldiers quite rightly rose to the occasion. Most of them had never had a photo taken, let alone appeared in a movie. This obviously added to the atmosphere of the day, and was a really good morale booster for the soldiers. All parades give participants a feeling of achievement, but in this case having the camera crew filming as well was the cherry on the icing on the cake. It was the full monty!

After all the speeches, when passes were given to every man and his dog, including ourselves, the powers that be laid on a special dinner for us all, troops and specialists. The two CIA types and their entourage didn't attend, and were last seen heading off to their aircraft. The dinner was a simple outdoor affair; but then, most things in Mozambique at this time were rarely anything else. When the troops were served a good helping of meat and a can of beer each, they *knew* they had élite status.

The meat-and-beer meal was the first surprise of the day. The next happened during the dinner. Colonel Rameka told the troops when their first operation was to begin — tomorrow! Strangely, there was no great response. I would have expected some sort of reaction but there was no cheering or 'bumping'. They just clapped a bit and got on with eating. Dead strange. Then one of the younger officers got the troops to give the Colonel three cheers. There was more reaction to that than when they were told they were to start operations. One would have assumed that they would have at least been given leave of a week or two so they could go home and visit their nearest and dearest, especially as they'd had none since the course had started almost three months before. The trouble was, I was still trying to assess everything on British terms.

However the troops took it, this operational bombshell was also a big surprise to the training team. We had no idea that ops were going to start so quickly after the Passing-Out Parade. What was an even bigger shock was that we, the training team, were expected to go along with them!

4

ON DEATH'S TRACK

Once again, the same rules applied as on the last threat of contact. 'We were not to get involved' — just as had been the case when it had been assumed that Renamo were heading south on to our position. This was strictly not allowed by London. We were only meant to act as advisors and not go on any military operations. 'It would be totally out of the question,' I remember London telling us via our in-country LO in Maputo the following day.

What London didn't know was that if we didn't go along on the convoy with the Special Forces, then the convoy commanders would refuse to as well. During the evening, it began to look as if we were scared of going with them, and from their point of view, it had nothing to do with London.

We were soldiers just like them. They didn't understand the political implications of us Brits mounting offensive operations there, let alone getting killed on one. Picture a tabloid headline in UK: 'Ex-SAS men working undercover in war-torn Mozambique. Two killed in Renamo ambush.' That would definitely cause questions to be asked in the House of Commons.

The long and short of it was that very early the following morning, the convoy of ten flatbed trucks, an old water bowser and an assortment of armoured vehicles headed north for Gurué, along with four of us Brits — Brad, Brian, Jimmy and myself — acting as 'advisers'. None of us wanted to be accused of cowardice!

After the 'last supper', all troops were ordered to help load the trucks with vital supplies for Gurué. For over a year Gurué had been cut off completely by road, and it was essential to the tea harvest that these supplies got through in order to feed the tea pickers and refinery workers.

There were irregular airlift missions flying in but these were very risky and, of course, becoming very expensive. The necessary supplies consisted of hundreds of sacks of grain and flour, and a real premium commodity, sugar. All had come via rail from Malawi some days earlier and had been stored in two huge warehouses in the town centre, under the control of the Mayor, and heavily guarded by his own militia.

When the trucks arrived outside our compound the following morning, I was amazed that they were still drivable. Eight were so overloaded that troops designated to ride with them had trouble finding spaces to sit. I didn't relish their job one little bit. They made easy pickings as far as any opportunist sniper was concerned.

The camera crew was there to film and wish us good luck. They really wanted to come with us but had more sense. It was hoped that they would still be 'in country' when — or if — we returned in a couple of weeks time.

For our part, we had been put in an untenable position. If we hadn't gone with them, all our 'street cred' gained during the past months would have been destroyed and more to the point, our personal security might have been jeopardised as well. Actually, if the truth be known, all of us were relishing the opportunity to go on operations and possibly get a crack at Renamo.

The only firepower, other than the rifles and RPG 7 shoulder-fired rocket launchers we carried, was: three AAs (Russian anti-aircraft guns) strapped down on the back of three Land Rovers, plus two lightly armoured BTR 60s, one at the front of the convoy and one at the rear, as protection.

The AAs were a real problem for the crews manning them. Over the previous weeks, we'd tried to secure these guns in the back of the Land Rovers, so they would stay stable and on target when fired for at least 100 rounds, but they would not. The recoil of the gun would shake the Land Rover so fiercely that the driver had trouble controlling the vehicle even when stationary. Firing on the move was a further problem because the gun's recoil would vibrate loose the makeshift wooden wedges jammed around the gun's tripod to lock the legs in position in a fruitless attempt to stop this happening. It became impossible to aim the gun with any degree of accuracy. In short, mounting this weapon on the back of the Land Rovers was a total waste of time.

The only advantage in bringing them along was as a show of firepower to the enemy. They were fearsome-looking pieces of kit. Renamo didn't know that they were incapable of putting down suppressive fire, nor could they know that they would jam up after every ten-round burst. Mounted on a Land Rover they looked the business and that alone would probably be sufficient deterrent for any Renamo unit thinking of mounting an attack. In addition, because the guns were relatively light and could be carried by three men, they might come to have a use in Gurué. There they could be taken off the Land Rovers and sighted on the ground, thus becoming very effective weapons indeed.

The convoy route was to take us along 100 miles of dirt track which had not been driven on for over a year. There was every reason to anticipate that Renamo had laid mines somewhere along it. It certainly didn't take the brains of a genius to work out that Renamo would have placed obstacles to slow us down, and probably trap us in an ambush. Because of the terrain and the natural obstacles along the way, we allowed between eight and ten hours to get to Gurué, a further three or four days to load up the tea, and then 12 to 14 hours for the return journey.

It all had the makings of a classic 'To-Hell-and-Back' journey. Our only hope was that Renamo had limited intelligence of our movements and didn't know on what day we would be travelling. Our own intelligence was non-existent. We had gained nothing from the latest reports sent down from Maputo; all we knew was that Renamo had been, and still were, operating about 20 miles to our north.

Their strength, weapons carried or methods of operating the units roaming our part of the country were very much unknown. We were very much aware that they were a pretty ruthless lot to their own people, and what they might do to foreigners, especially whites, was not a pleasant prospect. I could well imagine some of it! The best thing to do was not get caught.

The first ten miles were relatively easy going. This part of the route was well known to us all — we had driven over it many times — but as soon as we approached the mountains, the track started to turn and weave its way up, down and through old dried-up river beds. The drivers of the trucks had to drive almost blind because of the dust being kicked up by vehicles in front. Every 15 or so minutes we had to stop, dismount, and put out clearing patrols to check out the track ahead. At times there were rocks blocking our path, a possible 'come on' but more likely put there by kids, or a burnt-out tank or APC that had either been attacked a year earlier or just abandoned along the way.

The three middle trucks carried non-paying passengers who had hitched a lift to see family and friends. They rode high on top of the essential supplies. About 100 in all hung precariously on to the tarpaulin sheets which covered the trucks. As their vehicle braked, sped up, bounced and swerved as a matter of course, they sang constantly. A lot of vividly dressed locals singing in harmony was not the most tactical of approaches to adopt on this first convoy. I think it was their way of releasing the stress of knowing that they were likely to be ambushed. Maybe they assumed that we were the 'Force Invincible'.

The convoy continued at its almost unbearably slow pace. I had to be totally switched on, my eyes scanning every bit of open space that lay in front of us, anticipating the worst. It was like being back on the streets of NI, where a moment's relaxation could mean getting blown away by some sniper, or not concentrating where you've been stepping could lead to treading on a homemade AP that had been sited at an easy crossing place in an innocent-looking hedgerow.

I was incredibly hyped up, and my concentration was intense. This situation was bringing my military and personal qualities together for the ultimate test. It was about life and the need to survive. It was also about thinking, Why the *fuck* am I here? — a perception common to many soldiers over the years. Being in situations like this always reminded me of the saying, 'You're never more alive than when you're closest to death.' That's very true. All one's primal instincts, never really used in modern life, seem to come back and are greatly enhanced when one knows that Mr Death may rear his ugly head at any moment.

So far, things had been going pretty well, despite the fact that dust was constantly blowing into the Land Rover. Jimmy, now driving, had the worst job. Sometimes the dust was so thick that he had to back off or slow right down to see where he was going, which had a domino effect on the rest of the convoy. It continually stopped, started, and shunted its way forward. This added strain was not helped by the fact that our Land Rover was missing parts of its side windows so we could not stop the dust entering and swirling around us. And on top of *that*, the heat and humidity were constant discomforts.

We had passed a few small hamlets. On one occasion we stopped at a reduced village, as the people who elected to stay put and not to go off to the safety of the bigger towns were a constant target for Renamo. The population was less than one hundred, mainly old men and women. Renamo would come in, take what little livestock there was (sometimes only a few chickens), fill up with fresh rations, water, tomatoes, etc., and leave. It wasn't in their interests to wipe this village off the map, since the old people were no threat to them. Rarely had Frelimo visited this village in the past and we were the first to do so for such a long time.

We didn't stay too long — only long enough for those who so desired to top up with watermelons and water; and that was that. I wondered if this village would be here on our return journey, or would Renamo now wipe it off the face of the Earth because the villagers had 'collaborated' with us, the enemy? I seriously worried that our presence might be construed by the guerrillas as collaboration on the part of the inhabitants. I hoped not, since there was no way of avoiding the villages; no tracks skirted around them. We didn't really *need* to stop there, so why we did, I don't really know. I guess it was just common courtesy to say hello, yet in doing so we possibly signed the locals' death warrants. Still, this was a view I kept to myself. Certainly the troops welcomed these short stops.

Every time we came across a village or small hamlet, our soldiers would join in conversation with the elders, who would jump up on the trucks or run alongside them. In fact, we rarely stopped completely. The snatched conversations always centred around the possible whereabouts of Renamo. The standard reply was that none had been seen in the area for weeks. This was to be expected, there was no way these people wanted to take sides; in fact, most of them didn't know who was who. Ninety per cent of the population didn't even understand what the war was all about. All they saw were men with guns, some in uniform, others not.

At about the half-way point of the journey we had our first major stop, at a small town called Lioma, really nothing more than 40 or so buildings either side of the track. The inhabitants, 2,000 or so, turned out to greet us.

When I say they turned out to greet us, they weren't waving banners and cheering or anything like that. Most of them appeared just to observe us the Brits more than anything else. I felt unsettled. There were no smiles on their faces and most of them appeared very stand-offish as they trotted alongside our vehicles.

'Hey, have you seen any Renamo around here?' I tried to catch the eye of a bare-footed young lad of about 14 or 15, in the standard well-worn T shirt and jeans. He knew I was talking to him, but didn't acknowledge me.

'Hey you, you speak English, English? You want something? Jimmy, stop the wagon, will yer?'

The boy came up to the window and I held out four chewy fruit-pastille-type sweets I had got from a Malawi soldier. They were individually wrapped in white rice paper with twisted ends but tasted crap.

'For you. Speak English. Any Renamo?'

The lad looked puzzled at what I was saying.

'Renamo. Have you seen any Renamo around here recently?'

Jimmy was calling out to another lad with the same question, again to no response. Suddenly my lad took the sweets and ran off, followed by a crowd of children. I was left none the wiser, but very concerned. I still had this butterfly feeling in my stomach about being ambushed.

The troops didn't seem overtly worried, there was much bartering going on between them and the townspeople over the purchase of bits and pieces, mainly vegetables in exchange for personal items of issued kit, such as field dressings or water bottles. In fact, I didn't see any money changing hands. The troops had very little as individuals, and furthermore, money was no real use to these people. What could they spend it on, and who would take it in exchange? The team made a point of not getting involved — someone had to stay alert whilst the troops struck their deals for whatever. We always assumed possible danger and this form of apparently spontaneous activity could well have been a set-up.

We had been gradually climbing since leaving Cuamba, and now the area for miles around was flat and very fertile. Back in the 1970s Lioma had been (still was, to some extent) an agricultural town. As part of a much bigger aid programme, Brazil had at that time donated to Mozambique millions of dollars worth of all sorts of farming machinery and heavy plant, such as tractors, diggers, combine harvesters and baling machines, which all ended up there in Lioma. At the same time this machinery was delivered the war kicked off, so all this kit sat unused and rusting.

I was looking across at the fields which contained this equipment. The sight would have made even the hardest Young Farmer break down and cry: literally row upon row of tractors and combine harvesters, just lined up in a field, baking in the midday sun as they had done for 15 years or so.

Not one digger or tractor had been used — they had all just been driven into the fields and left. The original intention had been to give the locals training on how to use and maintain them, but as the war took precedence, the powers that be in Maputo took over the country's ration of diesel and petrol, so by the time Lioma received its share there was very little to put into the tractors' tanks. Through these bizarre circumstances, Lioma had become the world's largest graveyard for agricultural machinery. From what I could see, very few of these vehicles had been cannibalised; most looked as if they could be put to work with very little effort. I remember thinking that there must have been a strange kind of discipline instilled into the folks of this town, not to want to touch all this machinery.

Once the convoy had been refreshed and resupplied, we got it back on the road again. The rest of the route seemed pretty much easy going as far as the terrain was concerned. Lioma local militia told us that there was a small band of about 20 Renamo operating between here and Gurué, but they had not been seen for a week or more. However, their information was not to be taken at face value, so I was still very much on my guard. And that was just as well, because as we got about ten miles out of Lioma, the convoy came under attack ...

The story now continues with the events described in Chapter 1.

5

COVERING FIRE

As the laughter died down, Jimmy started to pull up his fatigues, and things were deadly serious once more. This was no time to look back on all that had happened since I first got to Mozambique — I had to live in the here and now. Everyone had to switch back on. It was a no-duff situation for sure.

After Jimmy's moon, the men settled down a bit, as did our nerves. They seemed to have enjoyed themselves; for most of them, it was the first taste of real action. They were pretty pleased, and rightly. They had performed well on their first contact, which had shown Renamo in no uncertain terms that these SF soldiers were not going to take any shit, and if attacked would retaliate with a massive display of firepower.

On approach to our final destination, the terrain had been slowly changing after the ambush. The track had become more hilly and the going a lot harder on the trucks. The landscape all around was turning more green. It was a sign that we were nearing civilisation. Suddenly the lead BTR stopped. I estimated that we were about three miles outside of Gurué. Both Jimmy and I got out of the Land Rover and walked up to the BTR. The rest of the troops stayed put and acted like they were playing the game for real. Only the hitchhikers got off their vehicles and mingled round, in anticipation of doing another runner into the bush. Surprisingly they had been pretty quiet since the ambush. I had not heard of any reports of casualties amongst them.

'What the fuck's up now?' Jimmy sounded irritated about stopping on what was pretty much the sort of open ground we had travelled across so far.

'Shit knows, but one thing's for sure. I ain't hanging around here too long. We're standing out like a big bag of red things.'

The radio crackled into life. It was Brad wanting to know what was the hold up. Jimmy put him straight and said he didn't know, but was 'sure as shit' going to find out.

As the dust settled I could see that the track ran straight ahead for about a mile, dipping about half way, then it rose up again and disappeared over the horizon. In the distance I could make out what had to be Gurué. I could see no buildings, but there seemed to be vast stretches of cultivation, which I took to be the tea plantations.

The troops and locals seemed to know where they were and were getting really excited. It was late afternoon, we had made good time. The sun was still up but a light welcoming wind blew across us. For the first time I could remember, I felt quite cold. Whether it was because it was cooler up there, or whether my body had just released all the tension it had built up over the past 12 hours or so, I couldn't decide.

'What's up? Why have we stopped? Who gave the order?' Jimmy shouted to the commander of the BTR.

'See the dip over there, Mr Jimmy?' The commander was pointing down along the track. His voice sounded stressed.

'Yeah. What about it? Gurué's just over the ridge, aye?'

'Yes, Mr Jimmy, I know, but this area ahead of us is where Renamo lay mines. Look, you can see the holes.'

He was right. There were a few holes caused by previously exploded mines and what looked like the remains of an old car. Renamo would normally lay more live mines in the old holes, since this would save them digging time — they could do the job in a couple of minutes and be gone. I got on the radio and told Brad and Josh of the possible mine clearance task ahead. They retorted that they were both coming up to see.

The area either side of the track looked relatively even, so the possibility of driving across country, thus avoiding this snag, was considered by Jimmy and myself. Then the other two turned up and joined in the debate.

Those troops designated as guards were off their vehicles and lying down, watching our flanks and rear, whilst the four of us plus two of the officers continued to debate tactics. The engines were ordered to be switched off and the rest of the troops were ordered down from the vehicles, to 'take five'.

It was during this Chinese Parliament, as all of us pointed in the direction we reckoned would be the best way to avoid the possibility of mines, that a roar of human voices suddenly came from the direction of Gurué. It was a tribal sound, one I associated in my mind with how Zulus might have sounded when they attacked at Rorke's Drift — an aggressive, spine-tingling sound. Then we heard a tracked vehicle coming from the same direction, and all we could do was wait for this 'thing' to break the horizon. I felt tension start to creep back. My thoughts tumbled over each other. Is this Renamo's main mechanised battalion? How many are they? What tanks do they have? What have we got to take them on with? Similar speculation must have seized the rest of the team. This was potentially the most threatening situation I had encountered since entering Mozambique. I was scared but not shaking, knowing we had a good unit behind us; anyway, if the shit did hit the fan, we could always do a runner. There were plenty of escape routes in the immediate vicinity.

At this time, we still had no idea where the population of Gurué was. The locals' usual routine was to disappear into the hills during the night. In the morning those who had to go back into town for whatever reason did so; then, before last light, they would take off to the hills again. An HF radio link was sometimes established between Gurué and Cuamba, but at the best of times this was hit and miss. Since there had been no way of establishing radio contact with the town whilst en route, we had no idea who was actually now controlling the town.

Meanwhile the sounds of the 'Zulu' chant and the tracked vehicle were getting louder with every passing second, but still nothing had broken over the horizon. It was an incredible feeling, waiting to see the first sign of movement atop the ridge. Brad had a quick talk with the force's captain.

'Captain! I want some kind of rapid movement of hardware up here ASAP, and I mean RAPID!' Brad was not a happy bear.

The captain did not reply — he merely obeyed.

There was a lot of shouting, and a couple of the vehicles started up and were reversing slightly. Where we had stopped the track was still very much single lane, giving little chance of manoeuvring the vehicles quickly if the need arose. Panic amongst the freeloaders was beginning to set in and as I looked around, most were ready for the 'off' again. This was not helping my nerves, either.

Brad had organised the two 20mm cannons to be up front, to line up alongside the BTR. The rest of the trucks were now slowly reversing out of sight. The force was organised in all-round defence, since the risk of being hit from behind and caught in a pincer-like movement was something we all wanted to avoid. This whole process took just a couple of minutes. Amazingly, it was difficult to persuade the hitchhikers to get out of the way. They seemed as keen as we were to discover what was heading our way.

A slight breeze started blowing directly towards us, bringing the approaching noise closer. It wouldn't be long before it broke the ridge.

'I spoke to the Captain. He says he's never heard of tanks or BRTs being stationed up in the town,' Brad said to no one in particular, indicating Gurué with his thumb.

As the four of us stood waiting, I realised how absurd this situation might seem to an observer. We certainly would have failed if this had been an exercise back home in the Brecon Beacons. We were not as ready as we should have been. We had no cover from view and, at that moment, no cover from fire either. Just observing, listening, waiting. The thought that this could be my last stand really did pass through my mind, and I started to worry about all the 'what ifs', all the things back home I should have made time for; particularly spending more time with my daughter. Should have done this, should have done that. Then I snapped myself back into the real world. *No way* was I going to die today! I gripped my rifle tightly, immediately got into cover and found a good firing position. I was now in overdrive, all my senses up. I checked the ground to my front, left, right and rear, and took notice of possible fire positions — and covered escape routes, should I need to crawl away.

Jimmy was close to me, going through his routine. It was as if, at a given time, a silent order had been given and we were all obeying it. Brad and Josh were doing exactly the same. They were working in pairs as well, on the opposite side to us.

Jimmy had grabbed an RPG 7 and a couple of rounds from the back of the Land Rover and was now making it ready. I went through my usual weapons and kit check. That was OK.

My actions were robotic. I constantly looked all around me for any signs that might affect the next few moments of my life, identifying positions of safety to move to, should we come under fire. I was also making myself aware of where the rest of the men were. Mind and body were in total overdrive. Sweat was pissing down the insides of my fatigues, and I felt a damp patch building up at the base of my spine as I moved my body from side to side. At least wearing a hat helped to soak up some of the sweat dripping off my face. It infuriated me, how much I sweated in situations like this, but it was something I had got used to over the years.

A burst of adrenalin ripped through me, making my body shudder. Wet through from all the sweat, I suddenly felt as if I was freezing. For a brief moment a tingling sensation erupted in my head then was gone. I felt warm again, aware that the sun was now beating down on my back. I felt confident I could take on anything. I didn't feel scared. I felt no fear. All of this happened within two seconds. Then I noted a slight grating noise from one mag when the spring was depressed, caused by tiny particles of dust inside the mag. Experience told me that it was nothing to worry about. I pushed the ejected round back into the top of the mag and pulled it slightly back with the tip of my thumb. Four tracer rounds, my usual selection, were on top and the first one out was on the left-hand side. This told me that I had a full mag and hadn't lost any. I snapped the mags back on to the rifle and released the working parts, happy with the noise the working parts made as they went forward under spring pressure. I picked up the first round from the mag, locked it in position and rechecked the safety, plus the rear and fore sights.

Lastly, I took the magazine off again and made sure that a round had indeed fed into the chamber. It had! I noted that the top round was now on the right, then snapped the mag back on to the weapon and gave it one last shake, just to make sure that it was secured in place. I also checked that the lengths of masking tape which bound them both together, and the tape which prevented the bottoms of the mags from dropping out, were all in good order.

All the time I kept an eye on the ridge line, still sweating buckets. I had taken cover behind a huge brown sandstone-type rock, and now shifted my position to make myself as comfortable as one can in a situation like this.

I didn't have long to wait. Figures broke the ridge line off to one side of the track, followed almost immediately by a large tracked vehicle.

'What the fuck's that?' Jimmy grunted.

'It looks like some kind of JCB! Can you see who they are?'

'Looks like a right ragged bunch of fuckers.'

My weapon was still held steady. The target was well out of range for most of us, but not for 20mms. Movement broke out to my left as the gun crews adjusted their positions and took aim at the oncoming horde. I could see no weapons as yet, but they were still bellowing their menacing war chant. This was the first time I'd encountered this kind of battle approach. I just imagined what it must have been like to be up against the British in previous battles, when the Jocks marched forward under the noise of the bagpipes. The enemy must have wondered, Who are these crazy fuckers coming towards us without rifles? I was having similar thoughts now!

Still they came, still they chanted, still we could not make out if they were armed or not. As they got nearer, about 1000 metres distant, it became plain that the tracked vehicle was a road grader, a kind of large JCB without a bucket on the front, it was used to level off tracks or roads before tarmac was laid. Behind it was that chanting mass of people, coming forward all the time.

Jimmy and I were still talking tactics when all of a sudden the war cries stopped and the grader and the mob behind it halted. Then there was an uproar. All the troops started cheering and shouting out to 'the enemy'. Jimmy and I looked at each other, worried looks on our faces, not sure if this was for real. Was it a staged ploy by Renamo or what? I'd learnt over the years never to take things at face value, especially in war; things have a habit of kicking you right in the balls when you least expect it. The entire team's attitude was never take the easy way out, so we stayed down while the troops around us carried on their cross-track screaming.

'Mr Steve, Mr Steve! This is our welcoming party! The townsfolk have come out to greet us,' the captain shouted across to me.

'How's that, Captain?'

'I got them on the radio. It's all clear. The town is all clear, the grader is clearing the route for possible mines. I've just spoken to Eugene, the Provincial Commander, he's an old friend of mine. He says it's all clear.' The Captain sounded positively jubilant.

The troops around us were cheering. It was the first time I had witnessed so much happiness coming from these guys. Everyone was getting well excited. Nonetheless, I stayed pretty much where I was, and so did the rest of the team. What I could not figure was why any of the force hadn't told us that they had a HF radio channel on which they could call up the town's commander? Well, it didn't matter now. Anyway, lots of things had happened during this contract which we had not been informed about. I put this down as just one more.

Slowly the grader made its way towards us. Brad gave the order that none of the troops was to go forward until the grader had cleared the route. Many of the civvies made their way across the fields, keeping well clear of the track, and I saw some of the crowd following the grader cut across the fields to greet our hitchhikers. The warlike chant (as it had earlier seemed to me) had now all but ceased. Both crowds were now singing and calling out to each other. If ever there was a hint of a party in the air, it was now. Our troops stood their ground with great restraint, I could feel it. They obviously wanted to break ranks and run forward to join in, but were still switched on, lying prone behind vehicles and rocks and still holding their fire positions. Every now and then some would get up and stretch, but they were swiftly ordered to get down again.

Brad had heard a rather bizarre (but probably bullshit) rumour about this chap Eugene, Mayor of Gurué, from one of the many briefings he had attended with the Frelimo commanders back at Cuamba. There were many accounts apparently, but the best one was about when he, the Mayor, and two of his militia men, supposedly held off an 'almost certain' attack from Renamo by shooting dead two Renamo 'spies' who had come into the town at night on a recce. He then supposedly cut off their heads and put them on spikes at the entrance to the town, to say to Renamo that this was what would happen if they attacked. Well, Renamo didn't attack that particular time, so Eugene was a hero in the eyes of his people. The people of Gurué were not really that bright anyway, most of them were illiterate tea-pickers who would believe anything this self-styled hero told them. Later, when Renamo constantly attacked the people of Gurué *after* this event, Eugene would always have a credible answer for them, even while they waited up in the hills as Renamo trashed their homes below.

From this tale we Brits formed our opinion of him. It might not be right to assess a person without actually meeting them, but we did; he was a complete arsehole, we decided. With that in mind, we all stayed pretty much under cover until the grader reached us. Even then, Jimmy and I didn't take part in the initial introductions to the townsfolk until we were completely satisfied that it was not a set-up.

By now it was very hard to determine what was what because everyone was patting everyone else on the back,

shaking hands, excitedly exchanging pleasantries. If this wasn't
a set-up, then these militia men who had come to mine-clear
the last part of our journey and to greet us like this were brave
fuckers. Funny there was no sign of Mr Mayor, though!

At this moment the grader turned on its axis and faced
back towards the town. On all four sides sheets of ten-
millimetre steel had been welded in place as mine-blast
protection — even the driver perched high up had steel-
plate protection. It looked like a huge World War I tank
painted a rusty canary-yellow. It really did the job, though.
Unlike a conventional mechanised mine-clearance vehicle,
which would have large flails — a bit like the cylindrical
cutting blades on a combined harvester — this machine only
had a metal contraption welded on to the dozer blade. This
would be scraped along the ground to detonate any mines
before the tracks of the grader reached them. It looked as if
it ought to work, especially as there had been no intelligence
that Renamo had ever used anti-tank mines, only anti-
personnel ones.*

Any possible detonation damage would have been contained
around the armoured blade. In fact, on the few occasions when
the grader *had* made contact with a mine, this is exactly what
had happened.

The convoy followed the grader until we were waved on by
its operator. Most of our hitchhikers had made their own way
into town so we arrived in Gurué looking like the military
unit we were, and not like a circus.

---

*These were very small, containing only about ten grams of PE. Their aim was
threefold: one, not kill but severely injure a victim, thus requiring two other people
to look after the casualty; two, tie up the enemy's medical support; and three, add to
the demoralisation of the enemy.

We were the first friendly force to make it through Gurué in over 12 months.

It was early evening. Hundreds of people turned out in welcome and we were treated as if we were real liberators. The scene of all these people cheering and waving flags was very moving. We felt like VIPs.

For me personally, it was also a very humble experience to be greeted in this way. Having gone through each of the last 30 minutes thinking that it just might be my last on this planet; once again wondering if I was ever to see my daughter again; and now, experiencing this frenzied, party-like atmosphere, emotionally I was in bits as we drove into town.

Women, children, the rest of the towns militia men, you name it, all were out in force. I imagined how the Allied troops must have felt when they rode into the towns and cities of occupied France at the end of World War II. It was a feeling I had never experienced before and don't think I ever will again. I couldn't even compare it to the feeling I had when I was one of the first troops to walk into Port Stanley, capital of the Falklands Islands, as a victorious paratrooper, before the official surrender, back in 1982. Then, the feeling of victory was one of relief — relief that it was all over. There were no jubilant crowds to meet us — they were locked away under house arrest, their fate still undecided. All there was then was a greyness in the air, death, and a battered, demoralised and defeated army. For me it felt like an empty victory, unlike the sensations I experienced now in Gurué. These people had been cut off from civilisation for almost a year. The odd aircraft flying in onto a make-shift airstrip to deliver vital supplies was the only friendly visit they had to look forward to. We were definitely a contrast to their other 'visitors'. When Renamo appeared, causing the people of Gurué to flee, they would crap in their homes and steal what little property was there. No wonder that the townspeople were happy to see us. As we drove along I wondered whether they believed we were here to save them. I had a suspicion they thought we were!

6

TEA ATTACK

Gurué is a brilliantly colourful town sitting on a vast plateau surrounded by thousands of acres of tea plantations. The hues of the trees and shrubs, and the views, are breathtaking; the different shades of green from the variety of shrubs mixed with the browns and reds of the trees made the place a definite setting for an artist's Garden of Eden.

This was especially so when we rode into the town this particular evening. The sun was slowly setting and its rays reflected off the tea bushes, as though the entire plantation was covered in a huge sheet of tin-foil. Very spectacular at the time, but I don't want to sound self-indulgent — like most of the wonderful locations I have served in, its beauty was soon forgotten due to the pressing circumstances of the operation.

The town was very like Cuamba, with old colonial-style villas. As we approached it, I saw for the first time what exactly tea 'on the bush' looked like — quite honestly, it was as ordinary as your suburban privet! The track cut through this plantation was only about one-vehicle wide. There was a one-and-a-half metre bank either side of it, and the tea bushes literally started on top of these then stretched out as far as one could see to the right and left. We were now on rising ground, leading to a summit where the town was.

Once inside Gurué we approached what looked like the centre, a large paved square with a make-shift wooden stage in the middle. On top, I sensed, would be Eugene. I was right. He was dressed in a very loud *Hawaii Five O* disco shirt, surrounded by a dozen or so of his armed militia men. As he stood up all the townsfolk stopped their cheering and waited in anticipation for what was obviously going to be a stunt for his benefit. Then both officers in charge of the Special Forces marched up to greet him. It was comical. They came to attention and saluted. Eugene saluted back. Then hugs and kisses were exchanged and they turned to face us, the convoy. Most of our troops had dismounted, including Jimmy and myself. However, we both stood close by the Land Rover, fearing our personal kit might go missing if we left it and moved forward.

A five-minute speech ensued followed by more cheering, back-patting and, once again, ego-stroking. We had to show our respect, too — after all, Eugene was the main man here and obviously commanded the respect of the town. No point in pissing him off at the start, even though our opinion of him was less than high.

He greeted us 'Specialists' one at a time, shaking hands and introducing himself as the Mayor and 'Protector of the People'. He seemed genuinely pleased to see us. What's more, he spoke very good English: That's a plus, I remember thinking. He was a big lump, about 6 feet 4, 18 stone and 40-ish. Not fat exactly, but not well-built either. I couldn't help thinking of the similarity between him and Idi Amin — the colourful shirts and the grin as wide as the Victoria Falls.

A lot of things happened in the following two hours, which was all the time we had before night fell. We organised the securing of the town by identifying sentry positions at the only three routes in and out, then secured the trucks and posted guards on them as well, tried to sort out some kind of intelligence on recent Renamo movements, and finally found a place to crash for the night.

For a town that had been on its own and out on such a limb, its people — and it was not for the first time I had experienced this in Mozambique — seemed quite matter-of-fact about their predicament. They were surprisingly organised, too. Eugene earned some brownie points off us, as he had sorted out a nice clean, well-secured villa for our stay, large enough for each team member to have his own room. It had hot and cold water, furniture, plus our own dedicated cook and two militia men to stand guard. Eugene had even fixed up a field telephone which ran down to his own villa, which doubled up as his operations centre, so that in the event of an attack we would — hopefully — get some kind of prior warning.

After sorting out the troops and driving around to familiarise ourselves with the towns layout, I decided it was time to get cleaned up, sort my weapons out, have a good scratch around and a pick of the nose, roll out the green maggot (sleeping bag) and get some shut eye. I was totally knackered. The journey up would have been stressful enough in peace-time, let alone during a war. But my idea of turning in early that night was not to be. We had been invited to a local bar for 'drinks' with Eugene and a few of the town's dignitaries. The invitation came through on the phone, as crisp a line as any British Telecom connection. Dress was to be civvies, but with guns carried if preferred. An unusual option if in normal circumstances, but then, Dodge City had fuck all on this place. I packed my pistol plus two mags. The rest of the team did the same.

Needless to say, there was no electricity at night. Come to think of it, there was no electricity during the day, either! So all the unloading of food, fuel and the rest of the supplies was done in relative darkness. The only sources of light were portable lanterns powered by petrol generators, which were only turned on during an emergency, as a rule. Fortunately tonight was deemed, if not an emergency, at least essential. Indeed, it *was* essential to have a quick unloading operation, getting all the kit off the wagons and into storage.

The petrol, which was stored in huge underground tanks, was at a premium. Everything that had a value was secretly cached. The shelves of every shop I peered in were empty. In fact, the locals did have stores, but they weren't kept in obvious places. The first time Renamo came in, they only slightly trashed the supplies they could not carry with them. After that, all surviving stores were taken away and secretly cached. It was just luck that Renamo attacked merely as a small force and stayed just for a couple of hours, otherwise

Gurué would have been short of essential supplies and wouldn't have been able to hold out for as long as it did.

There was probably some tactical reasoning behind Renamo's actions. Perhaps they saw Gurué as a soft target and realised that they could enter the town at their own discretion. So trashing their only source for a resup for miles around, especially food supplies, wouldn't have been, in the long term, the most sensible of tactics. Their most recent incursion, and their longest occupation, had been just a couple of weeks back, when they stayed for three days. This was enough time for them to find many of the cache sites, so when we arrived the town was down to its last bean.

We took two Land Rovers down to the RV at a bar called Bar Café Café. Our 20mm cannon had been off-loaded earlier, so Jimmy whizzed around the town, driving more casually than before. The roads were in good nick, large pot-holes appearing only now and then. Probably the lack of any form of transport using them in the last 20 or so years was one reason for their good state of repair. Many of the holes had been made by AP mines scattered by Renamo and detonated by the locals, more times than not by a child.

When we pulled up outside, Bar Café Café looked dead, but a faint glow could be seen through one of the curtains. It was a two-storey mid-terrace set-up, a single door with a window either side of it. The top two windows each had a balcony and once had had French-style shutters either side of them. These were long since gone, probably cut up for firewood. The brick had been painted in pastel green while the windows and door were a puce sort of colour, faded through years of neglect.

Then the door opened and we were beckoned in

surreptitiously, as if it was some illegal drinking and gambling joint. Inside were about ten locals, men and women, and, of course, Eugene, holding court at the bar with a couple of pretty young girls. It was a large place, to the left was half-a-dozen odd tables and chairs, and to the right was a small bar. At the back was a dancefloor arrangement flanked by doors: one toilet and one exit, I presumed. The room was lit by candles and the whole place had an eerie, sinister feel about it. I reckoned in its day it had probably been the 'in place', but tonight it smelt musty and used. More importantly, I noticed that the bar had no drinks, in fact, there was no sign of alcohol. Some invitation!

Beer eventually arrived, but it was the stock we had brought up for our own consumption — Jimmy had to go back and get it from our villa. That night we drank our entire stock of beer for four days between the lot of us. It worked out about three bottles apiece. It was just as well Jimmy didn't bring the team's emergency rations of two bottles of Johnny Walker as well. The night was a sober one, but I have never liked drinking with a loaded piece on me at the best of times.

Two days later an Old Antanov flown by good old Uri brought in supplies. If there was a beer resup on board, we didn't get to hear about it, since unloading was carried out by Eugene's men alone. We didn't even know there was an aircraft due in until we heard the unmistakable drone of its engines one morning.

On the outskirts of the town lay six tea-refining factories (called Upees — the word doesn't seem to have a specific meaning — and numbered 1 to 6), of which only two, Upee 4 and Upee 6, hadn't been sabotaged beyond repair by Renamo up to that time. These refineries, each covering about half the size of a soccer field, stood a single storey high. Very roughly covered in corrugated sheeting, they reminded me of very large Nissen huts. They were fitted out with pretty basic threshing machinery powered by electricity; each refinery had its own back-up generator should the primary generator fail, which happened more often than not.

Come first light the following morning, before half of the troops could be stood down, all of us conducted a search to clear these two working factories before anything else would be attempted. If there was one thing sure to happen during our short stay, it would be a contact staged by Renamo, if not directly at us, then at an innocent local, just to let us know that they were watching and waiting for us on our return journey. This was in the forefront of our minds. Unfortunately it was beginning to become obvious that the force did not seem to think the way we did. Discipline had begun to break down almost as soon as we entered Gurué. Drivers of the wagons had been carrying liquid gold, and they knew it — petrol. Fuel started to go missing, and other vital supplies for the town — and, of course, more importantly for us, for the journey home — also 'got misplaced'.

The troops might have liked to stay out here but we sure as hell didn't. So our major problem was containing the alarming fuel wastage. To make matters worse, a couple of fights started amongst the force, put down to the illegal siphoning off and selling of fuel. Officers and men alike had been trading, and the disciplined force we had trained so hard was now turning into a rabble. Something had to be done about this — fighting Renamo was not fundamentally a problem, serious though it was, but fighting between our own troops was wholly unacceptable. What's more, we felt responsible, since we had trained them.

The trouble was that these men had not really been let loose for over three months. Now they saw an opportunity to make a bit of money or to get something to make their existence a little more bearable, so I could see how easy it was for them to fuck around. I didn't agree with it, but I could understand it. A few were reprimanded, but this didn't help matters because one of the officers had been a main mover in the fuel details. Eventually it was decided that all the vehicles were to be driven out to the two Upees, leaving only the two BRTs in the town. Of course, our Land Rovers were driven out of town as well, and we made sure that we had enough fuel to cover any eventuality if the shit should hit the fan.

Jimmy and I opted to cover Upee 6, the more isolated of the two, with 30 troops. Whereas the other Upees were near to the town and had four or more entry and exit points via roads, plus many options to 'bug out' should an attacking Renamo force overrun it, Upee 6 was the furthest from the town, in the hills with only one dirt track leading up to it, and offered very limited 'bug out' routes. Furthermore, because of its location, it had become the most frequently attacked.

Upee 4 had 30 more troops under their own command. Josh and Brad would arrange that the local militia set up defensive positions around the town and acted as a roving patrol between all three positions, should Renamo decide to attack the town instead.

We were in constant radio communications with both locations and established a daily routine. During the day we would leave a skeleton guard-force at the two Upees to oversee the loading of the tea, whilst the rest of us carried out mobile patrols of the area, split between lying up in town for rest. At night all of us would man the positions and await possible attack.

Jimmy and I would place our troops in a typical British defensive position. The troops had dug their own trenches and were given their arcs of fire; trenches positioned so that these interlocked, thus covering all the ground around Upee 6. We also had the 20mm cannon mounted on the Land Rover which was located between Jimmy and myself.

The first night passed without incident. One problem was that half the troops either fell asleep whilst on stag or, worse, they vanished to go shagging in town, not returning until the morning. Another was that most of them now had civilian clothes under their uniforms, so that at the first sign of trouble they could strip off their uniforms and run off into the bush as civilians. This was very worrying.

So, come day two, we briefed one of the officers and the interpreter, who were loyal to the cause, to get a grip of their men and prevent a repeat performance. During that day, however, the fuel problem started up again. The force commander rounded up two of the ringleaders and had them publicly flogged. This seemed to do the trick. By the third night, Jimmy and I had our full complement of troops back in their relevant trenches, but nothing would stop them from falling asleep. It proved essential to creep round in the dead of night making sure that the troops were staying quiet and 'on guard'.

It was at around four in the morning of this particular day that we heard small arms fire coming from the direction of Upee 4. Crucially, the radio went dead for some time after the initial shots. That meant we didn't know whether Upee 4 was being attacked for real, or whether the troops there were shooting at 'ghosts'. Our answer came an hour later, when *we* came under attack.

A stream of tracer came towards us from out of the bush,

pinging off the highest points, the metal structures of the factory, and ripping through its corrugated tin sides. Sparks of light, caused by incoming rounds impacting and then ricocheting off those metal elements, showered all around us. Fortunately the attackers were firing way too high, and undeterred we returned fire back into the bush. Now the whole place erupted with the sound of small arms and RPG7 rounds exploding everywhere. My AKM was performing well and I fired off a couple of bursts to a position where I had seen the unmistakable muzzle-flash of an AK47. Next moment I switched my fire to a position some ten feet to the left, let rip with a few more rounds, then immediately switched back to the first position. Because we were in a semi-static position, every time I put a burst into the bush I got back down and came up firing from a different position.

This tactic normally works well when you have quite a lot of open cover to move around in. You can fire, go to ground, move maybe ten feet, then fire again. It prevents your head getting taken off should the enemy have his weapon trained on where you went to ground, waiting for you to rear your ugly head once more. I had only two or three possible positions to choose from, which allowed me to move just a few feet every time I fired. Still, this wasn't too much of a problem because my troops were putting down so much suppressive fire that only Rambo himself would have dared return fire.

I took stock of my situation, got down into cover and changed mags, and at the same time briefly looked across to make eye contact with Jimmy, who was still firing. Then I glanced further down the line of troops. Many, having left their original fire positions, were now standing up, jumping around, screaming and firing from the hip. It was total chaos.

Then the firing began to die down. I could see two of our troops preparing to fire a couple of RPGs, but they looked amateurish and panicky, so I screamed over to them to get a grip. At that moment they fired. An overwhelming *whooshing* sound filled the whole area. Jimmy and I watched as both rounds were fired almost simultaneously. One hit a tree somewhere in front of us, bounced off and exploded into a huge fireball, causing the bush to erupt and the ground around the point of impact to shudder. The vegetation caught light instantaneously as the high explosives detonated. The other round cut through the bush, narrowly missing some big trees, and exploded with a loud *crump* about 300 metres away.

The gun battle lasted for about five minutes, but it took both myself and Jimmy several more minutes after the initial contact to rally the troops into some kind of order and stop them from firing. They'd got out of their trenches, which could have been a very bad move. The whole point of 'digging in' was containment, to hold the ground you were supposed to be defending. By leaving the trench you make a break in the defence position's arcs of fire, thus (in theory) allowing the enemy to break through at a point not covered by fire.

Renamo had wanted to know what state of alertness we were in, and I think they got the message — our troops certainly knew how to turn bullets into empty cases. The volley of fire put down reminded me, in some ways, of the battle for Goose Green in the Falklands. To be fair, although our troops left their positions, they still fired in the right direction, i.e. away from Jimmy and me and outwards into the bush. Given the circumstances, that was as much as we could really have asked of them.

After getting a grip on the guys and putting them back

down in their trenches, I found that we had no casualties. This was good news, because we had very limited combat medical kits. Two field dressings were all that the troops had been issued with, and I was sure that most had used them for other purposes, such as firelighters or something to bargain with.

When first light came, Josh and Brad drove out of town to see how we all were. At the same time we put out patrols towards the general direction of the attack. It was at this stage that Upee 4 came back under attack. Josh had been talking to the local militia commander, who reckoned that the Renamo force numbered only about ten, so with that little piece of unconfirmed intelligence, we all got into vehicles and screamed off to Upee 4, leaving just the roving patrols and a static guard at Upee 6. It was a bit of a risk leaving all the trucks with the men, but actually there was nowhere for them to go if they did have any ideas of doing a runner. Their best bet was to remain calm and hope that the local militia's intelligence was good, and that this attacking group was not part of a bigger force. Brad decided that all the team should stick together on this occasion, and I was very glad of that!

It took us ten minutes to get to Upee 4, where the gun battle was still very much in evidence. It was difficult to work out how much enemy fire was being directed at it because there was so much firepower being unloaded by our troops. It was like a scene out of the film *Full Metal Jacket* as we disembarked from the Land Rovers and took cover along the side of the track with bullets ripping up the ground all around. It didn't help that the area on both sides of the track was densely overgrown with creepers, the odd tree and those infernal bastard bushes.

Upee 4 was now 30 metres up ahead. At the time I didn't

know if it was our own troops firing at us or the enemy — rounds seemed to be coming from all over the place. It was a mad, uncontrolled contact but it seemed to have done the trick. However, it wasn't until 15 minutes after our arrival, that Josh managed to get the officer at Upee 4 on the radio to tell him to stop firing, causing peace to fall on us at last.

Only when the firing stopped did we make our way warily up the track, taking cover behind the Land Rovers and the APC, firing the odd burst into the bush just to make sure no Renamo heroes were still alive.

Miraculously, our troops had suffered very few injuries at either Upee, the worst being a soldier who had two of his fingers on his left hand shot off. As regards the enemy, our troops recovered three bodies from the bush at Upee 4 and five from Upee 6, and also located a couple of blood trails. The men were ecstatic. So were all the townsfolk of Gurué; once again we were given a heroes' welcome and that evening they threw a big party for us. It was a nice gesture, but my mind was on a possible counter-attack that night and the journey back to Cuamba the following day.

By mid-morning we were on our way home. The grader had been out very early doing its stuff, and Eugene had ordered part of the militia to stand guard over the cleared track. Now, things had a habit of turning out very strangely on this job. Sometimes things you asked to be done never happened, other times things that you would never have expected to happen, did. This route clearance was an example. We hadn't asked for it to be cleared because it might have come across to Eugene that we were telling him to do his job, and that in turn might have caused him (or one or more personalities under his command) to lose face — never a good thing. Since we would be returning in the near future, we didn't want to piss off the next welcoming party by making any requests now that might be misinterpreted. So the clearing that morning was a pleasant surprise. What lay further down the track, however, was anyone's guess!

As it happened, the return journey was largely uneventful: no contacts, no flat tyres and no internal dramas between the troops, their officers or us. For my part, I was happy that the villages we had passed through on the outward journey hadn't been visited by Renamo in our absence.

Back in Cuamba, the tea convoys were now ordered to run about once every two weeks. During this period another selection course into the Special Forces would start. Half the instructors were soldiers we had selected as good men during the course. These would then form the backbone of the training wing, the idea being that within a year the entire unit would be self-sufficient.

I like to think that Renamo had had its arse kicked on our first contact and that the training we had given the Special Forces had not been in vain. If they'd learnt only one tactic from us, it was this: against an enemy such as Renamo, he who puts down a massive amount of firepower in the enemy's general direction will undoubtedly be the victor.

I was now nearing the end of my three-month tour and thinking about what going home would mean. Although I liked the people of Mozambique, and I had made a lot of friends there, I was keen to get back and sort the rest of my life out. Having spent so long dealing with other people's problems, it was time I paid attention to my own. I realised I hadn't thought of Lynn or even my daughter, Emma, all that much, and it scared me to think of what lay in store back in UK. In some bizarre way I had felt secure in this insecure African country; there were no problems here of mortgages, telephone bills or keeping up with the Joneses. No Sunday trips to the local trading estate to buy that prepacked wardrobe you dreaded putting up, just to appease your better half, or shopping at the superstore wondering if four loaves of bread were enough for the weekend. These are the only types of problem most of us face in the West. How mundane and how boringly conditioned some people are, I thought. I don't want that just now. In truth, I didn't really want to return home just yet! If it hadn't been for Emma, I probably would've gone walkabout around Africa.

Later, as the Dornier took off, I looked down at the town of Cuamba and all its people with some sadness. Having given serious thought to returning home, I was now happy to be leaving. My time here had been an experience of how the other half really live. I considered myself lucky having a British passport, which allowed me so much freedom. The people below were doomed to a life of poverty, famine and war, unless their government got a grip of the situation.

People can slag the UK off as much as they like, but one has to see and experience first-hand total poverty in a country such as Mozambique to get the other side of the picture. Mozambique was definitely an eye opener for me. Not even whilst I was serving in the Regiment all over the world had I come across such inhumanity.

I sat back on the inevitable sacks of cashew nuts with a headful of theme tunes. The heat inside the aircraft was not as bad as it had seemed when I had flown in, since I was now very much acclimatised. That didn't stop me sweating, however.

I started to nod off into one of those uncomfortable, half-awake-half-asleep naps. It was a mixture of a release of nervous tension, knowing that I was leaving a war zone (a feeling I used to experience when choppered back to Hereford after an operation overseas), and just plain tiredness.

Suddenly I woke and sat up sharply. My body was tense and ready but my brain was still in sleep mode. I thought a burst of 7.62 had ripped into the aircraft's fuselage and thudded into the sacks I was sitting on. I turned to look up front. My face must have been a picture when I eyeballed Henry's. I realised a split second later what he had done — he'd thrown a handful of the nuts at me, catching me smack on my face either to wake me up or just to needle me. Now he turned away and put his machine into ballistic mode for some unknown reason, climbing to about 10,000 feet. Then, looking back at me with a friendly grin, he said, 'Sorry about that, Mr Steve! I hope you still have your balls to do some fucky fucky with your wife when you get back to England.'

It never ceased to amaze me how little these people valued life, or how blasé they were about living or dying, even when they were as well-off as Henry. He knew all too well that the SOPs for taking off at Cuamba was to get as much height between us and the ground as the physical capabilities of the aircraft would allow, to avoid being a target for the roaming bands of Renamo, but once settled on his flight-path he would descend to an untactical height. Why? I can't think of any other reason than just pure boredom.

My imagined close brush with death and the image of a crash landing and the possibilities of an E and E in the wilderness below, sharply reminded me of the short letter I had received from Lynn telling me that she had moved out of my house and had gone to live with her new boyfriend, and how the situation I was in had tied my hands, halting reaction to this news. It was totally frustrating.

My mind was doing flick-flacks back and forth from inside the aircraft to my home-life predicament, wondering whether she had ripped me off for all my worldly possessions. Had she car-booted or smashed up all of my record collection in a fit of pique? I'd have to get a good lawyer if either proved the case.

I moved up behind Henry, pushed his headset to one side and said, 'Henry, just fly the plane, OK, and let *me* worry about my sex life!'

Some months later when I was back in the UK, a friend phoned to tell me that a documentary about Mozambique was due to be shown later that evening. To my amusement it was the one made by the film crew who'd visited us. They'd actually made a very good documentary. It seemed very strange reliving those hectic moments at a remove, sitting in an old armchair with a mug of tea!

PART TWO

Power tends to corrupt,
and absolute power corrupts absolutely.

Lord Acton, 1834-1902

7

THE LONDON SCENE

In civvy street, no matter how many bags of war stories you have, how many life-threatening situations you have found yourself in over the years, or how physically tough you think you are, one thing is certain — you don't get any brownie points for walking around town with your ugly head on. By that, I mean that no ex-service personnel should think that this country owes them a living just because he or she has fought for Queen and Country. There are a lot of hidden agendas outside the Services, and you have to adapt pretty fast if you want to survive. I've come to think that it's a lot to do with *who* you know rather than *what* you know. This is especially the case in one aspect of the Security Industry, the field of bodyguarding, or 'BG' as it's known.

There are a few powerful people around running BG contracts who haven't got a clue about the basic principles of their *own* personal security, let alone the knowledge to run a full BG team — and good luck to them, that's life. I'm talking, of course, from past experience and to those people who have yet to tread the streets of the BG world. My advice to ex-service personnel, and to guys from a similar background to mine, is to play down your experiences during a job interview and simply to look and listen, if and when you're lucky enough to get contracted onto a BG team. That means be on your guard for a full backstabbing session, and if you start to voice critical opinions about basic tactical procedures which aren't being adhered to, or about the everyday running of the job, be prepared to get kicked off the job.

In fact, in the case of the latter I'm not talking from personal experience, just relating what I have seen happen to many good guys who, unfortunately, have opened their big fat gobs and said what they genuinely thought of a particular tactic used, or suggested a better way some task should be carried out. It all boils down to a game of bluff, keeping quiet and juggling with people's personalities. It's not something that's taught on a live-firing exercise in the Brecon Beacons, that's for sure! To be frank, my *modus operandi* is never to educate anyone; if they say they can do the job well, I just wait and see, and don't even comment if they can't. I leave that up to someone else, or until they are seen to fuck themselves up.

I'm sure that not every ex-member of the Armed Forces would agree with me, but this was certainly the case as far as I was concerned. Unfortunately, it took a couple of years to get my brain around all this jockeying-for-position stuff, but I was lucky that I had a mate who had been around the BG circuit for many years, who pointed out the pitfalls of such work if I voiced my opinion.

Naturally I kept myself to myself a lot of the time. Anyone who has served in the Armed Forces will be aware of the 'Buddy Buddy' system, where you always look out for your mates because their lives and yours generally depend on watching out for each other. But for some reason, with a lot of service personnel, this approach seems to get handed back when they leave, along with their rifle and uniform.

Those of us who get out of the Armed Services to do something different with our lives have to learn to adopt a less brash attitude in order to achieve our aims. Some do, but a lot don't. Those who don't end up in large organisations which are very like that they have just left, where decision-making is in the hands of their superiors. That works well for some, but for me that was not a challenge, it was the easy way out.

Of course, this attitude was easy for me to take. I had no one to support, apart from Emma. (I don't say that in a nonchalant manner. Emma was living with her mother and was being brought up in a very stable home.) Yes, I had the everyday bills to pay like the rest, but after everything had been taken into account, I still had a pocketful of beer tokens. This gave me the freedom to explore other avenues and a breathing space to allow me to select the right profession. So that's what I decided to do once the Mozambique contract was over.

Select the right profession! This was wishful thinking — all I'd ever known was soldiering and security. When I really stopped to think about it, there was nothing else I was good at, or even had the inclination to do. It seemed I was doomed to be in the security industry, one way or another, for the rest of my life. If this was to be the case, then I was determined to learn all

I could about it: from working in the field (which was all I had ever done to date) to learning about the managerial and accounting skills needed to bring in contracts and run a successful business. This was the challenge I set myself.

Twenty-two, South Audley Street, Mayfair, London — aptly abbreviated to 22 SAS (not all that covert an address, I had to admit) — was where I started, the offices of the (now late) Sir David Stirling, founder of the SAS. I had met Sir David on many occasions, whilst working for his small but select company then called KAS, which stood for KA Stirling, so named, I believe, after Sir David's brother. Sir David (DS was how we referred to him) was truly a great man, and for me to give this accolade to an officer meant that I really thought he was the exception to the rule. My first-ever encounter with this living legend was when I was summoned to his Chelsea apartment to be formally introduced. Summoned was probably too strong a word — it was Dai, his aide-de-camp, who said I best visit him.

'He always likes to meet new members of the team, especially if they are ex-SAS,' Dai had said to me over the phone. 'No great dramas. Just come suited and booted. About midday should be fine, the old man will be up then.'

I had known Dai back in the Regiment. He had been attached to Regimental HQ as a clerk. A real nice guy, softly spoken and pleasant with it. I could see how he was the right man to be an aide to someone like DS.

I arrived at noon on the dot. Dai was there to usher me into the lounge where DS was sitting. All I could see was the back of a man's head sticking up from behind a high-backed armchair. I was nervous, but also felt honoured to meet this man. The room seemed fairly small and everywhere, scattered on small side-tables and the floor, were files and sheets of A4 paper. There were a few prints on the walls, but nothing to suggest that the occupant was from a military background.

'Excuse me, sir, Mr Devereux is here to see you,' Dai said in a loud but gentle tone.

A gruff, assertive voice answered from behind the armchair. 'Good, good, now leave us to it, Dai, there's a good chap. Oh! Dai, bring our guest some wine; white.'

During my time I have met many an officer and, in general, they seem always to bluff their way through life, whether in or out of the services. Many a time I have been to Remembrance Day and other military parades where I have seen high-ranking officers with a chestful of medals leading the parade and have wondered, How many members of the public actually know about medals? If they see a chestful of medals on an officer, they probably think, 'What a brave bastard,' without realising that most medals are awarded for service in a non-operational environment. Because that's how it is. The majority of medals are awarded for a job well done, not for acts of bravery. Sure, some are awarded for heroic deeds, but most aren't. For example, if you were a butcher attached to the Guards you might be awarded a MID for doing a good job. Contrary to what many civilians might think, an MID is not necessarily an award for storming a gun position against all odds, though, of course, it *could* be.

However, once in a while, it seems to me, a good Rupert comes along whose chestful of medals is a more accurate reflection of his valour. The military history books are full of DS's stubborn actions and unconventional methods — unconventional as far as the Army was concerned. His forcefulness paid off when he persuaded his superiors during the early days of World War II to go against the grain and got the go-ahead to form a new army unit, the SAS, which he used to full effect in daring, successful raids against Rommel deep in the North African desert. The SAS's history during the desert campaign inspired many of us when we found ourselves pitched up against the likes of Saddam Hussein during the Gulf War. The hit-and-run tactics we used were not dissimilar to those DS had used 50-odd years earlier.

DS had had his fair share of confinement, too. His stay at, and eventual escape from, the notorious German prison camp Colditz is well documented. It was a great shame that the powers that be in this country only decided to acknowledge this great man's many achievements by awarding him a knighthood a mere six months before his death in 1990. I thought that was an absolute disgrace on the part of past British Governments.

Why he wasn't knighted sooner was something I couldn't initially understand, but I was told — and this was the consensus among people I met who had known him for many years — that shortly after World War II he had told a few home truths to people in power, pissing them off. This voicing of opinion carried through subsequent governments. On top of that, there were rumours that he was secretly involved with the tragic Desert One operation of 1979, when the US mounted an operation to go into Iran to take back their hostages, but compromised themselves in Iran by crashing a C130 into one of their own helicopters. I guess that didn't help DS's case either. One thing I did know was that he didn't like to be addressed as Sir David, as a result of the knighthood. That was the kind of man he was. Nonetheless, I and the rest of the guys always addressed him as Sir, simply out of great respect.

On several of my visits to him he would be holding court with many a famous person. He would always introduce me and bring me into the conversation, as he would do with any member of his regiment, ex or serving. I met John Paul Getty during one of my visits, and when I had to drop some papers around to DS late one night I bumped into Sandy Gall, the famous newsreader and war correspondent. Another time, I was sharing a late-morning glass of wine with DS (which he forced me to accept, I have never been one for drinking during the working day, and *certainly* not before midday if I can help it) when the then Director of Special Forces popped around for a chat. Those of us lucky enough to meet DS were left in no doubt that he was definitely a 'soldier's soldier'.

KAS employed ex-SAS and Special Forces men on what seemed, on the surface, to be all sorts of exciting and dangerous missions. However, when I was asked to join, the company seemed to be in a state of confusion. Many of the dozen or so employees were cutting their own deals for contracts which were still being serviced by the Company. I had the feeling that I had joined a sinking ship. Did DS know what was actually happening to his company? I didn't know, and as the new boy, I opted just to look and listen.

The core of the KAS's business was anti-poaching work on the salmon rivers of Scotland. Other jobs were small and short-term. For example, it had a contract to supply a Swiss jewellery firm with bodyguards to protect their wares when its staff came to show them at one of the big London hotels, such as Claridges, or to individual clients such as the Sultan of Brunei in his penthouse suite in Park Lane.

There were many of these types of contracts, but they only

came in twice or maybe three times a year, and then only during the summer months. The anti-poaching contract was not a great payer, not big enough even to pay the rent on our Mayfair offices, let alone the guys, and not one person was dedicatedly out there chasing new business. Anyway, aside from the anti-poaching contract (which kept four of the guys away from the office for a couple of months at a time, unaware of the internal political struggle the rest of us were going through) there was only one other large ongoing job. This was to do with a London nightclub, Pinks. The job was new to the company, a bit like myself, and I found myself in the middle of it all. Acting as Operations Manager for KAS, I was thrown very much in at the deep end.

I have never really been one for rank or titles, I take people as I find them, but I did understand the need for the client (or *potential* client) to have a point of contact within the company whose services he or she was paying for. However, for a lot of the guys in the office on a daily basis, this didn't seem a particular concern. Anyone would pick up the phone and take a call. This would cause two things: one, the message would frequently not reach the person for whom it was meant; and two, the actual or prospective client would be very bemused as to how the company conducted its business. I know we missed out on a hell of a lot of contracts because of this basic lack of office procedure.

I sometimes wondered how the client perceived all this. Did he think, because he was dealing with a company run by ex-SAS men, that such an unconventional way of carrying on was a 'front' and that we knew exactly what we were doing? I suspect the answer was Yes, since a lot of the time this approach actually worked, but when it *didn't*, it was normally me who had to smooth things over with the clients, sorting out whatever cock-ups had occurred in the office. During this time I regularly felt that the only reason I had been put in as Ops Manager was to be a whipping boy, rather than as a guy who could and *would* do the job, whilst everyone else was cutting their own deal.

The blokes who I worked with were definitely the ones you'd want on your side in the SAS or on similar operations outside that required maximum physical force, should the shit hit the fan, but perhaps the successful transition from operations in the 'field' to the minefields of commerce and business practice was beyond some of them.

An example of how an almost certain long-term security contract was lost through the bad passage of information and blind ignorance occurred when the late billionaire Jimmy Goldsmith invited the company to do a security survey on his UK mansion (Ormerley Lodge in the Home Counties) and his massive ranch in Mexico. The survey on both went very well, and we were soon in the throes of signing the contract to run Mr Goldsmith's private security requirements for the Mexico location. This was to be a long-term contract worth millions, especially when we were asked to supply the equipment to complement the entire operation. So, of course, this is where it all went tits up.

A day before the contract was to be signed, one of Jimmy Goldsmith's executives on this project, had left strict instructions with me that *on no account* should the kit list and prices for the initial consignment of the communications equipment (all very special and worth a few hundred thousand pounds) be faxed to his office. This was not an unreasonable request, and was understandable for security reasons, too — someone might intercept it. He was to pick it up in person that afternoon. So I told Mark M, the signals expert, and he had no problem with it. But an hour or so later, one of the other company members asked why the comms requirements had not been faxed. Mark M logically said, 'For security reasons. Goldsmith's man is coming in to pick it up personally.'

It was an obvious statement, since we were all meant to be working for a specialist security company and knew the score; and the client was one of the world's wealthiest men.

However, that wasn't good enough for this particular guy. He faxed the document anyway — against my and Mark's serious objections. An hour or so later our contact was on the phone saying that he was very sorry, but that because of this breach of security KAS could not now be awarded this contract. It was as simple as that. A contract which would have put the company and its employees well on the road to financial success was lost because of one really basic security mistake. It never ceased to amaze me, the lack of security within this security company. One of the most frustrating things was that it was set up almost as an unofficial extension of the SAS. It was manned by ex-SAS members who were more than capable of successfully carrying out any SAS-style operations within the civilian world. If only the company had been run properly from the outset, it might have become a roaring success, providing an option for those members still serving to join when their times were up. But sadly I could see it wasn't likely to happen.

Over the next few weeks I must have upset a lot of the 'old and bold' as I tried to establish some kind of routine within the office, and some kind of accountability for everyone, especially where expenses were concerned. In recent years a ton of money had been going out on wages, equipment and expenses, and very little had been coming in. My feeling was that it might have been better for the boss man, an ex-SAS officer, to send the guys back home to Hereford and bring them down once a year for a pay rise!

I also thought that there had to be more to this company than met the eye. After all, how could it be financed when there was hardly any work coming in? This kept me wondering. Was this another one of these select security companies financed by the Government, to pick up jobs that the British Government could not be seen to be involved in, or indeed, to do its dirty work. It just *might* have been, but in reality I knew most of the guys, I had worked with them in the Regiment and I would have heard if this had been the case. The only secret you keep is the one you keep to yourself and don't tell anyone else about, and since there wasn't a lot going on in the office I didn't know about, I concluded that the company couldn't be one of those mysterious entities.

A contract which was easy to plan and administer, but which was screwed up, arose when a client who represented one of the ruling families in the Middle East came to the office with *his* client's problem.

The story was this. An Englishman who had worked for this particular sheikh as an adviser for some years had recently gone walkabout with over £200,000 in cash of the 'family's' money, and was now reputed to be living in the UK. The Sheikh's worst fear was that this so-called loyal employee of many years had done a runner, proving the old cliché, every man has his price. The client wanted us to source the whereabouts of this chap, follow him and build up a picture of his daily routine. I didn't get the full story as to why he had done a runner with the money; you never really do on these jobs, there's always a client's hidden agenda somewhere. I had the feeling that money

143

was not really the issue — more likely it had to do with the loss of face that explaining the theft to his family caused the Sheikh. After all, two hundred grand was not really a lot of money to these people. What probably preyed on the Sheikh's mind was his own bad judgement, and its repercussions.

The client had furnished me with up-to-date information needed to set up a surveillance operation: the man's passport details (the Sheikh had a photocopy of it) plus his CV; I was also given his last known UK addresses, a possible hideout in Germany, and an address in a Middle East country. Reading between the lines, I got the distinct impression the target was working for a business enemy of our client. He also supplied the target's passport number, photos of the target, the target's current vehicle and even a large cash advance — basically everything I needed to get a surveillance team up and running. In theory it was a doddle of a job, if, of course, the client's information was, as he said, only 24 hours old. Phase One of the operation was to identify and follow the target and report direct to the client ASAP if it seemed likely that he was going to visit his local BMW or Mercedes dealer. Phase Two could have come right out of a James Bond screenplay and, for sure, was highly illegal.

After we had found out where the target was, the client wanted a team to 'lift' him or spend time building up a picture of his movements and, if and when he was to show up back in the Middle East (a likely possibility the client thought), to formulate a plan basically to kidnap him, put him on a chopper and fly him out to a certain merchant vessel which would be hanging about the Gulf area somewhere. We were to supply all aspects of the contract, from the surveillance teams and equipment to the helicopter and its pilot.

On paper it was the ideal job; the company and everybody was up for it. We certainly had the skills and manpower to pull it off, that was never in doubt. This was exactly the style of operation we had all trained for in the SAS. Also, since the kidnap was to take place in 'friendly' territories, everything would be above board in legal terms (if there is such a phrase in this business), our client would fix that. The client had also said, 'What happens to the target once on board the vessel is not your concern.' That cleared the minds of any one of us who might have had moral thoughts about the target's fate.

I wrote up the meeting and got the ball rolling, sorting out a two-man team initially (Pete N and Tony D), which was what the budget allowed. For Phase One, there was no point in going over the top with manpower, saturating the ground with surveillance teams. I briefed them on what I thought was the best approach and pointed out the address where, the client thought, the target was the most likely to be at that moment — his parents' address in the UK, not far from London. As regards the rest of the intelligence from the client, in typical SAS fashion, the two-man team was left to do its own planning for the op.

Despite my tactical appraisal of the situation, they came up with the idea that the target would more likely now be keeping his head down at the German address. However, I respected the fact that Pete N had more years of SAS service under his belt than I did, and following the run of things, I had to let him get on with it.

'Well, it's gotta be the German option. No way would this jerk hang around his parents' basha. He'd be out on the piss and having a good time,' Pete chirped up.

'Yeah, and that's where we're heading for, too. We'll suss him out, even if we have to do all the clubs and pubs in Frankfurt,' Tony added.

'Well, that's down to you two. You know the score. It's a piss-easy job, so there's no need to rip the arse out of it, is there!' I left them to it, thinking that they were joking about Germany. But they weren't.

Contrary to the client's current information *and* my doubts, these two guys put themselves on the first available flight out to Frankfurt in hot pursuit.

My gut feeling was that the target was still in the UK and more than likely hiding out at his parents' address and I debated whether to follow this up or not. Late in the afternoon I made my decision; I was going to do a recce of that house. The thing was, I had to get one other guy to accompany me. It's a bit tricky doing this type of job on your own. It's not dangerous, but there are so many Neighbourhood Watch schemes now that it's always better to work in pairs. It helps make a cover story more plausible should the little old lady and her dog out for a walk, or whoever, take an interest in you.

Because of the 'little old lady' syndrome I always carried a couple of fake identity cards around with me, professionally sealed in plastic with a photo of me, making out that I was a sales rep for some made-up company. I would usually have this in full view on the dashboard of a nondescript Japanese saloon, and attached to it would be a chain so I could wear it around my neck, making my bluff that little bit more convincing.

I decided to give my brother Tom a call to see if he could knock off early and wanted to come along for the ride. Tom had never been on a surveillance and had no military background but you didn't need it on this job. The initial part of this surveillance was to stand off the target's parents' house and observe it briefly — for a few hours — to see if the target's vehicle was in the drive and whether there was any movement there, without causing suspicion. It's all basic common sense and very boring sitting in a car for hours, trying to look as inconspicuous as possible. Tom was up for it, keen to get out of his office and do something different. It took a couple of hours to get to the address, so by then, evening was drawing in. At the same time the other two guys were landing in Germany.

The area in which we had to work was a large cul-de-sac of 1920s mock-Tudor detached houses, each with a large sweeping gravel drive. The drives sported various vehicles, indicative of affluence: a Porsche 911 in one, a Jag in another, and a Rolls Royce in a third. Very much the stockbroker-belt style.

'Very nice, very nice, I wouldn't mind living around here,' Tom said.

'Fuck, this isn't for me! Shopping on Saturdays and the golf club on Sundays, talking a load of old bollocks with your neighbours over a very quaint dinner party — fuck no! Same shit different day, you can have this shite. I like a bit of spice in my life.'

As I retorted, I detected that Tom did not aspire to my way of life. We always have this type of conversation when we get bored and have nothing else left to say to each other.

Tom turned to face me. 'Let's just face it, Steve, your outlook on life is totally different from mine and everyone else's. The Falklands fucked you up, and as for the rest of this shit you do, call that a life?'

His comments made me rise to the bait, but at the same time I was still switched on trying to spot the target's vehicle without looking out of place to any possible onlooker.

'Yeah, right, you're right,' I replied sarcastically.

I wanted so much to say something, but instantly bit my lip as I spotted one of the reasons why we had come down here.

'Fucking *got* you!' I said out loud.

'You what?'

'The target's car. Don't look just yet, it's over there on the right. Three o'clock of me — we've just passed it. Quick, let me drive out. As we pass, see if you can spot any movement in the house.'

Our past conversation was forgotten, I could feel a rush of adrenalin about to come on. The target's car just happened to be in the drive. This was good news and a great first-time hit. I felt that Tom was beginning to enjoy a taste of this 'life that had fucked me up'. On any operation, big or small, it's always a good feeling when you get a result first time. It's like seeing that rod-tip almost bend in half and you know you've hooked a big fish. We were very lucky as this is not often the case. Of many such jobs, only on one other occasion had I picked up the target almost immediately.

There was some movement in the house but we couldn't eyeball the target, so we decided to stay, back off, and sit it out. We found a nondescript place in which to hold up and observe the cul-de-sac's comings and goings. It was not a particularly busy area apart from the junction with the main road, and, in fact, a regular flow of traffic along this helped us blend into the surroundings. We had an ideal lying up position and I was pretty sure that our man was here. It would be only a matter of time before we could confirm it.

I put a call through to the client and told him that I was in place, observing the house, and gave him the good news about the vehicle. He was really pleased and, like a lot clients who want surveillance and get immediate results, released a bit more information about the target. He said he usually caught the ferry after staying with his parents and was more than likely going to drive to Germany.

I often think that if the client is up-front with me in the first place about surveillance requirements and basic intelligence, then I could formulate a better game plan to achieve faster and more conclusive results, rather than having to think on my feet all the time. I don't mind doing that, but why hold back basic information that might be important to the success of the operation?

Fortunately, he didn't know that I had two guys on the ground in Frankfurt or he might have thought it strange, a waste of his money and unprofessional, sending two men there before checking the UK addresses. He was right, but at the time I was not strong enough in terms of authority to tell the German team to recce UK addresses first, since I was still finding my feet within the company. So I just let them get on with it, and after all, they were meant to be as experienced as me and know the score.

We carried on watching the house and vehicle, but nothing moved for some time. It was now getting late and Tom had to get up for work in the morning. As much as he wanted to stay, he had other commitments, so I had to pull off the job. At the same time I made contact with the German team and told them in no uncertain terms that I was doing their job because I had the target's vehicle in view and as there had been a lot of movement in the house, he was more than likely still there. Had *they* had any sightings? No. I asked them to pull off and resume the surveillance here in England as soon as possible, because I had to pull off.

I didn't explain to them the reasons why, and their request that I stay until they came to relieve me was a nightmare. I'd only come down on a hunch and was not prepared for the 12 or so hour wait until their arrival. I was ill prepared and would have probably compromised the job by not having a change of vehicle, at the very least.

On my way back to drop Tom off I got a call to say that the earliest the German team could get back was on a flight arriving at Heathrow at 07.00 hours the following morning. It would then be at least another three hours before they could get down to the location. The operation was beginning to turn into a big bag of rat shit. For a start I had to pull off the job to get back to London, *and* drop Tom off; that meant leaving the target with no cover for the duration of the night and early morning. Anything could happen during that time. It was unprofessional on my part to pull off, but this wasn't a life or death situation — I would have stayed had it been. This was no NI scenario, just a surveillance task fucked up by two blokes who should have known better.

So, the following morning I was at Heathrow to meet the German team and get them in place as soon as possible. The trouble was one of them arrived back drunk, having been pissing it up all night on the £300 float I had given him. What *more* could go wrong? There was no point in cross-examination now, but I had the feeling that these two were not taking the job seriously. I never worked out why. Maybe they just felt like going on the piss, I don't know. All I wanted them to do was what they were being paid for, and that was to go down and cover the target's vehicle ASAP. It took them over four hours (after doing a tea stop in the office!) to get down there, after which Pete phoned me at the office to tell me that the target's car had gone, presumably with the target driving (not that we ever found out). The entire job was blown and to top it all one of the guys later said, 'Let's get down to Dover port and see if we can pick him up.'

He really meant it, that was the worrying thing. I had just about had enough of this bullshit where people think they're still in the SAS, and believing somehow that they still had access to all the support elements and equipment to fall back on. I should have dropped him there and then but I didn't. What was the point? The guy knew he was a prick.

The ironic thing about this story is that the last I heard of this pissed-up guy, he'd got a job as a bodyguard with one of the most influential business men in the Far East — work *that* one out! And, of course, because the target got away, the client didn't get back to us for Phase Two.

The long and short of it all was that within several of months of my joining KAS, the company ceased trading. I didn't know the full story or indeed want to know. I'd learned one side of this business — how vital it was to know how to conduct oneself in the office environment. My time spent with KAS was a sometimes mystifying learning curve. Fortunately, I did get paid what was owed to me. Nothing unusual about that in the army, but in civvy street it's not always the same.

People not getting paid for work they have done is and has always been part of business. Shit happens, and it's no different in my industry. I would go as far as to say that it's worse than the building trade and, what's more, it's on the increase.

Quite recently I was introduced to a director of a large British-based airfreight company through a friend who wasn't connected with the security industry. This guy wanted to know if I could secretly find out what one of their competitors was up to, since his own company had just lost a lucrative contract to them from an overseas airline company, and he thought underhand wheeling and dealing was going on, or possibly a spy was operating inside his firm. He wanted it on the cheap but at least was going to pay cash.

I told him that I could have a go at getting info on the rival company (based at Heathrow) but there were no guarantees and I jokingly explained to him that while my industry was not like *The Professionals* and I don't always 'get the man', I was good at what I did. He took that on board. Because the contact was through a friend who vouched for this guy, I took a minimum advance on the job. The balance of £2,000 was, we agreed, to be paid after the operation; results or no results.

Generally I don't care how colourful their business card is, how fancy their address or how articulate they seem — I don't break the golden rule of this business, which is 50 per cent up-front when dealing with a new client. *But*, as a favour to my mate, I did this time — however, I made sure my minimum advance covered my time and any costs I might incur.

The following day I hired a white Transit van under a false name and driving licence, and half-filled it up with collapsible cardboard boxes I had scrounged off a mate working at a Park Lane hotel who was a supplier of packing boxes for a particular Arab family when they stayed there during their annual shopping spree. I then drove off to Heathrow with another old mate, One Punch Des as he was known because he was a bit handy with his fists. He got his nickname some years before during a Sunday afternoon riot with the Military Police in Aldershot Park. A load of us were just having a few cans and enjoying what was left of our R and R from Ireland when, without warning, half a dozen members of the mounted Military

Police Brigade decided to charge our position. We all bomb burst, but Des stood his ground and with one blinder of a punch landed square on a horse's head brought it down to its knees — and its rider got the same treatment as he fell to the ground.

On leaving 2 Para he had, until recently, worked for a major airline at Heathrow and knew the area like the back of his hand. He still had his ID and pass to get into certain areas of the airport, so with the aid of an electric security pass sealer I'd copied one up for myself, complete with a photo of me. He also lent me a set of his old company overalls, so I'd look the part.

Heathrow is OK if you're just there to catch a flight, but it's a pig's ear of a place if you're visiting one of the hundreds of companies servicing the airport. The industrial area where this particular concern was located stretched for miles, and you could quite easily spend half a day looking for any one name and the other half getting back to the M4, purely because of the volume of traffic coming in and out of it.

Des's local knowledge was invaluable. We drove straight to the company and did a drive past. It looked all normal, so within the hour we went back to target. It was a 1980s low block of offices with a contract security guard on the main gate. He let us pass after Des told him he was here to drop off some packing crates. Indeed, he wasn't too concerned and didn't notice as we drove past the main office entrance and pulled up behind the main building by the rubbish-bin bay, which to our luck was full. Any security cameras around? No. I opened the sliding door of the van and we loaded two of the four Biffa bins full of office trash in black bin-liners straight into the van. What we were doing was illegal, it was stealing. I wouldn't have liked to have ended up in court under a charge of stealing rubbish, *that* would have been a ridiculous charge to have on one's record.

Anyway, in about three minutes we were back at the security gate having a chat with the guard. When we told him that we would probably be back in a couple of hours, it prompted him to tell us that he would still be on duty, and he even volunteered that his shift change was not until 18.00 — six o'clock in layman's terms. This told us two things: one, as it was only eleven o'clock we had enough time to park out of the way, sit in the van and go through all the trash at our own pace; and two, the guard was probably ex-services or police since he was giving times out in the 24-hour-clock mode. It's a small thing, but you can build up a mental picture of someone by how they say things, and since I have a good working knowledge of the static guarding world, I can tell a lot about a company by the guard they employ. I was pretty sure that when we re-entered the premises, we only had to be polite and give him the impression that we were in a rush, just like most delivery drivers are. Like a lot of these guards, I felt he would want to chat away as much as a London taxi driver — because the job is so tedious, they positively crave conversation.

Having been given certain company names, employee names and dates to look out for, we worked like ferrets, opening binliners and putting to one side anything that might be of importance. We rummaged through dog ends, fag ash and half-eaten cheese and cucumber sandwiches; only one binliner contained what Des thought to be of any interest. I noticed he had stopped rummaging around and was reading something.

'What the frig have you got there — anything worth hanging on to?'

'Fuckin' damn right! Look at the size of these beauties. I love 'em all,' Des whispered.

He had found his true happiness. He was never short of a few cock magazines even when we were in the Paras together, and now it seemed he was no different. Des was perusing a well-read bumper edition of some porn mag.

'What bag did you get it from?'

'Not sure, I think it was from the one with all the sandwiches in. I bet it's a secretary's and I bet she's a les.'

'Hey Des, settle down will ya and give us a look!' I had a quick flick and chucked it back at him.

We retied the bags and went for the second pick-up. If what we were looking for wasn't in this load, we would be going back the next day. And as there was nothing in the second lot, that was just what we did.

In the first bag of the second morning we struck lucky — the names and a sheet of figures we had been looking for, even a copy of the contract bid from the company employing us. So it did seem that they had a mole. By now we also had a full intelligence scoop on this particular company; who was who, who was in charge of which departments. Nothing about who was shagging who, though! Still, recovering 20 or so pieces of useful information was a 'good hit', as we say in the business.

That evening I had arranged to meet with the client, for payment, in the Grapes Tavern, Shepherds Market, Mayfair. I showed him the information we'd got and he was impressed. As I put it all back in a carrier bag I expected him to make a move for his wallet. But he didn't. He said he would take the carrier and phone me tomorrow to arrange a meeting at his offices. That wasn't the deal as I read it, so I was beginning to get pissed off, and he knew it. I stood up and said, 'Let's take a trip around to the cash point.'

He wasn't keen to move but Des came over from the bar,

sensing he was in danger of not receiving his beer tokens for the day. He went straight for the jugular.

'Now listen, cunt, I'm not as patient or as articulate as old Steve here, but if you don't weigh us in I'll rip your arms off and beat you around the head with the soggy bits. Get my drift, fuck-face?'

'I think he means it,' I chipped in.

That was enough to persuade him that two cavemen outweigh a smooth talker. We frogmarched him to a bank on Curzon Street, just around the corner, where he drew out £1,000 on different cards. I took the money and kept the carrier bag, and told him to have the balance ready first thing in the morning. He wasn't happy, but a deal's a deal — I had delivered and I wasn't about to be fucked over by this dickhead.

It took me another two weeks to sort out trying to get paid. Even a trip to their offices, very plush premises just off Charing Cross Road, didn't do the job. I wasn't allowed past Reception. There was no need for me to kick up a stink about the situation — I knew what my next move was going to be. I just turned and walked away, found a post office and wrote an anonymous note to the MD of the company we'd done the job on. I explained what had gone on and who had instigated the affair and posted it first class, together with the contents of the carrier bag. It all went back to where it had come from two weeks earlier.

I gave the friend who had introduced me to this job a verbal bollocking, and next day by way of an apology he bought me a scoff at my favourite curry house, The Bombay, just behind Hyde Park Crescent, and handed over the outstanding balance out of his own pocket. Some weeks later I read an article in one of the tabloids headed along the lines of FREIGHT RIVALS IN

INDUSTRIAL ESPIONAGE PLOT, to the effect that these two particular companies were at 'pistols-at-ten-paces' with each other. Once again it just goes to prove that some people would have you over for the sake of a few quid, not realising the consequences for the big picture.

When one door closes, another opens. During the last weeks of KAS's life, when all manner of people came to the office to sort out the skeletons and pick on the bones of Sir David's boardroom and personal belongings, I met a man called Forester Darlington. He seemed to know a lot about Sir David's business and was keen to start up his own security company. I don't know if he had approached any of the other guys, but he asked me if I was prepared to work for him, basically doing what I had done before. Although he was definitely from the 'old school' of officers, a real ex-Rupert, he seemed an OK kind of guy. As I had no other plans, it seemed an opportunity I should take. I accepted his offer.

So Forester and I set up a new company, Cadogan Securities, based in Knightsbridge. The name didn't mean anything to me but I guess the thought behind it was that a specialist security company should have a name that didn't draw attention to its purpose. It was better than calling it SAS Limited or something.

The shareholders were all friends of Forester, a mixed bunch of very wealthy, middle-aged businessmen whom Forester had got to know during his time in the City. There were four of them, each with a 25 per cent stake in Cadogan: Forester; a banker from the Far East; a businessman who owned huge metal salvage factories in India; and another businessman who lived in the Cayman Islands. Apart from Forester, they didn't have a say in the day-to-day running of the company. They couldn't, living overseas. I presumed that Cadogan was one of many little businesses they held shares in. At the time I knew nothing about what shareholders or directors actually did. All I knew was how to be honest, work hard and do a good job for those who supported me. I was a bit naïve, back then.

Cadogan started off well. It took over the Pinks contract that KAS had somehow kept afloat and I expanded the company's involvement in it. This gay club had a problem, well at least the management at the time thought so. The problem was drugs along with rumours of all sorts of sordid sexual activities taking place on certain days of the week. The brief from the management was to find out exactly what was going on. So we mounted a long-term surveillance operation, inside and out, even putting one of our men in the club for eight months under the guise of Security Manager.

BS, a good mate, was the guy I needed for that job. He's a heavily set bloke, a real East Ender, one of the most loyal guys you could ever meet in this business. He's also pretty handy when it comes to 'dishing it out'! I knew he was the right man for the job, I only hoped he would take the position when I offered it.

BS had spent a lot of time overseas and after leaving the army worked mainly as a diver on oil rigs, but a bit of job stability was what he was really after. I told him I had a job in a London nightclub: flexi hours, no great heroics needed, acting low key was the order of the day. He jumped at it without even asking which club. He probably thought it was an up-market place like Stringfellows or Tramp! I guess he saw himself playing 'Mr Smoothie' with all the babes.

'Hey, Steve! Where's this club then? Annabels or what?' BS

eventually asked in his heavy East London accent. I had avoided giving him the name for as long as possible.

'Pinks.' I came straight out with it, matter-of-fact-like. That's all I said. It was all I had to say.

'That's a fucking queer club, mate. You gotta be fucking *joking*, for fuck's sake, they're all fucking queers!' BS has never been backward in coming forward.

'Only on certain nights,' I pointed out.

BS let rip with a string of obscenities, getting himself all worked up: 'How could you, my mate, even *think* of offering me the job? To think you had the nerve even to ask me!' Etc., etc.

I listened for a bit and then said, 'I take it that's a no then.' If he didn't want to do it, I said, there there was no problem. Secretly, though, I hoped he wouldn't turn it down. I needed this contract to work, especially since it was the first for Cadogan, and I knew that there was no one else from my background who could do half as good a job as BS would. When eventually I calmed him down, he reluctantly agreed to take it on.

'Listen mate, I'll give it a go, know what I mean, but if it's full of arse bandits every night then I'm fucking history, got it?'

'Hey, BS, relax, mate. You're always on about having a half-decent steady job so you can spend more time with Sue and the kids. Well, here it is. It's a doddle.'

'If it's a doddle, why don't *you* take it?'

'Because I don't *want* a half-decent steady job.'

'Yeah, like fuck you don't.'

'Hey, BS, you want it or not?'

'Yeah, I wannit.'

I was greatly relieved. Part of the deal with BS was that I had to visit him about once a fortnight, mainly on the gay nights when most of the drugs and shit went down. Not to hold his hand or anything, just to chew the fat and give him a bit of moral support. The immediate management didn't have a clue that I was working for their boss. They assumed that I was one of BS's straight friends who came and had a beer with him every now and then.

If you've never been into a gay club, you're missing something; it's well worth the entrance fee. I was amazed at the sorts you could find. There seemed to be two types. On the one hand, there are those who are just plain homosexual and, on the face of it, look no different from us straight men in dress and manner. They would sit up at the bar or in the lounge, talking to their mate and not really bothering to make conversation with others around, or get into the music that was always playing at the loudest possible level. (I don't mean to sound offensive to the gay community, it was just how I perceived the situation.) On the other hand, there are those who dress up in the most outrageous costumes and prance about like some failed 'background' artist, looking for attention. Complete nutters, I would think. Where the hell do they go home to, and what do they do for a living?

On one occasion, about four months into the job, I was talking to BS at the foot of the stairs to one of the bars when this old-looking black guy came prancing down the stairs, arms waving slowly and waiting for the crowd to acknowledge his entrance. He was dressed in a white wedding dress with a ten-foot train. Complete, over-the-top madness. He recognised BS and blew him a kiss. BS acknowledged with a 'Hi, Tina.'

I turned and looked at BS.

'It's alright, Steve, he's in here most Saturdays. He normally wears that dress.' I thought that BS was losing it. Maybe he had

had too much of this gay atmosphere.

Another memorable experience was witnessing what seemed to be one bloke getting stuck up another in full view of their mates. They hardly took any notice, like it was an every-night event. It happened in a small inner bar, where the biggest drug problem was.

This sort of thing would not be tolerated in any nightclub in the UK, and Pinks was no exception. Explicit reports were sent to the client. There's a time and a place for everything — consenting adults and all that — but it was too much to contemplate, even with my strong stomach.

During the eight months we had the contract, BS saw a lot of strange occurrences, including two separate robberies from the club safe, the biggest 'snatch' being £16,000 in cash. However, the contract finished when a new managing director took over.

I met with this new point of contact only once, when I was summoned to his office to explain just exactly why Cadogan was being paid all this money every month. In my opinion, this guy had a bit of an attitude problem. I tried to explain, but he wasn't having any of it. I guess he thought Pinks was just another nightclub. Sod you, I thought. We lost the contract. It was never awarded to any other company.

Over the following months I worked hard to understand the complexities of successfully bringing in business. Forester was keen, too, since he was taking some of the financial risks. Cadogan's set-up was small, all we had was a secretary. I, like Forester, worked five and sometimes six long days a week, when I would stay in a flat in Hertford Street. This was the size of a shoebox but being in the middle of Mayfair, it was very expensive. I chose this existence because I couldn't face the Tube journey back to suburbia that most people made each day.

I used to finish quite late, and by the time my day was over, my brain had been sucked dry of anything other than the desire to get a few beers down my neck. Even then, conversation was always about work, so it never stopped. At weekends I used to travel back to my house near Hereford and crash out. Very early Monday I was either driving up or travelling on the train. Some weekends work meant I never even made it home, as security contracts sometimes demanded that I stay up in London, just in case there was a problem. As in most BG jobs, the guys were employed as subcontractors and if you're not around to show a face, some start thinking they could do the job cheaper than the company employing them, and try to slip in between you and your client.

This happens a lot in the BG world, guys turning up on jobs with pockets full of business cards thinking that they can steal the job, but it's a short-term approach on their part. Often they end up fucking themselves, not the firm that gave them the job in the first place. Most jobs are seasonal, so the client–company relationship usually stands the pace until the next year, unless the company makes a humungous cock up.

Not all my work was BG. I had educated Forester (as if he didn't know already) that people from my background possess skills which are in demand, not only with individuals but with governments, too: the ability to procure any military equipment, and teach and train all aspects of a military operation, not necessarily just army ones. What's more, I had a personal portfolio of all sorts of highly skilled ex-service contacts: RAF fighter pilots; staff officers to give projects that seal of approval; communications experts. And if I didn't know someone with a certain skill, then I knew a man who did.

Forester agreed that we should spread our wings, giving the

company a much wider area in which to operate. My first main break came when I was approached, through a friend, by a guy claiming to represent one of the contestants for the rule of Liberia, a country on the west coast of Africa. At the time, 1991, it was experiencing a full-blown civil war. The two main fighting factions were busy chopping up both their country and their people into bits. My friend with the Liberian contact phoned and asked if we were interested in having a talk with the chap. I agreed, and some days later a guy under the name of Charles Von Douttenberg (which I later discovered was an assumed name) pitched up at the office.

He was mid-30s, fit-looking, with jet-black hair brushed back and held firmly in place by about two tons of gel and dressed in a well-tailored three-piece, double-breasted suit with a pocket handkerchief to match his tie, carrying a very expensive-looking light tan briefcase, the type top executives have, *and* a well packed out World War II ex-army hessian gas-mask bag. That threw my line of thought a bit; hardly an accessory I associated with the rest of his attire.

Without interrupting, I let him talk at length about what he wanted from us. He was very articulate, knowing a lot about Liberia and its internal problems. He said he had been over there in the past on 'other business' and had met and got on well with the now 'slightly' deposed leader. After an hour or so of trying to establish his credentials, he finally came to the point.

'Now listen, Steve, I'm sorry I've done all the talking. The fact of the matter is that I've been asked by the main man himself ...' (He raised his two index fingers either side of his head, like kids might do when trying to imitate a pair of rabbit ears, then bent them forward a couple of times, to mean that what he had been asked to do was through a friendly third party and was top secret. I gave him a minus mark in my mental file on him for that. Up until then he had been going great guns.) '... to stand by a team of SAS-trained guys just in case he needs a hot extraction from the field.'

I put another minus mark in his file for the American Vietnam War term — 'hot extraction'. A bit gung-ho and out of context for the meeting, it gave the impression that he had very little real tactical knowledge.

'Steve, does Cadogan have the expertise and ability to carry out such an operation?'

The answer was a simple Yes. It's what I and the people I work alongside are trained to do. It's no great drama for us, it's our job. The dramas come about when someone has to start parting with their money. A job like this, carried out by a team of professionals, never comes cheap, it never has and never will. Same as anything in business — you get what you pay for.

He wanted to know if we could mount an operation in the capital Monrovia to get the President's family out; not him, just his family. This all sounded very exciting, just the job for Cadogan. The sums of money he mentioned were huge, plus the benefits of any booty that this proposed 'snatch squad' could lay its hands on. At the time Monrovia was making big headlines, almost under fire from advancing forces and in danger of falling in a couple of weeks. Charles wondered whether we could we get a team together at very short notice, should the finance be in place. Of course.

One thing, though. I'd not quite made a judgement on this guy Charles. You see, anything can be done, but it can only be done at a price. Now, this operation was well risky. It would require a lot of planning and preparation, which meant time —

and that we didn't have much of. Men I could get at very short notice, that was no problem, but equipment and supplies were a different matter altogether. Still, if this man could get the cash — and we were talking a *large* sum of money — I was sure we could oblige. Just before the meeting came to a end, he asked me would I like to see $20,000 worth of Liberian currency, and he made a move on the gas mask bag. It was a strange request. I said, 'No, not really,' which, I think, blew him down a bit.

However, for all the superficially convincing things he said, I was not particularly interested in him at this stage. By now, I had met some extremely strange people in this business, and a lot of them turned out to be Chinese Knife Fighters with big ego problems. It was far too early for me to get cock-stands about an operation where my share of the profits would buy me a 60-foot Sunseeker yacht and provide the wherewithal to live happily ever after. I decided I would save my curiosity for the second meeting, scheduled for the next day.

For this, Charles arrived at the office bang on time in another expensive suit, but without the gas mask bag. We went to lunch over at the Grosvenor House Hotel. He paid, which was a good start, and we talked in greater detail about his proposition. The long and short of it all was that if we were to do something, I would have to get a guy on the ground to carry out a recce and to meet with the main man, ASAP.

This meant two things. One, it would show whether this operation had some 'legs' and whether his contacts were as good as he was making them out to be — Cadogan's man would confirm that. Two, that he was to finance the entire recce, up-front. Surprisingly, he agreed, saying that he had the sum of money I had asked for in cash; could we get on with things as soon as possible? He wanted to fly out to Liberia the following morning. (Actually, that wasn't possible. It would be at least two days before anyone could fly out.)

I agreed to all his requests, which weren't too numerous, and after 'banking' the cash, I called up an old ex-SAS mate of mine, Dave T, to confirm the job was a goer. I had touched base with him the night before to see if he was available for 'dodgy' fast-ball to accompany Charles on this fact-finding mission. Dave had said Yes.

So we were up and running. This was a real 'live' operation, and a very risky one, especially for Dave. All parties had been paid up-front. Unusual — but then, this was a *very* unusual operation.

The recce was to take about a week. When they had been gone three days, I still had not heard from Dave or Charles. The previous couple of days I had managed to gather as much info as I could on goings on in Liberia, so at least I had a working knowledge of the country's problems and would be able to discuss things with some degree of understanding on their return.

On the morning of the fourth day, I had just popped out of the office to grab a bite to eat from a local takeaway sandwich bar, when I saw Dave strolling towards me. On his own. No sign of Charles. I was gob-smacked.

'Jesus, Dave! You're back early! What happened? Where's Charles? Why didn't you give a call to let us know where you were?'

'The job's fucked! It was a total fucking *nightmare* from start to finish!'

I suggested we get a brew and a bit of scoff. Dave looked like he could do with a large injection of carbohydrates. I took him down to an Italian restaurant nearby for a debrief. He told me from the start how, when they boarded the 747 at Heathrow, there was only a skeleton crew aboard, all volunteers. The flight was to pick up the last ex-pats waiting to be evacuated at Monrovia airport.

'We basically had the whole fucking aircraft to ourselves,' he explained. 'I don't know who or what they thought we were. Idiots or MI6 or something, I guess. Anyway, the crew didn't quiz us, they sort of ignored us for the entire flight.'

Dave went on to tell how Charles had all these great get-rich-quick plans, and if we were successful the main man would be very generous, over and above our fee. On paper it looked the dog's bollocks of a contract. Dave went on: when they finally landed in Monrovia, Charles sorted out all their paperwork. He had, of course, been to Liberia many times before so at least Dave was not going in blind. Charles had pre-booked the hotel. Not many people pre-book hotel rooms in a city that's just about to have the shite bombed out of it!

They sat in the hotel for three days waiting to be seen by the main man. Dave said that being in Monrovia reminded him of how the Americans must have felt during the last days of the fall of Saigon in Vietnam. Almost by the hour, the sounds of battle seemed to get closer and closer. On the second day, Charles was trying like hell to get to see the 'man' but every time he was refused by his personal bodyguards. It appeared that Charles had no real clout with this guy at all. Meanwhile, Dave spent most of his time around the hotel swimming pool, kit packed, ready to bug out, as and when.

Should a rapid bug out be necessary, they had identified a couple of boats to commandeer for their escape. Dave was an accomplished yachtsman and said that there were many lovely-looking craft in the harbour, their owners gone by air long ago.

He also said that at the airport there were a lot of light aircraft, just parked up. To him they all looked airworthy but there was one problem — he couldn't fly!

Come the third day, the fighting was getting still closer. Too close for comfort so Dave opted for the IA (Immediate Action Drill), a rapid exit out of the country. By this time, Charles had lost all face in not being able to get the meeting jacked up and decided that getting out was his priority, too. Events had overtaken them far too quickly. Small arms fire was now being heard all around the capital. Soldiers, civilians and even kids were carrying weapons. In this desperate situation, they didn't have too many options. Rumour had it that the last commercial flight, an Air France 747, was due to land and turn around almost immediately that afternoon. At the time they had no idea where it was flying to; nor did they care. They managed to get on it just in time. Hours later the two rival factions fought each other to the death in the streets of Monrovia.

Dave had a lot of stories to tell about his time with Charles, some serious, some comical. He reckoned Charles meant well and that the job had actually been a goer, but they were overtaken by the events on the day. I asked Dave what he seriously thought about Charles.

'Well, on the flight back, all I wanted to do was to tell him to shut the fuck up, because I wanted to get my head down, I was so bollocked, but he kept on about how we could all make some money. He said that the "man" had a flat in Chelsea Harbour, London and that he knew the exact address. Charles said he had been there previously and that the "man" kept about eight million pounds in cash and jewels, in a safe, and that it was up for grabs since he was out of the country.'

'What did you say?'

'I told him, "That sounds great, but do me a favour first, go to the toilet, look in the mirror and give yourself a severe talking-to!"'

I never saw or heard of Mr Von Douttenberg again, although I did make some enquiries as to his previous history — just to log in the back of the brain for future reference, you understand. One lead I chased up (which in hindsight I should have done in the first place) was a business card Charles had given me from his recent, previous employer. It was a management company in London, quite a big one, too. I dialled the number. A lady answered and then put me through to a department. A moment's wait. Another lady answered. I asked if she could tell me a little bit about Mr Von Douttenberg.

'Is he still working for your company? If not do you have a telephone number where I could contact him?'

I detected a note of flirty amusement in her voice. 'I'm sorry. I'm not at liberty to disclose any information on present or past employees,' she said.

'But I have his business card, that's why I'm telephoning you, to see if he is there. I need to speak with him!'

She was very hesitant with her reply.

'Yes, Mr Von Douttenberg did work for the company for a short while, but I'm afraid he is no longer employed with us.'

Feeling that I was winning this voice over, I pushed her for a bit more information.

'Well, thanks very much for your time, you have been very kind.' I left a pause. 'Oh, just one last thing, would it be possible if you could tell me if he left on his own account or was he ..?' My curiosity was getting the better of me. '... or was he ... ?' I tried to think of a word more suitable than sacked. I stuttered, but no word came, '... was he sacked?'

'One second please,' she said.

She had cupped her end of the receiver but I could make out her talking to her female friend telling her that someone was on the line asking about Von Douttenberg. I heard giggles. She came back on.

'I'm sorry about that, I'm afraid I can't tell you any more than I have already. I'm so sorry, goodbye.' She hung up.

The tone of her answer was all I needed. I got the message. In my opinion, it was very plain that Mr Charles Von Douttenberg was seriously off his head. He's probably still out there, cutting around in his Armani suits impressing the arse off some other twat. God bless his little cotton socks!

8

THE ARAB
EXPERIENCE

D uring the Iraqi occupation of Kuwait in the early
1990s, many jobs came my way. One was sourcing vast
amounts of gas masks for the population of Saudi
Arabia. It seemed that Saddam Hussein in his wisdom might
have a go at all his Arab partners, one way or another, so the
Saudis, especially those close to the Kuwait and Iraqi border,
needed protection from a gas attack. This then became a
requirement for all of Saudi Arabia, since Saddam had the
ability to launch Scud missiles well inside the Kingdom. Every
man and his dog from Ankara in Turkey to Jakarta in
Indonesia, as well as Cadogan in London, was chasing the now
infamous gas mask deal.

The requirement was for three million masks with spare

filters, to be delivered immediately. It was a vast order and, potentially, there was a lot of money to be made even if we got just a small piece of the contract, so I started sorting out prices, checking availability and double-checking the specifications of certain models. I was in contact with some Russians who said that they could supply the latest military gas mask, the right quantity at the right price (whatever *that* was). I never actually got a quote from them, but in addition there were Danes who flew over especially with their samples, the Israelis with all their ex-army stock, and the Brits, who demanded an absolutely outrageous price for their old version of a particular mask that used to be issued to the British Armed Forces — the renowned S6 respirator — one of the best gas masks in the world at that time, later superceded by an even better version, the S10. I even sourced civvy masks from Korea. All the manufacturers had something to offer and were responsive to our requests, apart from the Brit who expected you to plead with them to return your calls with answers to your questions. I only experienced such arrogance from Brit companies.

My client contact was a Saudi Sheikh, their equivalent of a Royal, a Prince. I understood that there are hundreds of princes in Saudi Arabia but my contact was an HRH (His Royal Highness) and there aren't too many of *them* around. For most of the others, this applies:

Statement: 'I'm a Prince in my country.'

Reply: 'Not over here you aren't, mate!'

You have to know 'who is who' and once dealing with the right people, you also have to know, 'who *owns* who'. This was the biggest problem for all of us middlemen. Everyone thought they had the horse's cock of a client and no one else was in the running. It was like a game of poker. You stayed in the game as long as you could, or dared, trying to suss each opponent out to see if they actually had a better contact than yours or if you were actually sending your precious samples off to a competitor, thinking that they were the last in the long line of middlemen. Cloak and dagger stuff. Long-distance telephone calls were essential and some companies racked up bills of thousands of pounds chasing this deal. We did, too, about five grand's worth.

I guess greed was an important ingredient, we all thought we were going to make a killing. But, as I half expected in this 'what-the-fuck' business, the war took off at an astonishing pace, and the gas mask deal was dumped. Apparently, if the civvy population needed gas masks, the Americans would supply them. The client had played games with us, the dealers, and now no longer required us. The only winners were the telephone and airfreight companies.

Our contact in Saudi sent his apologies for not closing any of the deals. He did explain that his boss the Sheikh was the key player. I didn't doubt it — he sent one of his aides, from the Saudi Embassy in London, to the office with a cheque to cover all the 36 samples sent, and on top of that, had booked a table for four of us at Mr Kia's, an immensely prestigious Chinese restaurant in Mayfair. That night I ate and drank in style, but knowing that my 60-foot Sunseeker had once again set sail without me.

During this hectic time, I was also chasing other deals for Saudi Arabia: thousands of blankets sourced in the Far East; thousands of tents and battlefield kitchens for the UN who, apart from dealing with the refugee problems in the Gulf, were also working in and around the Kurdish regions of Northern Iraq. Once again, nothing was ever certain. I wasn't sure that our contacts were high enough in the chain of command, so I adopted a double-bluff policy of saying that we could meet and deliver under the requirement terms with a price that was well above what I knew I could get away with. In taking this stance I blew away all hangers-on who might have had their fingers in this particular pie. This worked well for a couple of deals, but it was getting increasingly difficult to keep a track of what was actually happening on the ground. Then the powers that be stepped in and dealt government to government, which in turn blew us middlemen away once more.

The illegal occupation of Kuwait by a million or so Iraqi troops was very much the talking point of the day. Newspapers were full of it, and most weekends when I was back in Hereford I saw that my mates who were still serving relished the thought of flying over into Iraq and getting stuck in. A part of me also wanted to get involved, and I pondered the lost opportunity of not going to war with these guys I had known for many years. Still, such thoughts only occurred briefly, and then only when I happened to meet up with them socially. To be honest, I was happy doing what I was doing. The notion of wanting to go off to war again was very shortsighted. War is shit, make no mistake about that, and war can get you killed no matter how glamorous and exciting the media make it appear. For the money you get, it just ain't worth it.

I had done my bit for Queen and Country many times and survived. This war was for those who hadn't experienced it in the past. If they had, then they would have had reservations about it. Yes, I was quite comfortable trying to make a living off the back of war, this time around.

One morning while I was in the office working on a proposal that might lead to equipping and training an Anti-Terrorist Force for one of the United Arab Emirates, I got a call from Tosh Ferris, another old para friend of mine who was working out of Saudi Arabia as an arms dealer. A good business to be in at the time. I hadn't seen Tosh for a couple of years since he moved away but we still kept in regular contact by phone. He said that he was in London with an 'Arab acquaintance'; could we meet for lunch? He suggested a meet in The Red Lion pub, Waverton Street.

Tosh and his Arab friend were already there up at the bar, a pint waiting for me. The other guy was a Mr Nassar Al-Khalhaif, a Kuwaiti who had recently escaped from his country. I took in his appearance: about mid-40s, greyish hair, quite tall, distinguished looking. Surprisingly, he was dressed in a suit and not in the Arab dish dash and yashmak, the traditional white one-piece gown and headgear. I hadn't got long to talk so I quickly finished my pint and arranged to meet them both later in Olivers, a downstairs bar on the corner of South Audley and Mount streets. There we would be able to talk discreetly about whatever they wanted to discuss — in fact, I'd adopted this bar as my second office. I gathered from Tosh's earlier conversation that he wanted me to do something with Mr Nassar Al-Khalhaif. I took it to be business of, shall we say, a delicate nature.

There were a lot of Arabs around London at this time, more so than usual, even though this was the traditional time for people from the Middle East to come on holiday. What's more, the Iraqi Embassy was just around the corner from the office and one never knew who was watching or listening in. Someone like Tosh arriving in the country with a Kuwaiti, whom I knew nothing about, and pitching up in the middle of Mayfair, might have attracted attention from certain agencies who might have been watching the area for 'known players' or 'suspect faces'.

It was always amusing to come out of the office at any time of the day and spot the 'Dick Dastardlies' waiting in cars, trying to look like chauffeurs and to blend into the ritzy setting in which they were trying to operate. Mayfair was, and still is, full of foreign security and private agents working on surveillance operations on anyone who was wearing a goatee, or who had a gold pen sticking out of their top pocket. It was a strange but exciting time. This part of London could easily have been a spies' training camp.

Once I bumped into an old friend walking down Curzon Street who I knew was still in the Regiment. We made eye contact but he turned away without acknowledging me, without doubt on a job. The last thing I wanted to do was to compromise him, or his operation, so I followed suit.

Tosh and I talked about old times and what each of us was up to now. I was wary of anything slightly Arab back then. Not because of prejudice but because I was still suffering from the large self-induced shot of 'Arab bollocks' over the gas mask deal and I was not particularly keen to repeat that kind of experience just to appease Tosh or his guest.

In business, many people can sit down with a prospective client and talk all kinds of shite. I couldn't and I still can't. To me, it's like a ritual that people get themselves tied up in. A lot of people just like to hear the sound of their own voice, telling the other person how great they are. They are basically ego-stroking each other until they both feel comfortable that each knows the other's weaknesses before they get down to talking about their real purpose. My style is more:

'Yes I can do it.'

'It will cost this much.'

'I can do it when you want.'

That's a rather simplistic way of putting it, but I tend to do a body swerve around all the other bollocks if I can.

Initially I was afraid that Tosh had introduced me to another Charles Von Douttenberg, and at that time, my time was at a premium. I was essentially a one-man band. Forester had no idea of the business he'd got himself involved in, and it was hard for him to work on this UAE project that needed my full attention because he knew nothing about the subject of Anti-Terrorism. So early on in the evening and out of earshot of the Kuwaiti, I had a quiet word with Tosh and asked him if he had made any money from any business the two of them had done. He said yes, lots of it; their particular contract was still ongoing and was worth well over two million American dollars. That was good enough for me. At least he was a player, not a time-waster.

I have known guys who've chased after wealth, especially Arab wealth. They have been wined and dined by them, experiencing the high-life only the very wealthy could afford, then been 'fucked off' at the airport when their use finally came to an end, never hearing from their contact again, and usually a lot worse off mentally and financially. Not even a *sniff* of a contract. So I was pretty cautious. Answering a question and then asking one.

Tosh had told him I was ex-SAS and that my mates were probably going to play a major part in the retaking of his country. Nassar seemed to like being associated with all this Special Forces talk, and in turn told me and Tosh how he had escaped from Kuwait with his family a couple of weeks after the Iraqi invasion. Taken at face value, Nassar was a nice guy, very articulate, with better English than most Brits I know. I immediately warmed to him. However, much to my concern, he openly came out with the fact that all his Kuwait bank accounts had been frozen due to the invasion.

Despite that, over the next few weeks I got to know Nassar pretty well. Tosh had gone back to Saudi but Nassar stayed in London. After all, he and his family, his wife and young son, had no country to go back to. They owned a large flat near Hyde Park and that was where he stayed. At least once a week he would call me up and we would arrange to meet up for a beer or play roulette at top London casinos such as Le Ambassadeurs Club, Palm Beach or The Rendezvous, then next to the Park Lane Hilton. He would play and I would watch. He couldn't have been that short of money with the amounts he gambled. When someone like me says they have no money, that's about the size of it. I might just have a few quid in my pocket. But when someone like Nassar says that, what he really means is that he is down to his last million or billion, you can never tell which.

Often when we met I would ask him about Kuwait and what he thought the outcome would be. He didn't really want to talk about it. I later found out why. He'd lost a brother in the first week of the invasion, the Iraqis had shot him dead. In fact, the Iraqis shot a lot of Kuwaitis dead for no special reason during their seven-month occupation. There were a lot of human tragedies happening there, most of which were never reported in the West and some still haven't been written about. I still find it hard to believe that even today there are well over 600 Kuwaitis being held prisoner in Iraqi jails — if you can call them that in and around Baghdad.

I learned a lot from Nassar, especially about the way Arabs are and how they conduct business. We all have this perception of back-handers openly being passed around for being awarded a certain contract or favour. This is their way, but it's not only the way of the Arabs. It's the way of many cultures, both in the Middle East and the Far East.

Here in the UK we still haven't learnt that. I think sometimes we Brits frown on this open method of winning business. Of course it's done, but it's done *under* rather than *over* the table. That's obvious — if you are caught 'on the take', then you're looked upon as some kind of villain. Why? I don't really know, because we all like cash every now and then. There is something excitingly sinister about the whole affair when you are handed a wad of vacuum-packed nifties in a brown envelope. It makes you think you've got one up on someone, or that you are getting something for free. But you haven't. It's just what you are owed. Nothing more, nothing less.

9

THE UAE AND THE GULF WAR

In early 1991 the anti-terrorist contract I had been pursuing so hard for months looked more likely to come to fruition. My contact, a well-connected (by family ties) serving officer in the UAE Armed Forces, had received a signal that I and one other (an ex-SAS officer) had been invited by the Government of the UAE to attend a series of meetings with their MOD to give a presentation of the project.

I knew the ex-SAS officer well. He was an old friend, but more than that, he was one of those rare officers who knew all the aspects of the anti-terrorist team task, from the ground level right up to talking turkey at ministerial level, since he had worked his way up through the ranks. Someone of high rank was very important to gain credibility with the UAE. In a game of poker, a Smith and Wesson will always beat four aces; just so, a colonel will beat a corporal. That's life, I know my place at the trough!

This was by far the most exciting piece of news I had received for a long time. To be officially invited by the Government was a giant step in the right direction. What's more, our company was the only one in the running. I'd heard that the client had two other prices from competitors but they were well over the top, even though the cost of my contract reached well into millions of pounds over the designated period, two years.

There are only a limited amount of guys trained in this particular field. They all happen to be ex-SAS/SBS men, and since they are few and far between, most are always in high demand. It's very hard to prise them out of their current employment without a firm offer of a contract. This was the problem for our competitors. They didn't really have the 'in' — a personal contact with these guys — as perhaps I did. Another factor was that our competitors would have no other option but to supply the exact same guys as I was. The client knew this, so he had a rough idea of the going rate that would entice them. Our edge was that we had small overheads and were very keen for the business.

I flew out and spent almost a month in a hotel waiting to give my presentation. Every day we would get a message to stand by to go to the MOD and every day it was eventually cancelled, and never before seven o'clock in the evening. The excuse was that the Minister was over in Saudi Arabia attending the Allied Forces War Cabinet. This was more than a pain in the arse because I could not venture very far from the hotel, just in case I got the call.

At one point I was invited to meet with the current Anti-Terrorist Team, the one we were hopefully going to train. In the past they had been trained by the Regiment, so when I got there I was greeted by the commander, a Brigadier, who introduced me to the team and went on to show me a complete demonstration and an equipment lay-out of all their kit. This was really interesting because it was very similar to what one would have seen back in Hereford, when it was demonstrated for VIPs and such like. As none of the other companies had been allowed this demonstration, I began to feel optimistic about the whole thing.

Meanwhile, however, things were really heating up. Every day the news carried speculative items concerning possible attacks on Iraq and there was talk of liberating Kuwait with a massive air and ground assault by the Coalition Forces. It was a strange time for me, sitting back in my hotel, watching the news, secretly knowing that my mates were probably on the ground carrying out intelligence-gathering operations. I had a gut feeling that the Regiment was working on the ground over in Iraq, but I couldn't be sure.

As the days passed, I was getting increasingly impatient about whether I was going to meet with the Ministers, since their priorities were becoming obvious. They had a possible war to fight and were probably not too interested in this contract at the moment. I'd asked the Ministry if I should come back at a later time rather than hang about waiting for a meeting that, in my opinion, was not going to take place. All I got back was the polite suggestion that I wasn't to leave the country. I took that to mean 'would not be allowed'. I believed that they were still very serious about the contract, however, it felt worrying that I was in some way held here in the Middle East. I was not too sure if it was against my will or not, and I didn't push the point. To a degree it made me feel important and gave some weight to the seriousness of their need for my services.

On the morning of 25 February 1991 I was told to keep the afternoon free; a car would be picking me up from my hotel. I had been called to give a full presentation of my contract to the 'Big Cheese', the UAE Armed Forces Minister — an unusual request in the sense that at all other times I'd been told 'not today, maybe tomorrow'. This got my mind in gear. This time I might get the chance to present my case.

The car picked me up on time and I was driven at speed through the city and into the MOD, met by an armed captain carrying a loaded H&K MP5, then escorted to the war bunker. Tight security had been commonplace since I had been 'in country', but today the security forces seemed to be in a higher state of alertness than normal. Hundreds of armed soldiers were running about the place. What they were up to was anyone's guess. I was almost expecting the air raid sirens to burst into life any moment. The last time I saw so many armed Arabs was in the film *Lawrence of Arabia*.

Inside the air-conditioned complex the usual military personnel were bustling around with an air of urgency. I was taken to an empty briefing room with a table that could seat 30 or so, a pencil and paper at each seat. There was a podium and screen to the front; no windows; food and soft drinks had been laid on. Very clinical.

I waited for about 20 minutes before UAE officers in combat uniform and other men in dish dashes started to fill the room. That gave me time to think what I was going to say. I'd had almost three weeks to get my presentation right but this little extra time was beginning to fill my stomach with anxiety. I tend to work off the back of a cigarette packet and make decisions on the hoof. All this pre-presentation stuff, I thought, hasn't done me any great favours. Then the Minister made his entrance, immaculately turned out as one would expect. All seated stood immediately, and I got the impression that he was life and death in this Emirate. So this was the main man. The man who, indirectly, had suggested I not leave the country for a bit. I immediately recognised him as the brother of an Arab prince I'd been bodyguarding a year earlier. The brother had a fantastic place in Knightsbridge and this guy had visited him on a couple of occasions. I'd no idea that this chap was indeed the brother of the Prince and realised I hadn't stopped to find out about this man. With so much to think about, contract detail and all that, I'd forgotten to research the main man; a very big mistake on my part if he recognised me.

I composed myself and started the presentation. Most of the time I addressed the Minister, wondering if he did recognise me. He didn't appear to, but then his mind must have been very full, with the pending Allied attack on Kuwait and Iraq.

I'd been told to keep the presentation down to about 40 minutes, which I did, though the question-and-answer session went on for another 40 or so. I gave it my best shot. I knew exactly what I was talking about, I felt confident, and certainly the Minister and his people seemed to be happy. Their questions, mainly tactical ones, were spot on and, surprisingly, there were no bone questions.

A couple of years earlier, when still in the SAS, I had given a similar presentation on the Anti-Terrorist Team, this time about demolitions and weapons to a group of visiting VIPs, government ministers and suchlike. I'd finished my talk and went into the usual routine of asking them if they had any questions. It all went quiet and I was thanked by the Armed

Forces Minister for an interesting talk and that, I thought, was that, when one of these 'chaps' came through with a real bone question. At first I thought he was joking, but as he was in the presence of his boss I realised he was deadly serious. He wanted to know what the trigger pressure was on my MP5. There is always at least one who has to hear his own voice. What a doughnut! I didn't have a *clue* what my trigger pressure was. I got out of it by saying that because I was heavy handed, it was 20 pounds. That got a laugh all round, and it came across as though this 'chap' shouldn't have asked the question in the first place. Unfortunately, I got the dagger look from the Brigadier. Hell, how was I to know? The question should have been fired at an armourer, not at someone whose only concern should be, 'Is this weapon reliable?' 'Does it go "Bang" when I squeeze the trigger?' and 'How many rounds can I fire through it before it starts to melt?'

Had I got the contract? I couldn't tell, but I knew it would be wishful thinking to expect some sort of positive response later that evening. In general, Arabs take an incredible amount of time to make up their minds on almost anything, in particular when they are parting with their well-earned *fluus* (Arabic for money), even when buying a pair of sandals.

All that was said was that a decision would be made very shortly and I was booked on the Emirates flight leaving later that night. It was all very abrupt and matter-of-fact, as though they wanted to get rid of me as soon as possible.

I was tamping! I knew they had a war to sort out, but I had spent *months* preparing for this pitch and it was all going tits up, big style. But there was frig all I could do. Shit happens, and here I was, part of it.

At about midnight we finally took off. On reflection, I was a bit sad to leave. I've always liked the Middle East and now wondered when I would return. At the same time, I was aware of a strange urge to be on the ground several hundred miles north of here.

'Bong.' Someone behind me had pushed the cabin crew button and a good-looking, black-haired stewardess hung over the back of my seat. Then I thought, No, this is a *much* better place to be, as I viewed her slim waist out of my peripheral vision.

'Can I have a glass of water, too, please?' I said.

'Yes, of course. Sparkling or still?'

'Still please, thanks.'

She was nice. Two minutes later she was back with my request.

On leaving the Emirates the aircraft was relatively empty, so I had a row of three seats to stretch out on. But a one-hour stopover in Dammam, Saudi Arabia, put a stop to that. There the plane filled up to capacity: mostly ex-pats, mainly Brits who had stayed as long as they dared in Saudi before they decided to put their sensible heads on and bug out of Saddam's main 'target area' pretty sharpish. Then a guy sat next to me. About 60-something, with a half-moon rump at least ten sizes too big for the seat, he was a huge man with thick red hair, sporting a rather large pimply boozer's nose on a face full of freckles.

'Alright, matey?'

'Yeah, fine thanks,' I replied, not sounding too distant.

As he sat down he cut one, a loud fart, without even batting an eyelid.

'Sorry, matey, it's all that lamb curry I had earlier.'

'No problems,' I muttered.

You dirty bastard, I thought. As I turned and look out of the window into the pitch black trying to hold my breath, he stuck a hand out to introduce himself.

'I'm Charlie but everyone calls me Geordie — from Newcastle, you see.'

'Steve. Pleased to meet you, Geordie.' As I took his hand, Geordie gave me a bear's grip of a handshake. It was an obvious macho move, to see who had the stronger grip. I let my hand go slack in his and with one last squeeze he let go. 'A man thing' for sure, it probably meant he felt he'd won this strength competition.

Geordie was alright for the first couple of minutes but soon I just wanted to tell him to 'wind his neck in'. He wouldn't stop talking. We hadn't even levelled out from our ascent, before I already knew his life story. I didn't think I could stand eight hours of this, it was worse than the interrogation phase of SAS selection.

I tried to nod in the right places as he droned on and then pretended to go to sleep but he kept nudging my elbow, not hard but in a friendly way; one of these 'touchy-feely' types. He had to be in your face all the time to make his point.

'Where have you come from, Steve?'

'Oh, err, all over.' Trying to sound bored.

'I've been all round the Emirates, fuckin' arse of a place. What business you in?'

'Contracts —'

He cut me short. 'Me, I'm in the construction industry. Put that fuckin' road in by Abu Dhabi airport, you know, the one that runs into the city, a while back. Shit, that was good money!'

You clever bastard, I thought, and all by yourself, I bet! He must have seen the dull look I gave him, because he grunted and changed the subject. I picked up the in-flight magazine, flicked through it and closed my eyes.

'A tax-free income was not worth getting a Scud up the jacksy for, and anyway, fuck the Arabs — I've had enough of 'em, dirty stinking ragheads ...' Geordie muttered to himself.

Flying has never been my favourite mode of transport and especially when the flight is packed solid. With not a spare seat to be had, and with 300 or so passengers on board and, from what I could see, a limited crew, this one had the makings of another flight from hell. We were five minutes into the flight when suddenly a voice came on the intercom. It was in Arabic at first, then the voice changed to English.

'Good morning, ladies and gentlemen, this is your captain speaking ...'

Then it went back to Arabic. Although the aircraft had levelled out and we seemed to have reached our cruising altitude, it was still quite noisy with the sounds of engine thrust, not to mention the racket of anxious passengers debating the Saddam situation. Suddenly those who understood Arabic gave loud sighs and the odd cry, which immediately heightened my and Geordie's awareness. This was obviously not the usual 'Have a safe trip' spiel from the captain. As I watched the air crew reassuring passengers, the aircraft's engines gave a final whine and it banked sharply to our left. My stomach dropped as we lost height, and I felt for my safety belt, making sure the buckle was fastened securely. The only thing I could understand from the captain's second address was the word *moshkleh*, Arabic for 'problem'. Not reassuring, given the circumstances.

'What the fuck's goin' on, man?' Geordie asked.

'Shush! Listen out, it's in English again!'

I was feeling as restless as the the rest of the passengers and there was bugger all I could do about it. I remember thinking, given all the different aircraft I've flown in, it's only a matter of time before one of them drops out of the sky. After all, it's a percentage game, isn't it? Aircraft *do* drop out of the skies, especially in this part of the world.

'We have a problem ...' The voice spoke good English with the calm you would expect from a professional, but 'problem' wasn't a word I would choose to use when addressing a plane full of passengers leaving a war zone. As he spoke, I tried to guess what he was going to say by the tone he used, but it was impossible. Suddenly, I remembered being in the last Gulf War, the one between Iran and Iraq. I was on board a supertanker steaming up the Persian Gulf when my mate (on another ship) was targeted by an Iraqi warship. I heard his May Day call on Channel 16 and listened to him giving his 'situation report' to a nearby American warship as he was actually being attacked. He'd been as cool as a cucumber and you wouldn't have known he was in a genuine life-threatening situation. He, too, was a professional.

'The Coalition Forces have started their attack for the liberation of Kuwait,' the captain's voice went on, instantly dragging me back to the here and now, 'so air traffic control has ordered us to turn back and fly south to Nairobi International Airport, Kenya.'

More panic filled the aircraft as the news sank into the English-speaking passengers. Geordie began to fidget even more as he adjusted his huge bulk around the two square feet of chair he was perched on.

'Christ! I thought for one minute we had a real problem and we were going to crash or somethin',' Geordie said.

'Yeah! I thought it was gonna be worse than that, but, shit, you know what the Yanks are like! I don't fancy being accidentally shot out of the sky by some triggerhappy F-16 sky jockey, either,' I said.

I left Geordie with a headful of possible scenarios to get on with, so he would pester one of the air crew for more information. I turned and pulled the shade up over the window to see the new day arriving. It was just turning light (we were well above the clouds at 30,000 feet, so the pilot said) and all I can remember was the sun disappearing out of sight as the aircraft was put on its new heading. It was an eerie feeling, knowing that six miles or so below me, the largest collection of Armed Forces of modern times had just been unleashed. It was the first and the last time I have ever flown *over* a war, usually I flew *into* them. I really didn't know if I felt envious of the experience I was missing out on or just plain scared of that F16 pilot.

Within a couple of hours, I was unexpectedly in Africa. We were some of the lucky ones. I was on the first diverted commercial aircraft to land in Nairobi that morning, but it was only by a matter of minutes — all other diverted Gulf flights were stacked up, waiting their turn to taxi and get allocated a parking place. As many as 20 could be seen in the distance. Besides the obvious killing and destruction in the Middle East, I thought of the more distant ripple effect on people's lives that this particular conflict would be causing all around the world. Not only the political repercussions, but how it would affect the day-to-day lives of, say, the locals in Nairobi who tout their wares in and around the airport. Certainly the ice cream and cold drinks businesses would profit from this unexpected deluge of foreigners.

We were shuttled off and into Customs. For sure, the Nairobi Airport Authorities had no idea what was about to descend on them. They were not geared up for thousands of unexpected arrivals. It was a nightmare sorting us all out, just those on our flight. Once again, I was grateful that I held a UK passport, it made my life getting through the red tape a lot easier. Eventually I made it out to the allocated courtesy bus which quickly filled up and drove off, leaving the airport in total chaos. Our flight was put up at the Nairobi Intercontinental Hotel for the night.

It was there, in the privacy of my room, that I watched this incredible war unfolding, courtesy of Emirates Airways and CNN satellite broadcasting. I say incredible for this reason: it was so visual. Apart from my Falklands experience, the last time I had seen anything remotely like what was being beamed into my hotel room that night was when I sat through the 'Ten Thousand Day War' video about the air war in Vietnam. But to see it actually happening *in real time* was awesome. We were given an almost minute-by-minute account. Teams of news crews stationed everywhere in the war zone (apart from Kuwait City) were each given a slot to report on what they thought was happening, mostly filmed against a backdrop of troops and tanks heading north, or the roar of fighter aircraft taking off with another load of bombs to drop on Saddam.

This sort of reporting, cut with actual footage of laser-guided aircraft bombs and SMART bombs meeting their targets with pinpoint accuracy, was extraordinary. I think all of us who watched the first few hours of that war could not help but be mesmerised by it. Certainly it kept *me* out of the bar that night.

1 0

THE WAITING GAME

Back in London, I found that the office was not the best working environment. We had little or no business, apart from waiting for the UAE contract. The days had now gone into weeks, and it was looking more like a protracted situation, which I'd dreaded from the onset.

It was inevitable that the allies were bound to win this particular Gulf war, now nearing its end. All the ground troops had to do was a mopping-up operation after the world's biggest barbecue. This might just get the UAE Government interested in anti-terrorist planning again, as they had been before Saddam moved on its neighbours. Meanwhile, though, Forester was having problems: with the company shareholders; with getting more credit from the bank; and on the home front. The stress was really beginning to build up. The UAE project had taken up a lot of my time preparing the 60-page contractual document — three months, in fact — and the flights and hotel bills for the three-week stay came to a small fortune.

We'd really stuck our necks out on this UAE contract and now we were paying the price. It was a recipe for disaster, with bankruptcy looming! However, there *was* one small deal that I closed during this period, a £30,500 project brought to us by Nassar. It was a small deal compared to what we were waiting for, but it was welcome money. It was to supply a couple of desperately needed bits of military software to the Kuwait MOD, which could not be sourced through the Allies. Nassar said that it was a 'thank you' deal for my hospitality during his and his family's most difficult of times.

The deal was struck in the Green Park Hotel, Mayfair. It was three days after the Liberation of Kuwait, a dark and rainy evening in London. I remember it all too well. I was running late for the meeting. Still, a cab would trim five minutes off my time. But I couldn't find one, so I had to speed-walk the distance. When I got there I looked like a drowned rat. I spotted Nassar up at the bar, with a group of other Arabs. Everyone was dressed in suits and was either standing or seated round small tables watching TV. Their Amir was on and they were listening intently to what he was saying. No one noticed my arrival so I found the gents, wiped myself down, stuck my head under the hand drier, squared myself away in the mirror, had a quick spray of the complimentary aftershave and walked back into the bar. The Amir was still speaking. I approached Nassar, who saw me and held out his hand.

'Ah, my dear friend Steve. So you have found us at last.'

He summoned a waiter.

'Yes, sir, would you like the same again?'

'Tut, please get my friend a Black Label, and change this ashtray, will you?' said Nassar.

'No ice, thank you,' I added as the waiter left.

The waiter responded immediately. He knew the Kuwaitis were on good form tonight, and his tips over the next few hours would probably amount to his weekly wage.

'Nice to see you, Mr Nassar. It looks like I've walked in on a bit of a party.'

'Yes, quite true. Come, come, let me introduce you to the General and to some of my friends.'

As he led me through the crowd I let him know that Forester would be joining us within the hour.

Nassar introduced me to many Kuwaitis, but he let me know that only two of them were part of the deal. They were government men and I could see from the respect the other men were giving them that they were 'big cheeses'.

There was a feeling of euphoria in the air. Quite natural — their country had just been liberated from a madman. The Kuwaiti spirits were really high and the Johnny Walker Black Label was taking a hammering, so the rest hardly noticed the four of us slip away into the lounge.

The three of them spoke in Arabic for about five minutes before the General — the older of the two men, a small, rotund man with a well-advanced receding hairline in his mid-50s — turned to me and gave a bit of a smile.

'Ah, Mr Steve, you were one of those SAS men, Nassar tells me.'

'Yes, sir,' I smiled. I didn't really know what to say.

'Your men did a great job for our country as indeed all the

Coalition Forces did. It was a great victory and I thank you.'

I attempted to bring a bit of humour into the conversation because I didn't know exactly what Nassar had actually said. He might have said that I was on the ground fighting, or anything like that to make the General feel comfortable. I couldn't be too smart and say that I was, because I wasn't — but, on the other hand I didn't want to embarrass Nassar if he'd said that I was. I boxed clever.

'Thank you, sir. I believe that Baghdad is very nice this time of the year!'

Everyone laughed, so I laughed, too. The ice was broken, then all three went back to talking Arabic whilst I fondled the thick glass tumbler of whiskey. Every now and then I heard my name being mentioned by Nassar; the General would turn and acknowledge me. The younger of the two, a captain or possibly a major, about 40 with the standard goatee beard, to whom I was never formally introduced, kept a very low profile and hardly acknowledged me. This didn't worry me. I showed him the same respect as I had Nassar and the General and if there was a reason I was not aware of for his reticence, well, that was fine by me as long as the deal went through.

As Nassar continued giving the background of the equipment, the General turned to me.

'Good, good, very well done,' he said.

I took this to be an acknowledgment of my assistance in quickly sourcing the equipment they so urgently needed. It was now in a bonded warehouse at Heathrow awaiting the arrival of its owners to ship it out. At the time I had this strange feeling that I was involved in some kind of shady dealings. Of course, it wasn't, it was strictly above board, but the way the meeting was turning out, I felt as though I was some kind of black-marketeer, and that any moment the police would storm through the entrance of the hotel and arrest all four of us.

For another 20 minutes I sat patiently waiting, on two accounts. One, for the payment — Nassar had said that it was to be cash — and two, for the arrival of Forester. Then I was asked to accompany the younger of the men upstairs to his room. I wasn't too sure about that. I trusted Nassar, but the situation had a sinister feel. It was still raining heavily, it was dark outside and I was around a bunch of people I didn't know. I'd worked with the Arabs in many countries, I even spoke and understood a little of their language, but all this mingling with powerful foreign government officials, plus the tone in which they spoke to each other (rather erratic, and sometimes sounding offensive to the English ear) created a very dodgy atmosphere.

Luckily the lift up to the room was big enough for ten men, so body contact was not a problem. I wasn't sure the 'Major' understood English all that well so I left out the small talk. When the lift stopped, the room was facing us. The 'Major' used his key-card to swipe the lock and opened the door, I could see that it was a grand-a-night suite, minimum.

'Please wait here.'

'Yes, sir.'

That's all he said as he disappeared into a back room, a bedroom. The main room was very well furnished with light oak-coloured cupboards and wall-panelling with a pair of large, heavy-looking gold curtains draped across two sets of windows and enough comfy chairs for ten visitors. The two large-screen televisions at opposite ends of the room looked out of place. A bowl of fresh fruit, mangoes, dates, grapes and oranges took my fancy, but I resisted it.

I looked around for any signs or clues as to who this guy actually was, but there weren't any. No uniforms or suits hanging up, no briefcases or papers lying around. The room was so tidy it didn't look as if anyone had used it. Maybe they'd rented it for just a couple of hours. That was possible, but Nassar had said that they were staying in the hotel, and there was no reason for me to think any different.

The 'Major' then appeared again carrying a brown envelope. With no messing I was handed the money for my part of the deal as he broke out in a bit of pidgin English.

'Please. Please check.'

'Thank you, sir,' I said.

Realising there wasn't going to be a sensible dialogue between us, I sat at a table and started to count. It was all there, in used notes, and as far as I could detect they were all pukka. I was unsure whether I was expected to give the odd £500 to the man standing over me or not. There was a pregnant pause which suggested so, but I didn't. A slightly tense moment followed as I put all the money back into the envelope and indicated that we should join the other two downstairs.

'Nassar and the General?' I said.

'Yes, let us go.'

During this time, Forester had arrived, as drenched as I had been. His grey suit was wrinkled and his face was red and puffy, like he was about to keel over. He looked well out of place and very much on edge. The 'Major' sat back down with no introduction. We shook hands.

'Hello, Forester, still raining out there?' I said.

'It hasn't stopped, old boy. I was just saying to the General about our typical English weather, it always rains.'

He had no idea I'd closed the deal and was sitting with the cash next to my heart. I could sense that he didn't want to hang around too long. He had the bank to go to, then a train to catch, and kept trying to catch my eye to see if the transaction had taken place. This was very embarrassing, not only for me but for Nassar as well. It was clear to all that Forester just intended to get the money and leave. He didn't understand the Arab etiquette which comes with a deal like this — a bit of socialising was expected. However, Forester had no time for that, so after a few more uncomfortable minutes I covertly indicated that I was carrying the cash. After a brief and polite excuse, I found myself with Forester in the gents.

'Now listen, Steve, did you get all the money?'

'Yes, yes, relax will you? Everything went alright, look — here it is. For Christ's sake, try and be a bit respectful in front of Nassar, after all he is my contact and he did set up this deal.'

'You can never be too careful with clients. Trust me, I've dealt with a lot of them in my time. Come on, let's have a look at the money.'

I handed over the envelope. He started to count the cash.

'You're not going to count it *here* are you? I've checked it. It's all there.'

'I know, I just want to be sure. Watch the door, there's a good chap. Did you get a receipt?'

'Christ, no! What do you think? It's a cash deal, you think I'm going to ask for one, then ...'

'Oh, very *well* then.'

Forester always sounded like he was talking down to me — he could be very patronising in the 'old school' sort of way. When we returned to the group, I caught Nassar's eye. He knew that something embarrassing was about to come from Forester, so with his own very clever use of English, he tried to steer Forester away from saying anything which might make Nassar lose face in this company.

'Mr Forester, are you OK? You look as if you could do with a drink; whiskey fine for you?' he said.

'No, thank you, Nassar, I'm fine. Have a train to catch at half past the hour.'

Nassar's intervention seemed to have avoided any unnecessary embarrassment for the moment. If you understand just one thing about the Arabs, it's this: causing a loss of face is about the biggest insult you can give them.

I didn't understand Forester's problem. He was on the brink of financial disaster, yet was just about to screw up a 'two-phone-call' deal and more business in the future. In addition, it had basically been handed to *me* on a plate, as a gift from Nassar, and not to the company. It was my *choice* to put the deal through the company. All this looming catastrophe, just because Forester had not received a receipt!

Then it happened. Forester asked for a receipt in a way unique to an arrogant Englishman speaking to a foreigner. The reply was short and sharp.

'Mr Forester. You have your money; Mr Nassar assures me that my equipment is in a bonded warehouse at Heathrow,' said the General. He spoke in a clipped educated English accent. A two-second pause was left before he resumed. It was obvious that he was going to continue talking and that he was not waiting for a reply from Forester.

'Now, if you would excuse me.'

He got up. This prompted all of us to rise, shake hands and exchange nods of the head to acknowledge everyone's part in the deal. Then the three Arabs moved off in the direction of the bar. I had a short conversation with Forester, who muttered some sort of comment about how the Arabs do business, said he would see me in the office tomorrow and scurried out of the hotel to deposit the cash, I assumed, into the company bank account and then catch the train home. Then I joined the Arabs. My obvious embarrassment about the way Forester had acted was alleviated by the General's comment:

'Don't worry, Mr Steve. You are amongst friends now.'

It was not until a few months later that I realised the real meaning of what he actually said.

I hoped that this entire episode had not affected my relationship with Nassar. He was, for sure, a 'main player' and in some way I saw my future with him. Not in the immediate term — he had his own personal family and business problems to sort out — but certainly in the long term.

Apart from that little deal, I was working with Nassar, through the company, on a potential contract of mine-clearing the blown oil wells in Kuwait. Nassar had jacked up meetings for us to attend with the KPC (Kuwait Petroleum Corporation) management at their London offices.

This was a contract which Kuwait urgently needed. Nassar's offices there hadn't been touched by the Iraqis during the occupation, so all that was needed to run the admin side of a project like this was already in place. The only problem we had (or should I say *Nassar* had) was to jack up these meetings with KPC and convince them that 'we' could do the job. Certainly I could call on the experts, ex-Royal Engineers and the like, to make the contract work. The equipment needed was not a problem, I had already begun to source it from manufacturers, and since Nassar's family name carried a lot of clout in Kuwait, the potential of pulling off a great job and making money was there.

Our point of attack was not to convince KPC that we were the answers to *all* of their problems, but, more to the point, that we could clear the routes to selected well-heads, those deemed by KPC to require the most urgent attention. In short, the ones that were spewing out most of the oil. Nassar had a friend on the ground in Kuwait who was constantly feeding us with real-time intelligence on what progress was being made. These reports reached us on a daily basis, so, for example, we were some of the first to know about the Kuwaiti soldier who nonchalantly strolled up to one of the oil wells that was gushing out thousands of dollars of crude an hour and just turned it off.

Things were looking good after the two initial meetings with KPC. I'd contacted an old mine-clearance friend and persuaded him to attend the third meeting to give his technical opinion on how to tackle the mine problem. He even gave some good ideas on the shutting down of those well-heads that had buckled and fractured castings, as a result of Iraqi plastic explosive charges detonating on them.

I could tell that KPC were impressed. Nassar had obviously done a great job in convincing them that we could do the job as claimed. For my part, I had convinced Nassar I could carry out my side of the operation. That was to supply a team of eight suitably qualified EOD (Explosive Ordnance Disposal) men and all the associated equipment needed to carry out the task competently. The only thing I wanted assurance on from Nassar, was that the team would have suitable living accommodation when on the ground, by which I meant that there would be a bed, clean water and something to eat. The guys in the team were a flexible bunch, not overly concerned about creature comforts, and their request was only for the basics that soldiers need to operate with. Anyway, the fee they were to be paid more than compensated for roughing it a bit.

It was a 12-week contract, which meant that we would have a foot on the ground and, for sure, were likely to win more work. The potential worth of further work, Nassar costed out, was well over ten million US dollars. Meanwhile, one more meeting with the cheque-signer for KPC would secure our little contract. This was a very exciting time, not only for me but for Forester, who could see the pound signs, and, of course, for Nassar, who was actually doing something as a Kuwaiti on behalf of Kuwait.

Not long after the liberation, John Major visited the Amir of Kuwait, in Kuwait. I remember so well watching the TV and listening to his speech about how the UK would help rebuild Kuwait. Here I was for the first time not actually being involved in a British war with my generation of soldiers but about to become very wealthy off the back of it. This I reckoned to be a first, because as far as I was aware, most of those who make money from any war this country gets involved in are those with a shareholding in government-sanctioned manufacturers of military equipment (probably owned or partly owned by past members of Parliament or the aristocracy), or those in the know as to just what military contracts the Government was to award to whom, and when.

The office phone rang at the same time John Major started discussing the problems of mines. It was Nassar: was I watching the Major report? I was. Then suddenly I was gobsmacked when our Prime Minister stated that Royal Ordnance, part of British Aerospace, was to be awarded the British section of the mine-clearance contract for Kuwait. This just about knocked all the stuffing out of me. It was the first time I had heard that Royal Ordnance, the former state-owned munitions manufacturer, was in the running. Of course I had heard about other mine-clearance companies trying to bid for part of the obvious contract, but they were not after our patch. They had been working through their own different contacts and channels.

In short, Royal Ordnance, who at that time were not geared up in the business of mine clearance, had just been awarded a contract worth well over £60 million to clear the designated British sector in Kuwait. The only thing Royal Ordnance knew about mines at the time was how to make them and not how to clear and destroy them. The entire episode was a farce.

Sometime later, Royal Ordnance invited us up to their HQ for a brief on the way ahead. I didn't go. I knew *exactly* what the format of this briefing would take. 'We have the contract and if you want to play ball, then you listen and do what we tell you to do' would be their attitude.

I was right. Forester came back from that meeting pretty much pissed off, confirming what I thought. No independent company was going to get a look-in. If we wanted to work for Royal Ordnance it would have to be on their terms. There was to be no subbing of any part of the contract. All those who wanted to work on it would have to work under the umbrella of Royal Ordnance, and, indeed, would be contracted to Royal Ordnance. That was that.

All that hard work and running around, knowing that we could've done a great job, was in vain. At the time, every ex-

Royal Engineer who was involved with mine clearance as a profession came out with the same old phrase: 'Royal Ordnance has no idea or experience in how to clear mines.' They were as shell-shocked as the rest of us.

I didn't relish the task I had in front of me but it had to be done. I had to tell the ex-REs lined up for our contract that if they wanted a piece of the action in Kuwait, they had to give Royal Ordnance a call. I gave them the number. Most of them did and most of them worked over in Kuwait. Some of the stories that filtered back through 'rumour control' were startling to say the least.

It doesn't take the brains of an archbishop to know that if you have such a large mine-clearance team as Royal Ordnance put out on the ground (well over 200 men), then you are going to get problems. Lots of 'em.

Although I'm no expert on mine clearance (the closest I've come to detecting live mines was when my platoon inadvertently walked through a minefield in the Falklands War), I have extensive practical training in explosives and booby traps and in their making, finding and detonation. Most British infantry soldiers are trained in some form of mine-clearance techniques, mainly the prodding method. This is where you prod, or rather push a rod (preferably non-metallic) down about a few inches into the ground in front of you. It used to be your personal bayonet! You do this at about a 30-degree angle until you feel something solid. It's a very slow process but good enough to get across a mine-field (if you're lucky!) What I *do* have is a practical knowledge of the problems a bunch of highly trained men, working together in a 'live' environment with just the basics of equipment, will encounter.

Reading the progress reports on how the Kuwait job was coming along, it seemed to me that those ultimately in charge of the operation had forgotten a fundamental thing: 'You've gotta keep the boys happy.' We all like to be stroked once in a while, otherwise you end up with bags of rat shit in the end. Especially if you bluffed your way into the contract in the first place and all your employed experts knew that.

Some days after John Major had given us the 'good news', I was debating what course I should take. Nassar offered an all-expenses-paid trip over to Kuwait, saying there were to be no guarantees but the potential was, on a scale of one to ten, about six and a half. This was a test for me. Forester and Cadogan were not going to be around for much longer if we didn't get any business. We were still waiting to hear back from the Middle East, reference the Anti-Terrorist contract.

Every week a phone call was made but we didn't get any further. They were still waiting to see the ashes of the war settle down. It could have been, as I told Forester, another year before we even heard from them. He knew I was probably right.

The Gulf War and Saddam had screwed up our chances of getting that contract, and subsequently our own Prime Minister had screwed up our chances of getting the KPC job! All we ever wanted was four well-heads to clear. KPC had agreed to that, but their government did not. From two potential multi-million dollar contracts to nothing; it was a great let-down. The company had a lot of potential but by now it was sliding down a very slippery road. I enjoyed the work and the buzz that this job gave me, of earning potentially more than just the flat rate, but the situation was getting very serious.

What to do? My choice was to stay with Forester. I have

never been one to chop and change. Forester had given me the break to be the Ops man for Cadogan, so the least I could do was see us both through this shitty period. Getting the company up and running was a challenge to me. It certainly had the 'legs' for it to work and I was keen for both of us to succeed.

During the next few weeks the finances of the company didn't get any better.

Forester had rather extended himself on all fronts. I knew that things were tight, because a few months before we had to give up much of the first floor to another company and move upstairs into the attic of the building.

One evening in June, when we were just about to leave the office, Forester suddenly broke down in front of me. It was a total surprise. I was really taken aback to have this self-proclaimed 'seen it, done it, doing it tomorrow' businessman in floods of tears, telling me how his young wife was having an affair with another man, and how he was forced to live upstairs in their big house in Hertfordshire whilst she got on with things.

His performance was outstanding. It deserved an Oscar. I don't know to this day if it was an act or the true thing. I was sure Forester was too hard to break down in front of me. What threw me completely was when he said he felt that he couldn't go on. 'I'll put a gun to my head,' he said. At the time I thought he was ready to meet his Maker, for sure.

I couldn't make sense of it all. It was the first time in my life that I'd met a man openly saying he'd had enough and was ready to pull the trigger. It was a weakness I hadn't perceived in him. With hindsight I should have picked up on this much earlier, but I didn't.

Nonetheless, I had to admit that Forester had some 'neck'. Maybe it's the way the rest of us have been brought up: accept your weaknesses; try and work around them and if you can, learn from your mistakes; then use them to your advantage. Don't just brush them under the carpet and kid yourself, 'I didn't really fuck up there. Did I? Yes I did, but I'm not going to admit it to any fucker.'

Anyway, a saviour, if that's the right word, for the company (and indeed for Forester as a man) was just around the corner, in the form of an ex-Royal Marine Officer called Alistair Douglas. Alistair had been living in Africa with his wife since leaving 'the Corps', but I'd met him on two occasions when he'd visited London. He ran a small but select security company specialising mainly in surveillance and counter-surveillance services to wealthy clients and corporations. They had to be wealthy to afford his fees, and from what I could make out from Alistair, there seemed to be no shortage of work over in East Africa for this type of service. Certainly I offered the same type of service, but no way could I command the sorts of fees which Alistair asked for, and generally got.

At the time the London market offering this sort of skill was awash with all sorts of 'Walters' offering electronic kits to clients, claiming that they could do almost anything. Once a few big companies and businessmen had been suckered by these types, it made getting business even harder.

A couple of times I was approached and asked if I could do certain things, such as break into an office, and de- and re-bug a certain room and area, or install a surveillance team to watch the so-called 'dubious goings on' of a particular individual. Of course, this could all be done at a price, but when many clients heard it they were shocked at how high it

Top: Welcome to Hargeisa, Somaliland. Note the rocket holes and small arms strike marks.

Bottom: A burnt out Russian helicopter that never made it off the ground, Hargeisa Airport.

Top: Welcome to the Hotel Hargeisa – destroyed by thousands of rounds of small arms fire and rockets.

Bottom: My first sight of the enormity of the task ahead. Live aircraft rockets and mines dumped everywhere.

These anti-personnel mines were injuring children daily. Designed to maim and so destroy morale, they had been thrown everywhere by the enemy.

Top: The road into Hargeisa. Note the pile of rocks on the left where the war dead are buried.

Bottom: Stockpiles of ammunition booby-trapped by fleeing Somali troops – we had to clear the area of mines and live ordnance.

Top: Big bombs, small bombs – all live.

Bottom: The camp protection – a Russian-built ZSU234.

Top: Migs at Hargeisa Airport. They had been vandalised in a hunt for spare parts.

Bottom: 'Chat' day in Hargeisa – a hallucinogenic plant chewed by Somalis.
The local economy is based around sales of the drug.

Top: A Hercules flies in stores and equipment. SAM missiles surround this runway.
Bottom: A mine clearance pioneer in the firing position with an anti-tank weapon.

On the road to Gurué.

would be. It sometimes shocked *me*, once I'd worked out how many men and how much equipment I would need to carry out even the easiest of surveillance tasks. And, of course, no results could ever be guaranteed. At least, not the sorts of results the client was looking for most of the time.

The movie industry has a lot to answer for as regards its portrayal of the world of surveillance. If you believe cop films and TV series, you would side with the client in thinking that just one covert operator sitting in a vehicle for a couple of hours was all that was required to pick up and follow the potential target without getting compromised. This, of course, was far from the truth. For an operation like this, you need many experienced bods on the ground with all sorts of vehicles and equipment, all properly briefed on what was what and what to do 'in the event of' (commonly known in the trade as 'actions on'). It's manpower-intensive and in and around big cities such as London, it's even harder, and very costly.

On one very memorable occasion I had just given a wealthy client (who had more money than you could shake a stick at) my costings for a five-day surveillance operation to follow two slippery customers of his. He was thinking of going ahead, then gasped at the final figure. Why was it so high, he demanded. Actually the price was costed to get any other business he might have wanted to put the company's way, so it was far from unrealistic. In fact, *his* shock shocked *me*. The only thing I could think of as a suitable reply was to ask, 'Sir, have you ever heard of a TV programme called *The Rockford Files*? It's an old American series about an ex-cop turned private eye, Jim Rockford.'

'Yes, of course. What's your point?' His reply was sharp, slightly arrogant. He was still looking down at my prices. Not once did he look up. I sensed no change in his irritation.

'Well, his charges were $200 a day plus expenses, and that was back in the 1970s.' I waited for his reply. I had tried to inject a bit of humour into the meeting.

He kept me standing whilst still looking over my document. I remember thinking, God, I *hate* the feeling of being in the hands of someone else. The company needed this contract and I didn't want to blow it, but being so subservient reminded me of being a raw recruit back in the Paras on pay-day, having to queue up and *thank* the officer for my wages, which I (and the rest of the platoon) had more than earned.

I was still standing in silence. About 15 seconds later he replied. 'This 50 per cent down in advance. Is this standard?'

He *knew* it was. He was playing the game.

'Yes, sir. That's 50 now and the balance on completion of the job. That's standard for this sort of job, and with all respect, we haven't dealt with you before.' Perhaps that last comment was pushing it a bit but the client didn't seem to be offended — at least, he didn't show any physical signs of it.

'OK. Since you mentioned dollars, I'll give you the 50 per cent advance in dollars and the balance in sterling. Are we in agreement?' he was now addressing me direct. Making eye contact.

I gave a three second pause before I answered. 'US dollars?' I said in a tone that implied I had accepted his terms. I knew he was talking in US dollars but even the mega-rich play these silly little games. He might have been talking in Eastern Caribbean dollars which were worth one and a half times less.

Business is all about the individual power we have over each other. It's an ego game, all about winning. We did the job. We did it well and got a result (which is not always the case), and we even got paid (which, in this business, is not always the case either!).

As I say, Alistair was successful in what he did. The second time he came to London we discussed what each could do for the other. Nothing serious, nothing written down on paper but a mutual respect for each other's skills and abilities. I liked Alistair. He was another ex-officer I respected and was a bit like me, still trying to make it in the world of business, a milieu very unlike the SAS or the Royal Marines, where your buddy was indeed your buddy and not the Grim Reaper in disguise, ready to stitch you up for a couple of quid; where your word was your word.

So over a long boozy lunch in Olivers we looked at how our two companies could benefit each other. I told him that at that moment we were waiting to hear from Abu Dhabi regarding an anti-terrorist training package that I had put together for the government there, and that through a Kuwaiti friend we were still hoping for a mine-clearing task for the Kuwaiti Government or for KPC. (At the time I wasn't sure who was holding the reins on this one. I still thought we had a chance with this 'live' project, since the Iraqis had blown up so many oil wells during their retreat and the routes to them had to be cleared of mines before the specialist teams of firefighters and oil workers could get in and stop the flow of oil. Royal Ordnance surely couldn't take on this entire contract, I thought. It would only be a matter of time before they subbed the work out. But that was wishful thinking, and I was totally wrong.)

We concluded by agreeing that the future between us

looked pretty good and if we could work together on joint projects, that would obviously be excellent.

Within a week of Alistair's return to Africa he was on the phone about a chance meeting with one of the project co-ordinators of an aid organisation in Somaliland (Northern Somalia), an old British Protectorate which was now another post-colonial mess.

This chance meeting happened at the bar of the Intercontinental Hotel, Nairobi. Just as any two ex-pats from the same country might in an overseas bar, they got talking, explaining to each other what they were actually doing there. This chap, Dave Morton, represented one of the NGOs (Non Governmental Organisations), specifically the IHA (The International Humanitarian Agency), who gave money to this part of Africa. It was his job to co-ordinate all the foreign workers involved with the distribution of aid, such as food, medical services, and the general 'hearts and minds' policy. He and his fellow workers were having a real problem with mines, anti-personnel ones in particular, and he had flown south to Kenya to have urgent phone talks with his people back in Europe. He desperately needed a team of Western mine-clearance experts to come in and sort it all out.

As Alistair related the story to me by fax and phone over the next few days, it became clear that Somaliland really did have a big problem. The country had literally just finished a long bloody civil war with the people in the south, commonly known as Somalia, in which well over 50,000 people had been killed, and whilst every effort was being made to bring in aid and get the country back on its feet again, aid workers and local people were constantly being taken out by mines. Every day 50 or so people — mainly kids — who had been mutilated by mines were brought into the makeshift hospital at Hargeisa with their limbs hanging off or blown off completely. The aid doctors could not physically cope with this added problem, and furthermore, two of their nurses had recently been casevaced, also victims of mines.

Throughout the country there were more than 1,000 deaths a day due to mines, out of a population of only one and a half million. It seemed extremely frustrating, as we waited for an answer, that here was a project I knew we could carry out with a great deal of professionalism, and in some respects, with relative ease.

I had a lot of experience in working in conditions like those in Somaliland. I knew all about how to run the hearts and minds side, getting the population on your side, getting them working not *for* you but *alongside* you, and I knew how very important that was to the success of any operation. I had the manufacturer contacts to arrange the technical and support equipment, and also the ability to plan and carry out an operation such as this, whilst Alistair had the local point of contact and was doing all he could in persuading the NGOs and others of our suitability for the project.

Because of our military backgrounds, both Alistair and I looked upon this operation as a great challenge and we put in as much effort as we would have done had we been back in the SAS and the Marines. It wasn't only the money. I have always got, and still get, a great personal pleasure out of working in these types of environments, a feeling of such satisfaction from being in a position actually to help people who have very little faith left in life.

Alistair had done such a good job of convincing Dave that

Cadogan was the right company to carry out the operation, that all we had to do was submit our costs. Because the urgency of getting a mine-clearance company out and on the ground was so great, we were told that we were not in a bidding race with any other company. Quite amazingly, no other company even knew of this contract! It was my bet that the other UK mine-clearance companies — which you could count on one hand — still had their noses well and truly stuck in the Kuwait trough. A dream come true, this was the answer to all of Forester's financial problems. Even better, funds from the NGOs and other aid organisations had already anticipated the situation in Somaliland, so had allocated funds for mine-clearance; this would cut much of the red tape which usually surrounds such organisations when they release funds.

So, here was a contract about to land neatly in Forester's lap. All of my costings and equipment lists had already been written for the Kuwait contract. All I had to do was to reconfirm the availability of all the equipment, check out the prices of radios, and change the name of the client on all the pages of the documents.

To be accurate, the mine-clearance task was slightly different, in that it was essentially a training task, training the local militia and/or population in mine-clearance techniques, rather than a definite 'hands-on' operation where you go out into the minefield with your mine prodder, helmet and body armour and perform the task yourself. My only concern was some friction between myself and Forester as to where we should recruit the team members from.

Because I was ex-Army, and this was to be a land-based job, my view was that we should recruit from ex-Royal Engineers (in particular 9 Squadron), the Airborne element, or the Royal

Artillery (or as it was called then, the Ordnance Corps). I had my reasons. I had worked with these 9 Squadron guys and they knew how to rough it, should the need require; and from reading the reports being sent back from Alistair I knew we would be working in a pretty hostile environment. I was convinced that these well-trained guys could not only do the technical side of the job, but would be able to hack it as well.

Forester, on the other hand, seemed to favour the Royal Navy option. I couldn't quite get my head around the fact that I'd never seen a minefield on board a ship. I'm not saying that the Royal Navy were not up to it — technically they were; but that was only half the job. There's no substitute for having worked out in the field, where the only luxury available was getting into the outdoor shower before all the hot water, heated during the day by the sun, had been used up.

Nonetheless, against my protests, Forester went with the Navy option. During this period I saw a considerable change in Forester's attitude, not only towards me, but also towards those people (including Alistair) who'd supported him during the build-up phase of the contract. It's strange that as soon as someone gets money, they seem to think they have power over the rest of us. I began to see this in Forester and it was something I informed Alistair about. He had to be made aware that Forester's main concern in all of this business seemed to be how much money could be made out of this contract. If that meant cutting corners and in turn risking the safety aspect of those on the ground, then in my opinion he probably would.

For over six weeks before the advance funds for this £2.5 million contract (some £250,000) arrived at Coutts Bank in

Mount Street, I hadn't been paid — the company could not afford it. This was my decision, to work knowing that I might or might not be paid, taken on the strength of believing that we *would* get the contract. I had every faith in the project during that time, and I was really keen to get to Somaliland and help these people.

It was a gamble that paid off, or so it seemed then.

11

MINE CLEARANCE, SOMALILAND

It was a really shitty flight from Charles de Gaulle airport to Djibouti. The aircraft was full to capacity and we must have flown through every bit of turbulence Mother Nature could have thrown at us. The smell of French Disque Bleu cigarettes didn't help either. The entire plane seemed to be smoking this brand. When I disembarked I smelt like I'd spent the past several hours sleeping in camel's dung.

My first night in Djibouti was spent sleeping on the floor of MSF's main HQ. It was a wooden four-bedroom bungalow, complete with outside loo, in one of the city's more upmarket districts. Having an outside loo gives you some idea of what century I'd just arrived in. Actually, the conditions were not that bad and I was made really welcome by my multinational hosts, mainly French, Belgium and Danish people. They had no problems in hacking it; why should I?

I'd planned to spend only two days in Djibouti organising the movement of the stores and equipment from a secure MSF warehouse on to the quickest and safest transport I could find to run it up into Somaliland. I was keen to start as soon as possible. Getting the mine-clearance admin phase up and running ASAP before the team flew in was my number one priority. You could say that I was the advance party for the operation.

My forward planning written back in London went to pot within hours of landing, so I spent two more valuable days running around Djibouti than planned. It seemed that no one had given any thought to transporting our kit into Somaliland. I'd been told back in the UK that all our equipment and stores were to precede me by one day and were being secured by some of the relief agencies, but this was not the case. They had no brief to guard it, only store it, and there was no way I could stag on for the duration over this mass of valuable, very expensive and attractive kit. Still, it was up to me to sort the problem. Thinking on my feet, I hired four of MSF's loyal local helpers to stand guard.

I had come across aid workers during my trip to Mozambique and they are a different kind of human being. Most are university-educated from middle-class backgrounds and they have given up earning a decent standard of living in order to help those in the Third World. In my opinion, these men and women are the unsung heroes of the charity world. They work in the shittiest of conditions for the most appalling rates of pay, year in and year out, all over Africa and the Far East. Yet we rarely hear about all the good work they do. I equated their working environment to that of the SAS but without the guns

— I guess that's why I got on well with them. Like them, I've never had any trouble in roughing it. It's nice to have all your creature comforts all around you, but you don't really miss them when they're not at hand. For example, no matter how many episodes of your favourite soap you miss, whether it's over ten days or ten months, you can generally pick up the storyline when you return to it.

Danish Dik, a lanky-looking 30-year-old who was one of the agency's field operators, took me out for a beer on the first night. The city reminded me of how Cuamba might have looked 20 years before, but without that Portuguese feel. Djibouti was a throwback to the French colonial days. There was a large French garrison still in residence, mainly the French Foreign Legion and support units. It could have done with a touch of paint here and there to spruce up the once-grandiose buildings on the main drag, and a touch of tarmac wouldn't have have gone amiss.

Dik took me to a couple of ex-pat haunts to see if we could bump into the crew of C130 Hercules transport aircraft chartered by the US aid organisation CARE, which had been flying food missions in and out of Somalia for the past few months. The idea was to try and get them to sort out my immediate transport problem. I wasn't really going on the piss as such, I was combining business with a bit of pleasure.

Since it was a Friday, the city was buzzing. It was still early in the evening but following Dik's recommendation we avoided certain bars where the Legion drank. That was OK by me. If they were anything like the bars in Aldershot where I used to drink as a young paratrooper, there was no way I wanted to sample their delights. Also, I didn't want to bump into any ex-

British soldier who for some reason had failed the 'all arms' P Company (the parachute course for any member of the British Armed Forces, reputed to be one of the hardest in the world) because he had to RTU and then had done a runner, gone AWOL from his unit and joined the Foreign Legion — all because his missus was being screwed by a Para. A similar story was once relayed to me about a Guardsman when I was stationed in Berlin. Having to do a fighting withdrawal with my new Danish mate out of a bar full of pissed French Legionnaires would be a nightmare. That's not my idea of a good Friday night. It used to be, but not now.

I'd had experience with the French Foreign Legion a few years back when I did my HALO free-fall course in Pau, France.*

There was a unit of Legionnaires based there and we jumped with them and often went on the piss with them. It had invariably ended in a fight of some sort. Nothing vicious, just soldiers having pride in their units and reliving past battle honours with a couple of gallons of beer inside them.

Eventually we ended up in the bar of the Hotel Europa after trawling three less riotous bars in pursuit of the Herc aircrew. Dik assured me that they, too, would be out on the piss, so we weren't on a wild goose chase. There was nothing else for the ex-pat to do out here, and really it was the only time when you actually got anything done. You would arrange to meet whoever in a certain bar and discuss the following day's or week's business. This was par for the course all over the world, the ex-pats' way, whether English, German or French.

Hotel Europa was more civilised and the class of women were a tad on the better side. I got on well with Dik. He, too, was an

* Described in *Terminal Velocity*.

ex-paratrooper, and since I had gone on a six-week exercise to Denmark with 2 Para years ago where we were pitched up against a bunch of very eager Danish paratroopers, we had a lot in common and much to talk about. It was all anecdotal stuff but he was good company, and like the rest of modern Europe, he spoke excellent English.

Soon, it was getting near 'Cinderella' time and I was finally giving up the ghost about bumping into this aircrew, at least that night. I was jet-lagged and the local lager was beginning to take effect and as the pores of my skin were continually pissing out this stuff, I was getting a bit agitated. All I wanted to do was get my head down. The bar was far too packed and noisy for my liking, especially for the first night in country. I didn't want to rip the arse out of it just yet, I normally do that on the last day, not the first. Anyway, we didn't find them, so Dik took me back to the basha the way we came, in the standard beat-up Japanese taxi, driven by a local nutter with a death wish.

Much to my surprise, the following morning I awoke bright and early, ready to attack the day. My first task was to locate all of the team's equipment and check that everything had arrived and was still secured; after that I would give a quick call to Forester to say all was well. I don't think he had any idea of how things actually worked on the ground, because he was constantly faxing me for progress reports, with questions like, 'How long will it take?' and 'Why do you need that amount of money?' Perhaps he thought that because we were English and we were over here to help these people out, they should be grateful. This was arrogance in him, but he just couldn't help himself. As it was, I didn't phone until I had some news.

Eventually I managed to meet up with the aircrew at the most obvious place — aboard their Herc. They were a mixed assortment of ex-servicemen all wearing bits of their old combat uniforms. The pilot was a chain-smoking Canadian called Baz; his co-pilot, a short aggressive-looking South African, was always ready to spin the odd war story or two, bit of a joker in fact; and the navigator, an American, was a dead ringer for the actor Bill Cosby. All three were old hands and had been flying missions of one sort or another across Africa for years. The loadie, Ted, was the 'new boy', an ex-Bootneck, which was really handy. He had only been part of the crew for just over a year and said that he really enjoyed flying with 'the old men'. Ted and I were about the same age and, like myself, he came from London. What's more, he was a Falklands vet and served with 42 Commando during the war, so we already had much in common, and it didn't take long before I had solved my transport problem. It was a chance in a million that the pilot had pretty much an open agenda — as long as he kept flying relief missions over Somalia, he was doing his job. Having to fly a bit further north on this occasion was no great drama.

Hercs are designed to land on makeshift airstrips anywhere in the world and because I was an ex-member of the SAS Air Troop, Baz and his crew were willing to land on my say so. That was good news and very trusting of him. How was he to know that I wasn't bluffing about being ex-SAS? I could have been any old Walter Mitty. Having said that, though, I did give him the strip landing dimensions of a C130 for a quick turnaround, straight off the top of my head when he asked for it, and there weren't too many people who could do that.

I had no idea of the ground up in the north, as I had not seen a map of it, apart from an old military one I'd acquired via a mate from the map store back in Hereford. That, however, was dated 1955. So I was still waiting for Dik to come up with a half-decent one. He'd assured me they did exist, but it would take a bit of time to track one down.

Baz the pilot knew the area of Berbera, a port on the east of Somaliland, quite well. He told me that there was an old Russian-built runway there, and once they'd bugged out of the country, the Americans came in and extended it for their Shuttle programme. It was one of a few such runways anywhere in the world, ready for use in the event of an emergency.

Altogether, through a series of very fortunate incidents, some things had just fallen into place. I was very pleased that now the team equipment was going to be flown in. What if the loadie hadn't been an ex-Royal Marine and a Falklands veteran? And what if the pilot hadn't once flown the SAS on an exchange trip to Canada back in the 1980s? Then I might have been sailing up to Somaliland in a vessel like something out of the movie *The African Queen*.

I'd arranged with Baz to call him up once I was in country ready and had secured a suitable landing strip, should the Shuttle runway prove to be covered in bomb craters. I'd also asked Dik to oversee the safe passage of the equipment from his warehouse to the aircraft, and had given Ted a complete equipment manifest of the weight and size of each piece of kit, so he could tick it all off as it was loaded. In addition, we worked out a few secure code words and call-signs for the flight, just in case a few bandits happened to be listening to our voice traffic.

The little Red Cross Cessna 172 circled the shanty town of Hargeisa, shuddering violently as it banked one more time. Both I (with my personal kit) and a relief doctor (with his) held on for dear life. I wasn't sure what the pilot was up to. It couldn't have been to avoid another aircraft because we were the first and last flight of the day, the only one the locals allowed to land, so the pilot had said in his pre-flight brief. Nor was it a manoeuvre to avoid any heat-seeking missiles because they would have hit us before we saw them, given the speed we were flying. I never did understand pilots. Maybe he just had a sick sense of humour. Africa does this to pilots. It seems to me that as soon as they're away from the rules of the CAA and normality, they take on a more blasé Biggles-like attitude to flying.

At about 200 feet we started to level out. Now for the first time I could see what appalling devastation lay beneath me, a massive bombsite, the like of which I had never seen before. The only way to describe it was like looking at those old Pathé News films of Blitzed London. Then I saw a series of runways with jet fighters parked up, Russian-built MIGs, and masses of people running to meet us.

We landed and the pilot taxied up as near to the end of the runway as he dared. We were to be met by a couple of the Red Cross doctors who had recently arrived to assist mine victims. Their relief programme had only been going for a few weeks, and it was because of reports they'd sent back to Europe about the horrendous injuries being inflicted on the people of Somaliland, in particular the town of Hargeisa, that the powers that be decided that mine-clearance experts should be brought in ASAP.

So there I was, about to embark on new ground as an aid/relief worker. It would be the first and the last time I would ever land in this part of Africa without a gun. Of course, I was very apprehensive about this, and now, looking at the vast crowd of locals gathering around the little aircraft, I was beginning to feel slightly naked without a weapon to wrap my hand around. It may sound melodramatic, but I've had a great deal of experience — in Northern Ireland and the Middle East for example — of how crowds could turn on an outsider like myself, even though they knew the outsider was there to help them. I had experienced this more than a few times.

There was no doubt that this was a war zone; the presence of the Mig fighters told me more about the situation than any intelligence reports I had in Djibouti. I adopted a more non-combatant air to suit the reality of the situation and as the Cessna slowly taxied towards the crowd I put my relief worker's head on and kidded myself that I didn't need a gun to protect me. I tried to imagine how the doctors were feeling. They didn't seem overly concerned, in fact, they appeared well relaxed, and if aware of the possible dangers, they didn't show it. I feigned a similar attitude, but I couldn't help registering all the possible escape routes from any dangerous scenario that might arise as soon as I disembarked from the aircraft.

The heat struck me, as it always did in this part of the world. It was like sticking your head in an oven for a brief second before I donned my baseball cap and what looked like a pair of designer sunglasses. In fact, these weren't the real McCoy, they only cost me £10, but if I had to give them away to appease some local I could always pass them off as the real thing. I was carrying four extra pairs just for that purpose.

We had stopped just short of the remains of the only serviceable structure left standing. It was the main terminal building, and the words 'Hargeisa International Airport' were clearly visible complete with bullet and rocket holes.

I was greeted by the two doctors, then by a local who turned out to be the Customs officer. He asked me for my passport and enquired if I wanted it stamped. This was a first for me, usually you don't get the option.

'Yes please,' I said. I thought it would be a nice talking-point when I got back to the UK. Who else did I know with their passport stamped 'Somaliland'? The Customs ceremony now taking place around the Cessna was equally strange. Two uniformed guards armed with AK47s gave a cursory glance — and a prod with their rifles — over our luggage and then leant up against the side of the aircraft, totally in a world of their own. They looked drunk. Curiously, they were both sporting a large callus-like growth on one cheek, as though they were sucking a giant gobstopper. I quickly turned away, trying not to stare for fear of causing offence. For all I knew it could well be some sort of cancer local to Somaliland; certainly I hadn't seen anything else like it in my travels. I felt sad for them. Had their deformity brought them together? I was curious to find out.

Later, I was told that none of the Western aid workers had an entry stamp in their passport. This was because they would frequently find themselves working in one part of Africa one day and the next being flown to another. And, like the world over, some countries will not let you in because your passport's been stamped by their warring neighbour. The north of Somalia, Somaliland, had no wish to be part of Somalia in the south and the south obviously knew this; after all, this was what the recent war had all been about. Getting into either country could be a right pain in the arse if you had the other's stamp in your passport.

As I was ushered to an open-back Land Rover (the usual mode of transport for this part of the world), I made out the fighters I had seen from the air, plus the masses of small but deadly anti-personnel mines, which were all over the place. It was as if someone had come along with a huge boxful and thrown them everywhere. The airport was *covered* in them, like confetti at a wedding. They looked like the screw-in tops of vacuum flasks and I knew exactly what they were — Pakistani-made jobs with nine grams of PE (Plastic Explosives) inside, activated by only a few kilograms of pressure. Nine grams of PE is enough to kill, but this nasty strain of mine was designed only to maim whoever stood on it, ripping at the legs and causing untold injuries to the rest of the body. As I've already noted, the design of anti-personnel mines is very clever, the appalling intention being to demoralise the rest of the troops or civilian population that witness the effects on their fellow men.

Apparently they weren't placed there by the local militia to keep the locals from ripping bits off the Migs; both the Migs and the mines had stayed there since the the end of hostilities. This is what happened, I was told. One day, shortly before the end of hostilities, pilots loyal to the south took off from Hargeisa, dropped their explosive ordnance on the very town that had hosted them — completely flattening it and its inhabitants — landed back on the airfield, then ran off into the bush and made their way down south. It was thought to be the first air strike in history where pilots from an airforce base-cum-civilian airport had taken off from it, dropped their bombs on the adjacent town and then landed on the same runway. This story came from a local aid worker as we sped off towards my temporary accommodation. I was really glad to learn it so soon after my arrival, it was a nice bit of recent history to get my teeth into and really cheered me up!

I was to see a lot more of this guy, Mohammed, who was to be my driver and my Mr Fix It. Although he stood well over six feet, there wasn't much of him to look at. He was very black and very skinny with short-cropped hair. His old army uniform was just hanging off his thin shoulders, and a month in a dentist's chair wouldn't have gone amiss. He was born in Hargeisa and vehemently despised the people from the south, especially those pilots. He was employed by aid organisations, one of the lucky people in this country with a job; that was because he spoke very good English. The job gave him a lot of street cred with the townsfolk, which in turn would make my job slightly easier in procuring kit that I had budgeted to buy in the country — essentially, petrol and paraffin.

My journey took only 20 minutes. Mohammed was a constant talker, pointing out all the sights of the war as we went, the vehicle bouncing as it hit every bump in the track.

'Hey, sir! Look over there, you see, big killings happened there recently, and, see that there, many mines, many mines. You need to clear them *soon*, sir. Much danger for the children,' he would say.

Although I was worried for my own safety, hanging on for dear life so as not to get thrown out of the vehicle and thinking about Mohammed driving over the odd mine, I made a point of looking interested in what he was saying. As I was, of course. I needed to get as much local intelligence on the town as I could and as fast as I could.

As far as I could see, there were hardly any buildings left standing and certainly none over two storeys high. All had some bomb or blast damage. They looked dangerous and uninhabitable, but were all lived in, while those who were not 'lucky' enough to have bricks and mortar made do with wooden and cardboard shelters on the sides of the road. London's 'cardboard city' had nothing on this place.

The devastation was almost incomprehensible, like nothing

I'd ever seen before. It was like travelling through a bombsite and a scrapyard at the same time. There were vehicle wrecks everywhere and hordes of people scouring around trying to survive. A lot of these people had lost an arm or a leg or both, due to many thousands of mines. Because the town was bombed flat, no luxuries were available. TV stations, newspapers and local radio did not exist. Also, all of its services — water, electricity and so on — had been knocked out, so there was the added hazard of open sewers running all over the place.

The stench from these open sewers mixed with a hundred fires the locals used to cook on would cut into my nostrils every now and again, causing me to retch and cough up a gobful of bile. As we slowed down or sometimes stopped to avoid hitting pedestrians, with Mohammed constantly on the horn, shouting and screaming at people to get out of the way, I really got the feeling I wasn't going to make my final destination. Indeed, I was beginning to have thoughts on what might be engraved on my tombstone: 'Here lies a man who was killed in a road-traffic accident whilst driving through the world's biggest minefield.' I pleaded with Mohammed to slow down and not crash. I didn't fancy spending one second in the hospital — if one existed — because if there was any disease to catch in the entire world, Hargeisa was the place to catch it.

There was one other thing which Mohammed kept pointing out to me all along the journey, as a child might: from the main drag from the airport and into the town, there were hundreds of piles of boulders.

'That's where the dead are buried,' he kept saying.

So you can imagine, with all these people living off a minimum water supply, no electricity, and with raw sewage running in the streets past dead bodies covered by rocks, in heat sufficient to fry an egg on the roof of the Land Rover, the smell was a bit tangy, to say the least.

My part place of residence for the next three weeks or so was the only building in Hargeisa with a new roof on it. (I had yet to source my main living accommodation. That would be dictated once I'd decided where I was to secure all the stores and equipment.) It was a single-storey structure surrounded by sturdy seven-foot-high metal security fence, newly constructed from scrap metal littering the town. There was enough space in the drive for three vehicles and, surprisingly, there was a small garden with yellow and purple flowers growing everywhere; a total contrast to what lay just a few feet the other side of the fence. A security guard-cum-gardener sat outside under a makeshift wooden hut.

Here I was warmly greeted by the two doctors, given a brew and offered something to eat. I declined politely, since my guts had been giving me shit for the past few hours. Instead I opted for a couple of glasses of Dehydralite to get them on the go. Then I was given a quick tour, shown where I was to doss for the time being, and left on my own. The doctors had their hands full and they were keen to get their newly arrived medical stuff up and running, so they left me to my own devices.

It took me a couple of minutes to tip the contents of my luggage out, to give it a bit of an airing, and then I went in search of Mohammed. I needed to make comms with Dik to see if there was any news of when Alistair was flying in, so I needed Mohammed to give me a quick lesson on the radio. There was very little I could do before he arrived, but the least I could do was familiarise myself with the area. So I asked Mohammed if he wouldn't mind taking me for a tour of the outside world.

'Mr Sir, I will be much delighted to show you around, we have many great sights here in Hargeisa,' he said.

'Thanks, but do me one little favour, will you, and try and keep to the speed limit? I mean, let's go *slowly* this time.'

'As you wish, Mr Sir, but if I drive fast, then any mines which go off will not hurt us.'

'I don't think that's strictly true. Who told you that?'

'It is true. I have seen it with my own eyes. It has happened to me only last month when I was driving over the tracks very fast — I ran over a little mine and all it did was go "pop" and break my back tyre.'

'Yeah, alright.' I nodded. I wasn't about to argue with him; he might even have been right. If it was an anti-personnel mine he had set off, then *maybe*; I gave him the benefit of the doubt.

I grabbed my small bergen, put a camera, some sweets in it and filled my canteen from a large water filter in the kitchen.

'Come on Mohammed, let's go. And do me a favour; stop calling me Sir. It makes me feel uneasy. Call me Steve, will ya?'

'No problems, Mr Sir, Mr Steve.'

For the next three hours he drove me around the vast, hill-less plains which surrounded the town. Everywhere we went the locals would wave and cheer, just as they'd done in Mozambique when we liberated Gurué. However, these people were fundamentally different from those in Mozambique. Yes, their plight was just the same, both having suffered the consequences of a bloody civil war, but the Somalians have a strain of Arab in them. By that I mean that their looks are very different from that of the Africans in the south of this vast continent. Their facial features are less pronounced and most have lighter skin because of their hereditary links with countries in the Middle East, such as Yemen, Oman and Saudi Arabia.

The scars of war were inescapable. Although we drove at a madman's speed, I still had time to take in many of the 'sights'. Along all the dusty tracks were burnt-out wrecks of old Russian-built war stocks. There were numerous T55 and T62 battle tanks, each graphically displaying war scars; wrecks of tracked AFVs (Armoured Fighting Vehicles) mainly BMPs; and lots more of the armoured troop-carrying versions of the wheeled BTR. There were as many military vehicles just in and around Hargeisa as I'd seen during my whole time in Mozambique.

What really caught my eye was not all these, but another piece of kit which RAF pilots used to call one of their worst nightmares if ever they had to fly over one — the notorious ZSU 234s. These tracked vehicles were about the size of a medium battle tank but without the long barrel sticking out of the front; instead they had four 23mm machine-guns to spit fire at enemy aircraft at a rapid rate of knots. They've always been thought of in the West as an awesome piece of kit, and here I was, seeing them for the first time in all their glory. I'm not some kind of anorak when it comes to military equipment, but like most British soldiers, I've spent many hours in the classroom studying Russian armoured fighting vehicles and aircraft, never expecting to come face to face with any. So it was quite an experience to see these.

We passed several remains of downed combat aircraft — two Migs and one other burnt beyond recognition — and two troop-carrying helicopters, a Hook and a Hip, both damaged well beyond repair. We couldn't get near them because they were well off the roads. There was also another vehicle that I couldn't really get a good look at, but nonetheless made me turn my head. To most people it must have looked very much like an old burnt-out flatbed truck, but I noticed it was an eight-wheeler carrying some kind of crane gantry on the back. I concluded it was probably a vehicle which could, or did, carry a surface-to-air missile. If that was the case, then there was probably some serious high-explosive ordnance lying around. That was some serious shit if anyone came across one and accidentally let it off.

The tracks we were travelling on had only recently been cleared of mines, not by experts but by ordinary people just walking over them and taking a chance. Most ended up dead instantly or, wounded by secondary fragmentation, died later through loss of blood or shock.

Along one track I felt the vehicle accelerate slightly. I didn't think it could go much faster. I thought Mohammed had already been driving flat out.

'This track is where I popped off one of those mines I was telling you about. We go faster,' said Mohammed.

'Why did you bring me here, then? To show me how you pop mines off?'

'No, no, Mr Steve, it's the way back to town. We have to go here. I have travelled it many a time and it is much safe now.'

I held on for dear life as Mohammed tried to follow the tracks in the dust of previous vehicles. Whilst doing so, I consciously pulled my bergen underneath me, to act as added protection to my manhood — not that a waterproof sack would hold much defence against an exploding mine.

In reality, *no* area was safe until formally searched, but since most of the mines which lay scattered around were the anti-personnel type, then as long as Mohammed stuck to used routes we were relatively safe. There had been no reports of vehicles running over the bar-type anti-tank mines (although designed to take out or at least immobilise tanks, a soft-skin vehicle will quite easily set one off), but I thought that was because very few vehicles were driving around at all. I only hoped Mohammed was as switched-on to the situation as he claimed.

Sobering though it was, the tour was just what I needed, in that I got a good feel for the plight of the people. Not what they had gone through, nobody could make sense of *that*, but how they seemed to be coping now. Several times I asked Mohammed to stop so as I could speak with people. Most of the time Mohammed had to translate, not because they didn't speak English, but because it was spoken in an accent that I couldn't readily understand. They were friendly enough and pleased that the war was now over. Like Mohammed they seemed to have an immense hatred for the government of the south but a sense of relief about, and great expectation of, the newly formed Council of Ministers, the government of the north. Was the price worth paying for their independence from the south? There was no doubt in their minds that the answer was yes.

Every mile or so we came across a checkpoint. These took the form of two or three soldiers presiding over a makeshift wooden barrier across the road and half a dozen bullet-ridden, 50-gallon oil drums filled with rocks and earth to act as traffic cones (presumably to double up as targets when the soldiers got bored). At every one I tried to have a polite chat with them and Mohammed explained what I was here for. At one checkpoint we skidded to a halt. These armed guards were much younger than the previous lot, probably not more than 17 or 18, all in new-looking uniforms. All four approached us. I was beginning to think we had strayed off the beaten track just a little too far. Then Mohammed stood up and shouted to them in English as they trotted over.

'Hey, my brothers, I have a visitor for you. Come, come.'

'What's going on?' I asked.

'These are my brothers, well, my brother's children. They are good boys,' he said.

Mohammed got out of the vehicle and greeted them all in a sort of communal hug. I stayed put, not sure of the rules of local etiquette. Anyway, I have learnt never to leave the vehicle if possible in certain situations. This might just turn out to be one of those 'certain situations', I thought. I gave a cursory wave to them all, but though they waved back they did not come over. After a few minutes of laughing and pointing in my direction, Mohammed got back in the driver's seat, the barrier was lifted and we drove through. As we passed them, one of the lads yelled out.

'Gazza, Gazza, Gazza, good football Englishman!'

'Paul Gascoigne, a top man,' I called back.

'They like football, they are *crazy* on it. They listened to the World Cup on the radio, the BBC World Service,' Mohammed explained.

'Ah yes, of course.'

I remember thinking that even in the remotest parts of the globe, the BBC World Service is listened to by many, a rich source of information for those who have very little to look forward to in life.

Mohammed seemed to know every one in Hargeisa, but there was something bothering me, and it wasn't a military thing. All the soldiers I had met had this gobstopper-like growth on their cheek, just as I'd seen at the airport. Mohammed put me right on it. It wasn't a cancerous growth or anything like that. Their mouths were full of the local 'weed', the root of a plant that they call chat. Looking a bit like spinach, it was sold in small hand-size bundles and chewed raw, the leaves as well as the roots. Apparently it was a mild, aniseed-tasting drug which over a period of time made you 'kick back', and was very addictive. Chat was now starting to be grown in the town, but because of the war most of the chat I saw being sold came in across the border via Ethiopia.

Apart from sugar, chat was the only stable currency on the 'vegetable counter'. It was sold in huge quantities every day at 12 o'clock sharp at chat markets all over Somaliland. Only the men took it, and it was the only thing to look forward to in the current circumstances. They would sit around for the rest of the day chewing the root into a large ball and storing it in their mouths, as a hamster might do with nuts, waiting for its hallucinogenic effect to take hold.

Word spreads very quickly about the smallest piece of gossip in a place like Hargeisa, especially when people have very little to do with their lives, and around late afternoon on my second day I got a typed invitation to meet with the newly established Government and its 'main man', a Mr Abdel Rachman. The invitation was very formal, like one to an Embassy bash, and I found its neatness curious.

Alistair had arrived during the day, so once he'd got himself settled and had a quick recce, we got ourselves cleaned up and went to visit Mr Rachman and his Council of Ministers for the Government of Somaliland. As we approached the main street where the government building was, we noticed lots of people running everywhere. There was also a warlike chant which got louder as we neared the Ministry. Mohammed had no idea what was happening, so as we turned the corner on to the main street he slowed down and asked a guy what the problem was. Alistair and I held our breath, hoping that this wasn't a coup. In such circumstances our invitation would tar us as friends of the 'old government', and as a result we would probably face death by firing squad. Quickly I ditched any evidence of the invitation by setting light to it in the front of the Land Rover. Then Mohammed said that everything was alright, there was no coup going on just yet.

'It's the people, Mr Steve, it's the people! They are very angry. They are very angry that one of the ministers has been talking to the government of the south. They are demanding that Mr Rachman hand over this minister.'

That's *alright*? I thought. 'Jesus Christ, Mohammed, you're kidding me. What sort of shit have we just run into!' I said.

'No, Mr Steve, I'm not kidding. We must get out of here, quickly!'

Everything seemed to be happening in slow motion. We were in the middle of a horrendously dangerous situation without a hope of escape. We couldn't drive fast or even manoeuvre the vehicle away because of the crowds. However, they didn't seem to take much notice of our vehicle as they were too intent on getting to the Ministry gates. At this point I thought I should have made getting tooled up my first priority on landing here. There certainly was no shortage of weapons, everyone had an AK 47 slung over their shoulder. Right now, I could have done with a nice little PPK pistol and a couple of mags of ammunition. Alistair was of the same opinion.

Mohammed quickly found a place to do a U-turn, but as we did it the crowd blocked us in and we were left at 90 degrees across the road, facing the government gates. The crowd was growing larger and noisier by the second, then they started to rock the Land Rover. Mohammed was silent, so was I, so was Alistair. It was like being taken over by a swarm of bees. Some of the crowd started to try and open the doors but we held them shut. Others clambered over the bonnet, yet others were hanging on to the outside. Then I realised it was not us they were interested in, but what was happening over at the gates. People had started to scale the security walls and in a few seconds the gates were open. A few shots were fired, and that was the signal for every man who had a weapon to fire a mag into the air. There was a big scuffle from the gate area, then my vision was blurred by this mass of bodies all wanting to get a piece of what was happening.

Suddenly the crowd parted in the middle, forming a gap of about ten feet. Here I saw one of the funniest but saddest sights I have ever seen in my entire life. Given the seemingly very dangerous situation we had found ourselves in, it was understandable that my bodily functions and emotions were doing all sorts of flick flacks. So I found myself laughing, but for the wrong reasons. Although what I saw looked funny, I was really laughing because I was very nervous.

The crowd had parted to reveal what I presumed to be the disloyal minister. Stripped totally naked, he was now being pursued with great haste down the road and out of town by a horde of women holding up what was left of his clothes. The crowd was roaring with laughter — not the laughter you associate with watching a good comedy, but laughter with sinister undertones, a sarcastic kind of laughter. Some were still rocking our Land Rover in their frenzy, and small arms were still being fired off into the air as they let rip with their emotions. Then, without any obvious reason, the firing stopped just as quickly as it had started and they broke out into full melodious song. The rocking of the Land Rover stopped, too, and the rest of the crowd gave chase. Then everything was silent. Suddenly, from a crowd of 300 or so, half a dozen armed guards at the gates were all that remained.

Alistair and I agreed that we'd had enough excitement for one day and told Mohammed to return to our basha. I asked Mohammed what would happen to the ex-minister. He just shrugged his shoulders.

'Mr Steve, the people were very angry today, you saw how they reacted. They thought of him as a traitor.'

'What will they do to him, send him back down south?' I paused. 'They won't kill him, will they?'

'Yes, of course,' he said, quite casually.

Whether that meant 'they' would send him back down south in a box or not, I never found out. It was left to my imagination to think the worst. I was in Somaliland, Africa, not Surrey, England.

Two things happened later that day. One, I sent Mohammed around to the Ministry with our apologies and to try and arrange a meeting for another day; and two, I persuaded Mohammed to take me to a man — every town has one — who would sell me something more useful than nervous laughter and a supercilious grin to protect myself with.

In the safety of a faintly-lit market wig-wam affair, and with the provocative aroma of hashish lingering all around, I found that a set of questionable designer shades and an American ten-dollar bill bought me a serviceable Makarov pistol, 50 rounds of ammunition, and a woman. I politely declined the offer of sex so, as a substitute I was then offered a box of 500 rounds for the pistol. These I also had to decline because I couldn't carry them all, and anyway, this was meant to be a covert deal, with no one meant to know that I was carrying.

Over the next few days Alistair and I had our work cut out.

First of all, we'd received a signal from the UK saying that six guys, the first of the training team, were due to arrive in country in four days' time. This put us under pressure to arrange the collection of the equipment up at the port of Berbera, where the landing strip was, and make the 350-mile round trip back to Hargeisa in time. We also had to locate where we wanted to establish the base camp and then liaise with the local militia chief Abdoli to arrange accommodation for his 400 or so men. These we were going to train up as the mine-clearance force, a force which I named the Pioneers. Timings were critical, it was going to be tight.

Early on in the second day I called up Baz on the radio to see how he was fixed about flying in, and to go firm on a RV with him at some spot up at Berbera on the afternoon of day four. He replied that he and his crew were all ready and told me not to worry about the loading that end, they had it all under control. They were definitely up for it.

In the course of my short time in country I'd already met with Abdoli and cemented our friendship with another pair of snazzy sunglasses. He was a short, thin, wiry man who looked 60 but I reckoned he was only about 40. Fighting for his country had certainly taken its toll. For sure, he was an experienced mine-clearer. So were his men, whom he had personally trained up. They were still responsible for clearing all the major routes in and out of the town of mines. Abdoli was also responsible for educating the kids not to play in areas his men had not yet cleared, but unfortunately, his warnings usually fell on deaf ears. It was not uncommon to hear the muffled explosion of another mine being detonated by little feet — in fact, it was a daily occurrence. His efforts had been acknowledged by the Government and because of this he was a well-respected figure about town. Not the type of guy to piss off, even though he might be wrong on a point or two during a conversation. Anyway, I liked the guy. Although he'd had a lot of shit in his life, he was still prepared to do something constructive for the good of his people. I could see it would have been easier just to sit back with the rest of them and plod on until the aid organisations flew in, but instead he got on with what had to be done to tidy up his town.

During our meetings with him, Alistair and I realised that he thought we were here to teach *him* how to clear mines. We told him no, we were here to teach the *men*, whom he was going to supply to us. Luckily, he was happy with that. We needed this guy on our side because he knew a lot more about the goings on and who was who than we did. We had to secure our relationship with him for the good of the contract. In addition, he had relieved us of one of our major problems, the site selection of base camp. He was adamant that the best place to train the team of Pioneers was the main army base, now deserted, just outside of the town. His men had cleared it for just that purpose: rockets, bomb, ammunitions, mines, the lot. We couldn't really argue with his choice, so once our quick recce was carried out, we had to agree.

In one meeting I got the feeling that Abdoli was a lot more powerful than he made himself out to be, and that somewhere there was a hidden agenda. I couldn't quite put my finger on what it was and didn't care to dwell on it too much, but it was something to do with the tribal culture in this part of the world. Since half the Pioneers were coming from afar, from another tribe, I could only surmise that there was going to be a clash of the chiefs further down the road. It was therefore good sense for Abdoli to argue the case for having the base camp set up in Hargeisa; if fighting were to break out, he would be on home territory.

From the outset, Abdoli had stuck very close to us and wanted to know what our game plan was. It was pretty difficult to tell him that, because we were taking every day as it came, almost making it up as we went along. The game plan kept changing because of the unstable situation.

Petrol was our main concern. We were very much governed by how much there was in Hargeisa and how much we could draw on at any one time. It fluctuated daily from one gallon to ten. Without petrol there was not a lot we could do. The few warlords with wheels basically controlled the fuel supplies, but that was where Abdoli came in. He had become aware of the problem, so had dropped a word in someone's shell-like, and sorted out our fuel problem. More importantly, he had also arranged for us to fuel up for the journey up to Berbera and back, on the understanding that he took a cut of the petrol ration. I had no problem with that, it was part and parcel of the operation, and an ideal example of the hearts and minds programme I've mentioned elsewhere.

The journey from Hargeisa to Berbera took us through some of the most inhospitable terrain I have ever travelled across. Abdoli's men, an armed posse of about 20 of his best mine-clearers, accompanied us. Bandits were all about us so I kept my pistol cocked and very close. As it took us the best part of the day, we arrived at Berbera late afternoon. We were greeted by the MSF project co-ordinator for Somaliland, a young, thick-set Belgian guy who called himself Frederick, Fred for short, who'd made Berbera his capital. He seemed pleasant enough, with a charitable brain in his head, and he turned out to be a good laugh after he had got his head around the fact that his home had just been invaded by a couple of British ex-servicemen. We stayed the night in his apartment which was a newly converted shack with all mod cons: a TV and video, hot and cold running water, carpets and new-looking furniture. Berbera was a lot more upmarket than Hargeisa and in general the people were much better off — though one couldn't go more downmarket than Hargeisa.

That evening Alistair and I went through the following morning's game plan with Fred. It was important to start as early as possible, and that would allow us to start our return journey equally early. That way, we wouldn't get caught out in the wilderness during the dark hours. I didn't relish getting into a firefight with a horde of roaming cutthroats, with or without Abdoli's men. I also needed to get out at first light, if possible, because I had to recce the airstrip before Baz and his team flew in — we had gone firm on landing at about 05.00 hours. I also had to meet up with the man in charge of the trucks we were going to hire. Back in Hargeisa Mohammed had said that there would be no problem getting transport, because the port was the only area in the whole of the country where truck owners could find work. Fred confirmed that. However, I wasn't thoroughly convinced, and had to see the trucks with my own eyes before I was 100 per cent sure they existed. But that would have to wait for the morning.

In typical Belgian style, Fred invited us out for dinner. I thought he was kidding; where the hell was there to go? But no sooner had we arrived, once I had dumped my kit on my bed space, I was bouncing, with Alistair, in the back of a Toyota Land Cruiser, heading towards the big lights of the town, without even so much as a splash of water over my face to take the day's grime away. Here we could sample the delights of downtown Berbera and God knows what else.

It was dark when we entered the town, which was nothing more than a large market-place made up of about 100 wooden stalls, all set up in an 'organised-chaos' way. Lighting was available only to those wealthy enough to afford a fuel-run generator or small, sweet-smelling paraffin-type lamp. The big lights I had seen from Fred's basha, which I had thought marked our destination, were actually those on the dockside, and we weren't anywhere near them.

The market had a vast array of fresh vegetables and fish — and some not so fresh! Sweet, acidic spicy smells wafted all around us. The place was jammed with traders and hawkers out on the hustle, and thousands of bargain hunters all shouting at each other. It was a prime example of a place you shouldn't go after dark, but here we were.

There were people out eating, but not as we might do back home, sitting outside a restaurant on a hot summer's night; these people were eating on the ground. There weren't any tables, apart from an open-area eating house where we were heading. It was the only 'restaurant' I could see with half-decent lighting — a dozen or so strings of light bulbs precariously suspended from a series of long poles, though all but three were blown.

Our waiter for the evening was a big, wart-faced local. I didn't think he was from these parts but none the less still had the usual ball of chat stuck in his gob. He was dressed, not in a waiter's uniform, but in a ragged, faded white T-shirt and a pair of jeans that had seen the arse-end worn out of them a long time ago. As he approached our table, I noticed that Fred and Alistair were deep in conversation.

'Can I see a menu?'

'Sorry, man, we have no menus, only one dish, meat,' the waiter replied.

I felt slightly embarrassed for even asking. Fred looked up and laughed.

'Three of the specials, then, and some water please,' I said.

'Excuse me, sir?'

'Food for the three of us, that's great,' Fred replied.

We all burst out laughing at what I'd just said. It wasn't that I was trying to be funny, I just wasn't thinking. How was I to know that there was only one dish available?

What he brought us was a great scoff of goat stew served up on an old but clean-looking metal canteen tray — the sort you get in the army or prison — and washed down with lumpy, very sweet guava juice, and for afters, quite amazingly, we had a dollop of homemade ice cream. Where that came from or how it was made I had no idea. Actually, it tasted like a very cheap vanilla-flavoured ice cube, but still, it was appreciated. Later, Fred told me that the goat had been slaughtered in the old 'bash-it-to-death-with-wooden-clubs-where-it-stands' method, a tradition in this part of the world. That would have accounted for the bits of splintered bone and grit in every mouthful. Again the people were very friendly. A few stopped and talked to us while we ate but most just stared as though we were some kind of new breed of circus animal. They did seem happy to see us, though. Fred was a great host, and he chatted away to the locals in their half-Arabic, half-African lingo. By the end of the evening's festivities I was pretty sure Fred had 'gone bush' while living out here.

With no hangovers the following morning, we were all up and at it, and by first light we were standing on the end of one of the longest runways in the world, only to be confronted by a quite extraordinary, eerie sight. As the light broke through a high cloud base, I had this strange sensation that I could have quite easily been on the front line of the first Russian offensive at the start of World War III, if we were still experiencing the Cold War. In front of me stood well over 200 SAM missiles, some sited on their ground-based launching pads. Many were at their launching angle of 45 degrees but most were lying down, as if ready to take the place of those due to be fired. It just blew me away. They were all of a late 1950s–1960s model and had been sweating here in the blistering sun since the mid-1970s, ready to 'cock off'.

I stared in sheer amazement, wondering, What if the Shuttle has to use this runway and the pilot's a bit bleary-eyed from his descent and crashes into the lot of them? Some fireworks display for sure, probably it would vapourise the entire port of Berbera. As difficult as it was, I put the thought of the SAMs out of my mind and got on with the task of recce-ing the landing strip, but every now and then I kept glancing back at them, just to reassure myself that this was not a dream.

Apart from a few lumps of rock and wood left by the locals, the landing strip was all clear. I picked a spot for the Herc touchdown where the sun had not burnt into the tarmac too much, then called up Baz. He was in the air and on time. When I told him about the landing strip and the SAMs, he just laughed. I guess it was a standing joke among incoming pilots and the people of Berbera.

The distant rumble of a Herc's engines getting closer always sends a shiver of excitement down my spine. It's a great feeling if you know it's coming to pick up from a mission or to drop a resupply, and that morning was no exception, as the sound told me that Baz and his crew were spot on time. Of course, a different feeling of warm nervous tension enters the body when the ramp is lowered at night at 28,000 feet and you know you have to jump out of the thing.

The Herc landed in a great ball of dust and for a brief second I couldn't see it, but as I heard the massive engines in reverse thrust it reappeared magnificently and taxied towards us. It took us an hour to unload, by which time the four hired trucks had arrived. They were old Russian wrecks, but not as bad as those in Mozambique — at least these had some tread left on their tyres! With the help of some locals we loaded up in no time, but now we had a problem. The drivers were unwilling to drive all the way to Hargeisa because of talk about recent bandit activity. Even though the trucks were loaded and the drivers had known of their destination the day before, no amount of persuading by Abdoli was going to get them moving — so I had to offer more money. By the time the haggling had finished it would have been cheaper to buy a truck, but at least I got it sorted. Once that was out of the way, we were off, heading back west.

I swear they must have had the current year's Hertz price list, the amount it cost: US$180 per truck in the end, and that's how they wanted it, not in local currency. I didn't blame them because their currency wasn't worth a bean; that amount in local notes wouldn't have fitted into the boot of an average car.

Over the next two weeks things really got going. First I set about establishing the base camp and setting up some kind of routine so we didn't get every Tom, Dick and Harry roving about the camp on the ponce. The trainee Pioneers were arriving daily and were sorted by Abdoli and his men, and all of our team had arrived safely from the UK. There were six of them, plus myself and Alistair; that made eight.

They were a diverse bunch. One guy, Stuart, had just recently left the Royal Navy after six years and this was his first civvy job. Two more, both young, were ex-SBS, and another was an old hand, Vic, who had been around the bomb disposal business for many years, and the last two were ex-Naval guys. On initial appearances they all seemed switched-on and looked the part. We settled in no probs, since we were all used to roughing it from our Service days, and on top of that they were being paid a big wedge of £200 a day for an initial six-week period. In addition, the organisation asked us to find a further guy to monitor the team on their behalf (a rather unusual request), so JJ came on board.

It took us a week to get the camp into some sort of order. We pitched our new tents in military-style lines, dug shit pits and invented makeshift showers, which were refilled by means of an old water bowser I had commandeered, and secured all our equipment under lock and key. Everything was going fine. We were getting on well with the locals and really gelling with Abdoli. Through him I eventually got a meeting with Mr President himself. Everything was very amicable, and if there was anything the team required, all we had to do was ask. It had the makings of a great contract.

One night, about three days before I had to return to the UK to liaise with Forester, JJ wanted a chat with me, reference a 'delicate operational point'. He told me that he had a few reservations about some of the team's experience in clearing land mines. Who did he think was not up to it? I asked.

'All of 'em,' he said.

I asked him to explain this pretty serious accusation. And

over the next hour or so I found myself living my worst nightmare. There was a bit of bitchiness in JJ's tone, but fair play to him, it needed guts to come out with it all. It transpired that all the guys were very experienced clearance *divers*, but the four Naval guys had minimal hands-on experience in any form of *ordnance* disposal. Disposing of under-the-sea missiles with just a bit of hands-on removal of mines on land was not enough. As for the two SBS guys, they had less mine-clearing experience than I did. They were more used to putting mines on ships, not taking them out of the earth.

JJ continued to express his doubts, constantly apologising for not wanting to drop any of the guys in the shit. Everyone had to earn, and £200 a day was a lot of money to lose; on the other hand, he wanted to know that the team he was going to work with was all on the same wavelength.

He went on: 'It's not like you can bluff your way with these mines, it's dangerous shit. Abdoli's men, they do know a few things about mine-clearing, be it slightly less orthodox than the way I've been trained.'

It wasn't till the following morning that I briefed Alistair — I'd wanted to throw a few things around in my head before I spoke to him. Not surprisingly, he was as shocked as I was. In fact, he was furious.

We decided not to mention anything to anyone and went about our business as usual. Operationally this was not a problem because the team was still waiting for all the rest of the Pioneers to arrive, so there was not much to do apart from familiarisation with the local ground and personalities.

The next few days I couldn't help thinking, Why hadn't I been stronger in putting my case for an all-Engineer team? How could Forester make a balls-up on such a momentous scale? Of course, I knew how! He didn't have a clue about the business we were in — but I knew that anyway, it was I who wrote up the contracts and sourced all the necessary equipment for the job — and he sure as hell didn't understand the logistics of working on the ground in a hostile country, otherwise he would have listened to what I had been telling him.

'You have to know the beast,' I would say. I'm not being derogatory, I'm referring to 'us', ex-Special Forces people. Whether we like it or not, we are a different breed of soldier — I know that because I'm one — and I know how my people tick. Forester didn't. Putting an unqualified team on the ground compromised us totally. The people who you are trying to help lose all faith in you, quite rightly so, and that's when you get *big* problems. Hearts and minds go out of the window because the locals see you as a bunch of bluff merchants. You lose all street cred and, worst of all, you could end up losing your life. In this part of the world, life is as cheap as a five-quid blow job. As it turned out, the day I left Hargeisa was the day I left Somaliland for good, but none of the team was to know that, and neither was I. My intention was simply to go back and brief Forester on the situation, resolve it by putting the right guys on the ground — the ex-army guys I'd wanted in the first place — then return.

As a matter of course for anyone flying back to civilisation, I was handed a shopping list of things the guys couldn't buy locally, mainly small items such as washing and shaving kit and torch batteries. One item jumped out at me — *ten* big boxes of Kellogg's Corn Flakes with a name scribbled by the side of the order! It was a request by the guy who had just got out of the Navy. It's usual on such jobs that on the first ration supply a few goodies are thrown in, a couple of boxes of cereals or a few Mars Bars, but that's your lot. It's normally a one-off gesture because they're non-essential. Bulky items such as boxes of cereals are usually the first things to get ditched because aircraft space is always at a premium. Anyway, cereals go soft within a few hours of being out in the heat. It did bring a smile to my face, despite all the worries, when I knew that I was right about the drawbacks in picking an all-Navy team because of their inexperience in the field. It left me thinking, What the hell was this sailor's last posting — the Good Ship Lollipop?

Back in London I voiced my concerns to Forester, in particular his selection of team members. He should have listened to Alistair and me. My other point, which he failed to take on board, was that we couldn't just arrive in a place like Somaliland with a shedload of all-singing, all-dancing boxes of brand-new equipment and shiny things, then start to train the Pioneers, who basically possessed shit all, in the art of land-mine clearance, and not recompense them with a half-decent wage.

During the drawing up of the contract I had addressed precisely these problems, plus the need to build in a lot of 'fat' for any unforeseen events that might happen during the contract, such as hosting the President and other important people who would be crucial to the smooth running of the job. But Forester disagreed with me, taking the line that we were out there to help them, not party with them.

'Now listen, Steve, I don't know how you guys accounted for hosting parties when you were in the SAS. I bet you had to pay for it yourself, no doubt.'

'Well, Forester, you seem to know what's what, but actually we had a thing called a Squadron Fund which was part of the budget and took care of all necessary parties. You mean to say you didn't have a similar thing when you were working in the City?'

'Yes we did, but it was all strictly accounted for in a business-like fashion, by way of receipts.'

There was not a lot I could say about his comments but, with hindsight, I should have. Since he had the money in the bank and held the purse strings, it seemed to me at the time that he preferred to choose profit before professionalism. It was my opinion that he thought that he was dealing with a bunch of, as he put it, 'idiots' who didn't know, or care to know, the difference. I was convinced that the profit had gone to his head and now he was slowly losing the plot through his own sense of greed.

'You come back here and tell me that the men I've sent out are clearance divers and not land-mine experts! *Ha*! You're just trying to scaremonger and throw a spanner in the works. Now I know *exactly* why your wife left you!' Forester yelled at me.

I blew up. 'Well fuck it, that's it. Sort me out the money you owe me, and make sure that includes all my commission on all the equipment I sorted out — because *you* didn't have a fuckin' clue about jack shit, and I'll leave you to it.'

'I'm paying you only what we agreed, and that's the daily rate times the time you were out in Somaliland; not a penny more.'

Now, as you can imagine, on hearing what he had said about my ex, I was spitting feathers. I was *shaking*. He had now made it very personal and that particular conversation has stuck with me ever since. The money, well, I just had to write my commission off and put the episode down to experience.

As a man, I could have done one of two things. My first thought was to jump over his desk and slit his big fat belly and watch him slowly haemorrhage to death. Or I could clear my

desk and simply walk away. With emotions running high, I did
the latter, just turned and walked. If I hadn't done, my life
would be rather different now. I might still be doing time for
murder or at least attempted murder; worse, I might have had to
flee the country and go on the run, never to see my daughter
again. I was so raging with anger that on the drive back home
to Hereford I wrote off my mother's Audi at Oxford, the pride
and joy of her life as my late father had bought it some years
earlier; *that* was a fate worse than death.

Having thus severed my links with Forester completely, I was no
longer involved with this contract in any way, though I did hear
that he got hold of someone else to run it, keeping the same
guys on the ground.

Some months later, a friend of mine who worked for the UN
sent me an eight-page confidential assessment document that
the UN and other agencies had written about the working
practices of Cadogan in Somaliland. On the one hand I read
through it with great delight, but on the other I felt a great deal
of sadness for the people of Somaliland. They'd desperately
needed this operation to work.

It was a scathing attack on Cadogan's inabilities to carry out
such an operation. Criticisms were many. Examples: one, the
'in-country' team was not qualified to carry out or train others
in the clearance of landmines, the whole point of its being
there; two, the team members didn't keep records of areas that
had been cleared by the Pioneers once the contract was up and
running, which is basic, drummed into every student on day
one, week one of any landmine clearance course; three, there
was an inadequate amount of remuneration for the Pioneers,
and no insurance policy to pay them in the event of accidents

(hearts and minds); four, there was inadequate 'in-field' medical cover — again, another basic. The list of bad points went on.

In another document attached to the assessment was a quote from a guy called Yusuf Hussein Diria, a 27-year-old former mine engineer in the Somali National Movement, and one of the founders of the Pioneer Corps:

'When Cadogan came here it seemed that they came to learn, not to teach. They were asking us questions.'

There was also a list of the dead and injured as the contract got under way: one Cadogan team member seriously injured; seven Pioneers killed, and over 30 injured.

To sum up from the same article, there was a piece which read: 'After continuing strikes by the Pioneers because of one thing and another, mostly over pay, and, believing that the Cadogan team were about to leave the country without paying them, they surrounded the team members' living accommodation and held them at gunpoint, and only when government officials intervened did the Pioneers lift their siege. This allowed the Cadogan men to make good their escape and flee the country for good.'

Some time later, I found out that Cadogan had disappeared from the old offices, never to be heard of again.

Alistair and I still keep in touch from time to time. He, too, thinks he was stitched up like a kipper by Forester and he told me he was seeking legal advice about his situation. The rest of the team I have not seen or heard from since I left Somaliland.

1 2

VIPs

ost Cadogan, I took a bit of time out. My brain was totally mashed because of what had happened in Somaliland. I'd seen another great opportunity wasted because I didn't have total control over what was going on. It wasn't that I thought that I was always right, that I was the all-singing, all-dancing know-it-all about security; I don't, and never would, say that. But there are certain things in life where you instinctively know what is the right way to do things and what is the wrong way. I was no different from any other professional person who had been taught by the best in their particular field.

So, in order to control my own destiny and to put into practice what I thought to be the best way, I set up on my own. With the money earned from the Somaliland job I set up shop in a small office in Curzon Street. Although the rates were pretty high, this being Mayfair, I was right in the centre of prospective clients who might need my skills the most, and who could pay for them.

My main strategy was to pursue the annual Arab family bodyguarding contracts. These amazingly wealthy people lived out of the big London hotels, such as the Intercontinental, the Hilton, the Mayfair and the Dorchester, for weeks on end during the summer months. That was where the money was, so that was where I pitched.

During the first weeks, I worked all hours getting my name around the circuit and establishing my credibility as an operator. Some nights I would catch the train back to my brother's house in North London, but most of the time I slept in the office. It wasn't the most comfortable of options, but then again, my life has never really been that cut and dried.

My first big break came when I was working on the security team for Prince Khalid, commander of the Arab forces during the Gulf War. He had recently rented, on a five-year lease, a large Georgian mansion in a very select area of London. It was rumoured to belong to the Queen Mother.

The BG team who went with him all over the world were all ex-US Secret Service or Special Forces guys, and good to work with. It was during their first trip over that the team leader asked if I could take on the static security of the house whilst they were away, and when the Prince came to visit, would I supply the extra qualified bodyguards, so his men could get a rest. This was to happen at least twice a year, for about four weeks each visit. Of course I could! It was the break I'd been looking for.

The Prince was an OK guy. He didn't say much but because of his military background he knew the score about security and looked after his bodyguards. It was the first time I'd experienced the vast wealth such people possess. This mansion cost several thousand pounds a *day* to rent, on a minimum five-year lease. That didn't include the security, the live-in butler and the house maid. On his first visit he had plans drawn up for a £20 million refit of the inside. The outside, as you would expect, was listed and couldn't be altered. It was certainly a good contract while it lasted.

As in a lot of these jobs, when your point of contact (in my case the Prince's head BG) changes, so do the people below him — as they say, a new brush sweeps clean — so my team of guys were replaced and the contract was then run in-house by the new operator. I wasn't too concerned at the time, since I had had a good few months and had earned well from it.

A year later, in 1995, I was working for his elder brother, the three ic of Saudi Arabia. I was part of a six-man team for his seven-week summer trip, working and living out of the Hyde Park Hotel, Kensington (as it then was — now it's called the Mandarin Oriental Hyde Park). I really enjoyed working for the man. He was polite and never gave us any security problems.

By contrast, there are some clients who would just leave their room without warning, so the corridor security man would have to radio through quickly to the BG team. Then half of the team would crash down the corridor to pick up the client, whilst the other half would be running around the hotel securing the lifts on room level and ground level, calling up the drivers to get ready for a pick-up. Sometimes it would transpire that the client might only be going down to the hotel restaurant, so the BG tactics had to be changed, and the drivers stood down and someone then had to secure the restaurant. The usual form was that half the team got split, since most of the time orders sent by the BG via his radio transmissions as he descended in the lift came through broken up. With a good team you could usually pre-empt the client's move, but even so, it was always prone to a cock up or two.

However, we had no problems like that with this Prince. He would always tell us well in advance when and where he was going — not that he went anywhere much, but it was nice to give the team a bit of warning beforehand. When he did go out it was generally out for a walk in Hyde Park or to a high-class Lebanese restaurant. He never went shopping, never met with people outside the hotel. If people wanted to meet with him, they had to make an appointment through the Saudi Embassy and visit him in one of the rooms on the fourth floor of the hotel, which he took over for the duration of the seven-week stay.

To give you some idea of the wealth these people have, he spent over a million pounds just on the rooms and service alone. That's wealth! One of his small daily expenses was this. The Hyde Park Hotel's original front entrance was, in fact, its back, which faced onto the park. To have access in and out of the hotel's park side (commonly known as the Queen's Entrance) it cost £800 a day — just to have that door kept open. Another fascinating thing: every day, ten or so boxes of dates would be flown from his own date farm in Saudi. They were the best dates I've ever tasted, really sweet and gooey. I ate a ton of them on that job.

One day when I was stagging on in the corridor, the Prince's personal BG, a colonel in the Saudi Armed Forces, approached me in a slightly uneasy way, which struck me as odd since he was usually pretty up-front, with a do-as-I-tell-you attitude.

'Hello, Mr Steve. Please, I have a request.'

'Hello, Colonel.'

'Mr Steve, the Prince wants two gazelles.'

'Two gazelles!' I stepped back in amazement.

What would the Prince want with two gazelles? Was he going to keep them as pets and fly them back with him to Saudi, to leap about in the desert with his camels? I didn't know.

'There is a party tonight and the Prince requires them for his guests.'

'Oh, OK, Colonel, now I understand — he wants to eat them.'

The Colonel looked at me, as if to say, What else would the Prince do with them, you stupid security man?

'Yes, there is to be a party tonight in the Royal Suite.'

'Leave it with me, sir, I've got a contact, I'm sure he'll help us out.'

This, of course, was complete bullshit on my part. I had trouble trying to hold back my laughter. I didn't have a clue what a gazelle actually looked like. Still, I'd have a go. I had no idea where to start but then I remembered a posh butcher's down on Mount Street which always had fancy game hanging in its window. They said that they were fresh out of gazelle that morning (I got the feeling that that they were taking the piss in a friendly sort of way) but they did put me on to a farm in Scotland. The long and short of it was within four hours the Prince's personal chef was preparing two juicy gazelles in the kitchens of the hotel.

After the party (it was six o'clock in the morning when the last guest left) the team was given the pick of the leftovers. Now that might come across as though we got the scraps, but that's not the case. It's a traditional Arab custom always to cook more than enough, so for ten guests they would sometimes cook as though for a party of 40. This derives from when they were Bedouin, living in the desert. Because they wouldn't see people for days, sometimes weeks, at a time, when a lone traveller did pass by, the host would cook a huge meal and the guest would stay for a couple of days to pig out on goat and rice. The amount of food served was generally an indication of the host's wealth. Well! For breakfast that morning I had my first taste of gazelle and a couple of sheep's testicles, washed down with Arabic coffee — a bit different from a 'Greasy Joe's' I know, but it had to be done!

As I said, in general, the job was problem-free. There were no incidents and no attempted breaches of security. All in all, a good job which tipped extraordinarily well.

One morning the Prince got up and wanted to go for a picnic. He didn't know *where*, but he wanted to go for an hour's drive out of London, and he wanted to picnic in a park by a river. That was our brief. We assisted the Saudis in organising everything, from selecting the picnic location to sorting the food and the extra transport needed. He wanted a couple of special coaches for himself and his entourage. One guy on the team had a contact with a London coach company and got their best coach sent to the hotel, but when it arrived the Prince's aide-de-camp said that it wasn't good enough. I couldn't see the problem — it was the poshest coach *I'd* ever seen. It had everything: three TVs, videos, telephones, a fridge and freezer; and was fitted thoughout with leather and deep-pile carpet. It was the bollocks of a vehicle, but it didn't have a half-moon sofa on which the Prince could hold court, so it had to be sent back. The only coach then in the UK which met the Prince's specs was up in Birmingham, of all places. An amount of cash was agreed and the coach was driven down in time for the entourage's departure.

The chosen picnic site was a park not far outside London. We arrived just as the park was closing and it was getting dark.

A £200 tip to the keeper was enough to keep the gates closed with us inside. The Prince ordered the vehicles, eight in all, to form a circle facing in and, with the aid of dipped headlights, the Prince and his party started to eat. The spread was typically Arabic, a huge carpet was thrown on the grass with everyone sitting cross-legged on it. The scoff was all piled up in the middle: the best cuts of lamb, China's rice ration for a day, lots of fresh salad and fruit and a ton of dates. Without any warning, the Prince called us over to come and join him, but we had to decline his invitation, we were after all his BGs, there to do a job. Then, in a calm and official tone, he *demanded* we join him, so who were we to object? Six of us sat down with the three ic of Saudi Arabia in a park on the outskirts of London whilst his own Saudi bodyguards stagged on.

A couple of summers ago I ran the BG contract for the Royal Family of Qatar during their stay in London. They were a bit late in arriving for various reasons. They'd decided to spend three extra weeks in Switzerland, and during this time a power struggle took place between the 'old man', who was out of the country, and his eldest son. Calling it a bloodless coup would have been too strong a word for it. However, the family flew to London nonetheless.

Unlike in our Western culture, Arab men are allowed more than one wife, and my client had three of them — though only two arrived on this trip. It was the general rule that they stayed in different hotels, out of sight of each other; watch out if ever the twain should meet, and all that. The split was between two local hotels, the Intercontinental Hotel on Park Lane and the Mayfair Hotel just around the corner, off Berkeley Square.

Because of this situation I divided the team of 12 BGs, six with me on the younger wife staying at the Mayfair, six with the

First Wife. We also had four corridor men stagging on at the two locations, two on during the day, two at night. This gave us the ability to sanitise the floors which the family took over in the two hotels.

The BG team also stayed in the hotels and on the same floor, to be in a position to react, should an incident occur. We put a 24-hour cover on both wives for the duration of their trip, which was to last several weeks. Only rarely did I give them time off. It's expected on these types of jobs in order to keep the continuity of the team and not to give the 'principals' (the common name for the people BGs look after) an added cause for concern by having them see different faces every time they went walkabout.

Because of UK gun laws we weren't allowed to carry guns, and this applied to any other form of weapon: knives, stun guns or telescopic truncheons, for example. The only specialist pieces of kit we carried or legally had access to were our personal radios, explosive sniffers and metal detectors, the last two for use by the corridor men. No one — principal's guests, members of the entourage, not even the staff of the hotel — was allowed to enter our floor unless cleared through the corridor men first. Certainly no letters, packages or food entered the principal's room unless it had been given the once-over. That was usual SOPs.

We developed our own radio procedure and code names for every entrance, exit, bar, room and restaurant, and for every eventuality. We closed down all routes in and out of the floor, including dividing doors and service lifts. The fire escapes were the only exits we had to be aware of. Since we weren't allowed to seal them, for obvious reasons, we somehow had to cover them with the corridor men. The idea was to deny access to anyone who wasn't supposed to be on the floor but, in the same breath, not piss off the principal's daily routine with her own people and, more importantly, not interfere with the smooth running of the hotel and its staff. When working in a hotel environment, hearts and minds are a big part of the bodyguard's role. And just as the BG team was on standby 24 hours a day, the drivers of our four stretched Mercs, plus those of the back-up vehicles, had to be as well, and were briefed about keeping a 24-hour watch on their vehicles.

One particular incident happened at the Hyde Park Hotel I mentioned earlier, but with a different client, a Yemeni businessman who thought he owed someone some money. That was the brief I got from my contact, but even when I pushed for a bit more info he wouldn't elaborate. We had to take the threat factor as fucking high, so a team of four guys was soon living in the hotel and working around the clock. The client was picking up the bill for everything, and that included three meals a day and as much tea, coffee and mineral water we could drink. Problem was, he had forgotten to organise the laundry. Just with the tea and coffee business, four guys lazing and standing about 24 hours day can easily rake up a bill of over £200, just for room service, so the usual form is for the team to chip in, buy a kettle and some brew kit, and brew up in our ops room (normally my bedroom) to save the client a couple of thousand. On this occasion, though, the client didn't want this to happen, for whatever reason. Now, because he was a very busy man and he was financially looking after us big style, I could hardly go up to him and say, 'Hey boss, the guys love the £250-a-night rooms, and have you eaten at Marco Polos yet? The steak is well tasty! But we got a problem — you haven't paid for our suits and shirts to be laundered!'

That would have gone down like a death at a birthday party.

So I set up an arrangement with the in-house laundry man myself. He would do all our laundry for a 'ton' a week. Now that was a good deal. Everything came back just as clean, crisp, fresh and neatly individually packaged as they would have done if we were paying guests. But, of course, one guy had to rip the arse out of it. Unbeknownst to me and the other two guys, on his day off, he decided to bring in all his clobber and dump it on our laundry man — four binliners full! It was, of course, duly laundered and returned, but this time he had his own bill. He tried to back track and made the usual excuses: 'I thought it was OK.'

What a twat. Some guys just can't stop themselves from taking the piss out of a nice little arrangement. When he finally parted with six crisp nifties I kicked him off the job and then went to do some damage limitation and a hearts-and-minds job on the laundry chap. Though I won him over, things weren't the same, but he finally came around after the job when we invited him and a few of the hotel staff (the security people, the room service and floor staff) out for a drink to say thanks for their help. No doubt one of us might be staying in that hotel again in a couple of months' time. Doing little things like that goes a long way towards making the job run smoothly and thus giving you street cred with your client or principal.

As I've said before, you rarely ever get the true story of why someone like this requires such a level of protection; it's the nature of the game. On this occasion the job came to an abrupt end when the client simply came up to me a fortnight into it and said that he had 'sorted out his business, thank you very much, it was nice knowing you, you and your men did a great job'. Fundamentally, 'Thank you and goodbye.' That's how a lot of these jobs finish. If you're lucky you may get 24-hours' notice. It's not an industry in which you can plan long term, that's for sure.

Contrary to popular belief, being a bodyguard in London is not as risky as it may seem. Certainly, crime in the West End (an area which we rarely worked outside) is pretty high, but the threat of our principal being taken out, or snatched by a terrorist organisation or a grudge merchant, was relatively low. Our main concerns were the tosspots, scumbags and wankers cutting about the streets, who all of us have to put up with in everyday life.

I've been involved in many an incident caused by these types. It's a big problem for the BG in London, especially when working with the Arabs. Every second I'm out with the principal I'm always waiting for that lone gunman, the 'shoot past' by a guy on a motor-bike, or the closet terrorist dressed up with a full-face veil to let rip — but, in reality, it's always the twat with a can full of extra-strength lager in his hand or some street vendor who makes a scene. They're probably quite innocent and mean no harm, but for some reason I just happen to attract these sorts.

I could be walking unobtrusively down Regent Street with my principal (no point in playing the big hard man, that's not doing the job; if you do, you're asking for someone to take a pop at you) when someone like the relentless beggar out of *The Life of Brian* tries to get in between us, or worse, tries to touch the principal, in a vain hope that they might be handed a slack handful of pound coins. The pavements are usually crowded as it is and I and my team have enough problems trying to assess the threat situation, and work out what shop the principal is heading towards, without these added interruptions.

It takes a very good BG with quite a few jobs under his or her belt to sense and disarm a situation like this. You have to turn it on its head. You don't say anything in front of the client, or anything which he or she may hear. Your job is to let them get on with whatever they want to do, without them feeling they're being BG'd. You speak only when you're spoken to, and *never* chew the fat with them. Arabs can be very strange people, they have different mannerisms and ways of doing things and addressing each other, sometimes in a tone that comes across as rather offensive to Westerners. Trying to get close to a principal to gain some 'brownie points' is not professional and generally gets you kicked off the job. If you're the chatty type, the BG game is not for you — trust me.

The point is, a good BG should be by the principal's side and *not* be by their side, if you see what I mean. Not invisible, because that takes away the whole point of your being there. You're there to be seen by others, but rather like a baby, you should be seen but not heard, ready to react to any threat or situation with the least amount of hassle between you and the third party. I always make sure that I have a few pound coins with me to give away, because once you've given them a quid, they're off you and on to the next punter, and that's where you want them — away and out of your face. When I give them the 'tip' my eyes are usually telling them, 'If you start to hassle me and my client when I come out of this shop, then I'm gonna hassle you and I don't give a fuck about my job.' It's a mutual respect between two professional people working together in unison. It works.

On another Arab job I had two occasions which could have turned nasty. The first was when I took the principal shopping at Selfridges. Because my Sheika dressed in her native gown (so did her three sisters), I naturally stood out like a sore thumb, which can attract attention. Some bloke suited and booted, walking around with four Arab women in the ladies shoe department could could only be their BG. (It is not unheard of for clients to want female BGs but it's still rare — it may have something to do with the attitude towards women in some societies.) We were going up the escalator, the Sheika first, then me, then her sisters. I always give a one- or two-second pause at the base of escalators, just to put a bit of space between me and the Sheika before the next person gets on. Sometimes this can cause a bit of whingeing from the person behind me, especially if they're in a rush. On this occasion, a woman, late 20s and very smartly dressed, came pushing her way up and passed us. I had pinged her previously, hanging around at the base of the escalators, partly because she had no handbag, which I registered, and partly because I'm a man and she was a good-looking chick. I managed to protect the Sheika without touching her by shouldering this woman away from both of us as she passed. But, because the escalator was quite narrow, and because of the gravitational effect of 200 pounds hitting about 100, the woman bounced off me and was almost flipped over the edge. Luckily she managed to keep her balance and shot passed us. The Sheika was not overtly disturbed by this incident because she didn't know what had gone on, or the reason for it. As the woman reached the top of the escalators, she gave me the finger and shouted down to me, 'You fucking baldy twat!' and ran off. Very ladylike, I thought, and from behind the Sheika's back — and very unprofessionally — I gave her the wanker's sign in return.

I knew exactly what her game was. She was a bagsnatcher. They work all over the West End in the big stores, Harrods, Harvey Nichols, Selfridges, and the like, in teams, sometimes as big as 12. Usually they go for women's handbags. Their MO is to identify a rich-looking victim, suss out when to hit them (usually away from the security camera or guards) and, once the bag has been snatched, in all the confusion it might go through two, three or even ten hands, depending on the situation, before it's out of the store. Hitting someone on the escalator gives them a softer target than on the ground. It just wasn't this girl's lucky day. Tomorrow she would be back, with a different hair style and colour, and dressed in a totally different outfit. (All credit to Selfridges' in-house security, incidentally — they were right on the case.)

The other episode when my heart hit the floor was when the Sheika decided to do a left-wheel off the pavement and crossed the road just outside Harrods. Normally, most principals like to drive round London but this particular Sheika was a bit of a fitness fanatic. She walked everywhere, but didn't use the Green Cross Code. I was close beside her, looking right, left, right for the both of us, when a motorcyclist came screaming down one side of the traffic the wrong way, obviously in some kind of rush. It was all I could do to grab the Sheika's arm and, in a semi-violent sort of way, yank her back out of the path of the crazy shit. She said nothing and we carried on crossing the road. When we got to the other side I apologised for being a bit rough and said something like, 'That was close!' She would have had it for sure if I hadn't pulled her back. She might have met her Maker riding on the back of a Kawasaki 750, and I probably wouldn't have got paid. Because she had said nothing, I thought that I might have offended her, but she thanked me shortly after, which put me at ease. No man touches a wife of the Amir back in Qatar; that was the Amir's job. If they *did*, Allah have mercy!

Incidentally, a much less serious — indeed, almost comic — incident happened some days later. We were in John Lewis on Oxford Street, buying up half the store's bedding and cloth. We were there for well over two hours, so all I had to do was stand close by while the sales team ran round collecting her orders. Ten grand here, two grand there, fifteen grand on some special cloth or something. It was pretty boring, but I still had to stay totally alert. It was mentally and physically mind-blowing, and my feet were killing me. Every now and then the Sheika would turn about to see if I was still with her and give me a smile as an acknowledgment. If she wanted my opinion on something she would ask me, which was nice since it wasn't the norm. Going shopping has never bothered me, unlike most of my mates who just can't stand it. If you hate it, don't work with the Arabs, because this is half the BG's task.

Anyway, all the time I was hanging around trying to blend into the background when customers started coming up to me, thinking that I was a salesman. This was probably because I was dressed in a dark suit and just standing there. The first time a woman came up to me and asked if I knew where the deli was. I said that I was sorry, I didn't know. The second time someone questioned me, I said the same thing. The third time, by which time I was getting a bit pissed off with it all, I just stood upright and forced a little bit of saliva to dribble out of the side of my mouth without saying anything — this got rid of *that* one! I guess she thought I was mad. Next, a lady in a well-cut designer outfit with a Sloane accent demanded to know where the lifts were, in a really pompous and patronising way. I was taken aback by her complete rudeness, so I put on my best Spanish waiter's accent:

'I speaka na Engleesh, no comprende, no comprende.'

She went off in a bit of a state, talking to herself. What I *didn't* know was that the Sheika had heard me and turned around. She grinned and said that she was not going to be much longer (Christ, I hoped not! We'd been in the store for well over four hours), rather as a wife might speak to her husband — a trait in her which I found quite endearing.

During this trip I went everywhere with her. Twice a week, for example, down to Panache in Knightsbridge to buy £1,000 worth of sweets on two trays, which she gave to us when they had had their fill. We did every designer shop possible more than once, bought a £600 pair of kid's shoes from a shop in New Bond Street, did 12 grand on an antique vase estimated at four at Sothebys, which I bid for by waving my paddle in the air. This Sheika, along with her sisters, was young and very pretty — no more than 30, she still had 50 years of shopping in her, and she could certainly shop! She shopped till *I* dropped, and as the job was coming to an end, I was really looking forward to some rest.

My daily routine was up and at it and out of the hotel by ten, walking around one of the four parks in the West End, then straight to the shops for a few hours, back in for two hours during the afternoon, then back out again to visit friends — or *more* shopping!

On the last day of the job, there was a quick change of plans. The family had arranged to fly to France on their own personal 747, so we organised all the vehicles — six stretch Mercs and two trucks for the shopping — for a run-up to Heathrow, but an hour before we left the hotel the Sheika decided she wanted to travel on the Eurostar train so we had to 'all change'. The car I'd previously sent ahead to liaise with the VIP lounge up at Heathrow now had to go to Waterloo Station. I didn't know if Waterloo had a VIP lounge or any procedure for VIPs. A quick call to a friend who worked for British Rail confirmed they did, so he then jacked up the introductions for me and secured the VIP lounge for a party of ten. When we arrived at the station we were met by the station's management and everything went like clockwork. Very soon the Sheika and her party were safely on the train and the Qatar security people were satisfied with the handling arrangements at the other end.

My job was finished when the train had disappeared out of sight. Now as I've said before, tips on these jobs are not the norm. If you get one then you get one, and if you don't, well that's the way it goes. You should never expect it. The custom is, the day before their departure, both principal and their two ic will sit down together and go through who should get what and how much, starting with the hotel staff departments through to the drivers and then the BGs. The money is put into individual envelopes, initialled and sealed. This is the way the Arabs do it. You might be forgiven for thinking that because they are VIPs they wouldn't be too bothered with the whole process of 'bungs', but they are and they take it very seriously. They are very well aware of the wealth they possess and know how we mere mortals tick. Why not give the people who serve you a wad of the nifties, especially if you've got more money than you can shake a stick at?

After this process, one of two things happens. Either the client will give the envelope to you personally or (and this happens in most cases) their aide hands them out and, nine times out of ten, the contents aren't in their original envelopes when we get them. A 50 here and 100 there stacks up to a little nest egg after 20 or so envelopes in half a dozen countries have been tampered with. I've seen the old envelopes left in the bins before, because one of the jobs of the BG team, after the principal and entourage have left the hotel, is to keep secure all the rooms the party may have used: one, check to see if anything has been left behind in the rooms (and unofficially, rob the fridges of all their goodies) and two, we're on duty until we get the nod that the principal's flight is actually airborne and they haven't changed their mind. That has happened on a couple of occasions — I've had to re-book the rooms or find another hotel. They usually go back to the same hotel which is only too pleased to have them back, even though they might have trashed the rooms and floors every time they stay. Even if you won ten million on the lottery tomorrow there's no way you'd be able to have the lifestyle of these people. Well, that's not strictly true, I suppose your money might last a couple of months.

Over the years I've worked for many Arab families, some good and some not so good. I don't consider it an honour or a chance to suck up to someone whose least worry in the world is the size of their bank balance. I do it because I actually like the Arab culture, their way of life and especially their food; and what other job allows you to stay in the world's top hotels and sample the culinary delights of the best restaurants for nothing?

A small but, in my opinion, misguided group in the BG circuit believes that the Arabs haven't done a good day's work in their lives and have only got their wealth because they were lucky enough to have oil. Well, these guys should check themselves. They should look at an aerial photograph of Dubai. Back in the 1960s there was nothing but sand and desert, yet look at it now, a real humdinger of a place. It's home to some of the most modern hotels in the world, grand modernistic shopping centres that put ours to shame and, on top of it all, has brilliant weather and fantastic beaches. A great place for a holiday, yet all this rapid expansion, built up in less than 40 years, has left their millennia-old culture intact. I don't think other nations could have kept up with this explosive change of pace in the way the Arab culture has.

13

LIAM AND PATSY

Sometimes jobs come from the most unusual of people. One in particular was from an old friend of mine, also in the security business, who'd let his ego get the better of him over the years. I broke off the friendship because he was cutting around London telling anyone who would listen to him that he was once in the SAS in order to drum up business. I have no problem people bluffing normally; if they kid themselves that that is what's needed to get on in life, then all well and good. Sad bastards — still, a man's gotta do what a man's gotta do, and it's the perfect line to say to the uninformed client because it's an area in which people are often too apprehensive to ask questions. If they do, a bluffer can reply, 'Can't say too much, you understand, because what I used to do was Top Secret.' If the bluffer's good at it (and this guy tells a good story) he can have you believe it. So, if you ever come across someone who says this, just ask them, 'What Squadron were you in, and when?' I've met quite a few bluff-merchants and many are convinced that they were once in the SAS, even though I know they weren't.

Anyway, this particular guy asked if I would do a BG job for him. It was looking after Liam Gallagher, of Oasis fame, and the actress Patsy Kensit, whilst they were staying at Blakes Hotel on their honeymoon. I like Oasis as a band and quite fancy Patsy, too, and since it was only a short job I decided to bury the hatchet.

I hadn't done too many stars. It's not because I hadn't had the opportunities, but rather, I was kept busy either with the Arabs or doing surveillance jobs of one sort or another. I'd read in the press that Liam could be a bit punchy, but then again, who wouldn't be if you were 20-something and had been shot up the ladder of fame with a few million quid thrust into your sky rocket? I know I probably would have been, and anyway, I looked forward to meeting them.

For a few days before the wedding the press was speculating about the location of the honeymoon. It was all the tabloids were full of during early April that year. It wasn't until Liam did a bit of his own PR (not that he needed it, I guess it was more fun for him than anything else) that the press finally got the location of his hideaway. He'd contacted a showbiz journalist and revealed their location, so that was that. The cat was out of the bag and by way of a thank-you the journalist sent the happy couple flowers and champagne for the tip-off.

Set-ups between a star and their favourite journalist have always been a way of manipulating the media, and getting the press on your side if you want them. I wasn't above this type of game-playing either. I'd recently had my first book, *Terminal Velocity*, published and reckoned it would make an ideal wedding present. There's nothing like a good book to read before you get your head down, so I took one with me on the job. Totally unprofessional, but you've got to take windows of opportunity when they present themselves. As long as it doesn't compromise the tactics of the job or piss off the principals, there's no harm in it.

The job was fairly routine as far as BGing went. I was pleasantly surprised by how level-headed Liam was, and how gorgeous Patsy really is. They were no problem at all and, as you can imagine, they didn't venture further than their bedroom for a couple of days. When they did they were pretty casual, polite and laid back. It wasn't until the world's press turned up outside the hotel that the circus really kicked off. I was shocked to see so many reporters and pressmen waiting outside. I didn't think two people could attract so much media attention. I was wrong.

There was much speculation about what Liam and Patsy were up to (I thought *that* was pretty obvious, considering the event). What room were they in and when were they coming out were just a few of the questions thrown at me as I came in and out of the hotel. The media stagged on all night in the hope of getting that 'one' picture or hearing a bit of verbal from Liam that might earn them some attention. The newlyweds, however, were having none of it; they kept their heads low.

There was also a bit of rivalry between some of the newspapers, and Liam's reporter had a plan that he wanted to put into action. He asked if he could set up one of his rivals and the other papers by pretending that *he* was Liam. I had no problems with that since he apparently had Liam's ear. In order to carry out his prank he hung out of one of the hotel rooms and only exposed his arms in full view of those below, making out that he was Liam. It seemed a bit childish but he obviously knew what he was doing, because several front pages the following morning showed a photograph of 'Liam's arms' not knowing that they weren't really his. The prank also had the effect of drawing them away from where Liam and Patsy were actually staying, which was on the ground floor out the back, in a sort of private Spanish villa affair. It helped us with security, since any budding paparazzo or desperate fan would be put off the scent.

On their last day, word got around that they were leaving so the mass of people doubled. Pressmen on chase vehicles like motor-bikes and little mopeds were starting their engines, ready to cut through the traffic and back alleys to follow the star's vehicle at speed. Flashlights popped every time there was a bit of movement inside the hotel. They were all fired up for the happy couple's exit.

Liam and Patsy wanted to leave by the front but those outside didn't know what exit they were to leave from, or when; only Liam's reporter contact and his people knew that. I think they both quite relished the photo opportunity and wanted to give the photographers and fans something for their efforts. I've often wondered what it must feel like to command so much attention, having thousands, *millions* of people hanging on to see what you're going to do next. What power! In my job it's quite the opposite. Most of my life has been spent trying to look inconspicuous, playing the 'grey man'.

Once they were ready, one of the team sent a decoy vehicle around the back with a couple of lookalikes in it. This was just to fire up the press and get rid of some of the more gullible ones. Those who knew their business had all the options covered, so as not to miss anything.

Standing inside the hotel with Liam and Patsy next to me was how you imagine boxers feel, just when they make that walk from their dressing rooms down the corridor and into the arena packed with crazed fans. Liam was slightly rolling his shoulders to and fro, Patsy stood silent. I was going through all the 'what ifs' in my head. What if a fan tried to make a grab for either one of them? What if the car was a few seconds late and we were stood around waiting while hordes of people chanced their arm and advanced? What if this became a re-run of the John Lennon affair?

This last was Liam's main concern, quite rightly. Oasis were frequently compared with the Beatles, so it was seriously plausible that some nutter might come out of the crowd and spray the happy couple with a quick burst of 9mm — and me and the team, too. That's why I planned it that I would lead Patsy out. She and I would go first, then following me really close behind but off to a slight flank would be Liam, surrounded by the rest of the BGs. This would achieve two things. One, it would make for a good photo shoot; and two, it would be the best way of protecting them without making out that we were surrounding them totally and playing it over the top.

As we continued to wait for confirmation that the decoy vehicle had left and taken some dupes away with it, and for the signal from the real vehicle's driver that he was 30 seconds out, Liam chirped up.

'Hey Steve, what'ya think? Are there gonna be any problems out there? I mean, I've heard there's a lot of press out there. I don't want no hassle, know what I mean!'

'You're joking, aren't you? They're all your fans out there, the decoys worked, and besides, you've got the A Team with you.' I tried to calm him down, not that he looked nervous. He was more used to it than I was, but I guess this John Lennon thing played a bit on his mind, and on Patsy's.

'The only problem we'll get is if you lamp one of them,' I said jokingly.

That seemed to break the ice.

Then the radio clicked in — the driver was 30 seconds out. I asked if everyone was OK, then led off. We took a slow walk out. Some of the hotel security had managed to hold back the crowd for the best part, but as we appeared a natural surge brought the crowd closer. My eyes were everywhere. Patsy was close and I was aware of everything around me. My senses and heightened awareness were working overtime. I took everything in, looking at the crowd, through them, behind them, for that one individual who might have been wearing a mad person's face that day. Then I was aware of the Merc pulling up, and all the pops and clicks as a thousand cameras and flashes worked.

I'd briefed the team that only the near-side door was to be unlocked and that I was the one to open it. We neared the Merc. The driver stayed in the vehicle as briefed. Mentally I picked up on all the central locking devices on the door. They were down, good, and as I put my hand on the rear near-side door, only that door's locking mechanism sprang open — the others remained firmly locked as intended. Quickly I helped Patsy in first. As I did so, the crowd saw that this was the last chance and broke ranks, but they were too slow. Liam was now getting into the car. I had to bundle him for the last bit, and in doing so trapped his left trainer in between the door and chassis. As quick as I draw a pistol, I took out my wedding present, threw it inside and slammed the door shut. Immediately it was locked from inside by the driver and the car was speeding off, followed by little hatchbacks and motor-bikes.

It was a good clean job. Everything went well. No one was pissed off and no one hurt; Liam might have been suffering from a bruised ankle, that was all. Later that day the BG team convened in a pub just around the corner from Blakes where we met up with the reporter Liam had contacted, who had promised to get the first round in. He asked me what I'd thrown into the Merc. 'My book, of course!' He wasn't aware that I had written one, so he demanded one, too. He also wasn't aware that he had just witnessed one of the best BG teams in operation working the London circuit.

The Monday after the newlyweds' honeymoon, a tabloid got in touch saying they'd received a call from a businessman who'd read an article about the whole episode and required a similar level of protection.

One of the paper's writers had taken a contact number for him and passed the enquiry directly on to me. It was nice of him to do that, because I've learnt that, in general, nobody in the media ever gets in contact with you to pass on info which they aren't likely to get something out of themselves. For some reason, newspaper people and publishers always have a million things to keep their minds occupied during any one day (like the rest of us don't, of course!) so I was pleasantly surprised by this call.

The paper hadn't vetted this man, but there was nothing wrong in that — vetting was up to me, checking him out to see if he was genuine or just another Captain Bullshitter with a dog's breath of an attitude. I decided to make the call the following morning. I dialed the mobile number and a well-spoken Brit answered.

'Yes, speak,' a rather sharp voice bellowed.

'Hello! Steve Devereux, you called the ...' I was interrupted.

'Of course! You're the guy who was looking after that Oasis chap and his wife, interesting. Thank you for getting in touch. Are you in London?'

'Yes.'

'Oh good, that's great, so am I. I wasn't sure whether that reporter would pass on my call. One knows all too well what the press can be like.'

He was very friendly but not to the point. He kept talking, as though he was trying to beat me in a verbal contest or liked the sound of his own voice. I didn't have a chance to interject. I've always been a bit hesitant in dealing with someone through a third party, especially over the phone. You can never tell if they are serious or just want to chew the fat; they could even be a hack searching for a follow-up story, in this case about the honeymoon. So I let him talk, that's always the best approach. That way you can at least get the feel of whether they're full of shite or not.

My first thoughts were: a Rupert; middle-aged; probably fat through years of a high intake of 'business lunches'; used to strutting around shouting at people and making himself feel important. I had a feeling that he probably worked for an Arab or some wealthy guy from the Far East. I don't know why, it was probably something to do with all the foreign business connections I'd met through Nassar. Most of these highly successful, extremely wealthy Arabs had a middle-aged city type, usually an ex-public school boy, running around after them, advising on financial deals or educating them on the

Brit way, whatever *that* was. Really they were just highly paid handbag accessories who enjoyed the prestige of their boss, whilst as far as I could see, not really giving much in return, other than being part of this country's old boy network — which, as we all know, can open City doors.

It transpired that his boss (not *his* word, I think he used 'business associate' or something — typical of this type, always wanting to be in charge) had got himself into a spot of financial bother with a bank and wanted to know if we could meet soonest and talk through a possible security scenario to look after his wife and daughter whilst his boss conducted business dealings with a series of banks in the City of London. It would require 24-hour cover — was I interested?

From his use of the term 'security scenario' and mentioning 24-hour cover, I surmised that he was ex-forces; definitely a Rupert. That would explain his rather pompous manner when talking to me, like the way an officer would address his men on the parade square. A less likely thought was that he'd had dealings with other security companies in the past and had picked up on the lingo. I don't think so, though — my first theory felt correct.

I might be critical of my prospective clients but sometimes these forms of introductions do pay off, so during the conversation I managed to force my choice of venue for the meeting, since he was coming across pretty much like the 'man about town'. I suggested a discreet table in the bar at the Lanesborough Hotel next to Hyde Park Corner, a place I knew well. I would be a lot happier meeting in familiar surroundings on my patch.

'You know it?' I added.

'Yes, I know it well, let's say about two. Is that OK for you?'

I looked at my watch. Only 10.30. I got the impression from his tone that I had managed to jump in with the location before he did, and that's why he quickly suggested a time, a sort of one-upmanship. It came across arrogantly, but these Rupert types always do! However, I wanted to reduce the time before meeting him. From his tone I figured out that he'd never been to the hotel and I didn't want him to do a recce.

'I can't make that, I've something else on.' I tried to push his hand. 'How about 12?'

After all it was *he* who wanted *me*, and actually I did have something planned. He agreed. All this might seem a bit too tactical, too much like thinking on your feet, but a lot of people — clients especially — expect it. It bores me to death, but I still have to go through the routine of it all. It's par for the course in the security business.

The trouble is, sometimes I just can't help feeling very cynical about this entire line of work. I've learnt so much on the bodyguard circuit and it always seems that this side of the business is full of people living on another planet in one way or another. If it's not a member of a team who thinks he's a budding Jean Claude Van Damme or Dark Destroyer, strutting about like they've got a bore brush for an 84 anti-tank weapon rammed up their arse, then it's some of the clients, who never cease to amaze me with their inability to take advice from their personal bodyguard. Maybe they've seen too many movies and live in that world where everything ends up perfect for the good guy.

Anyway, I made the RV at the Lanesborough, and so did the client. It was a meet that was to bring all my skills as a soldier, BG and businessman into play.

But that's a story for another book!

PART THREE

You can never plan the future by the past.

Edmund Burke (1729-97)

1 4

THE DIANA TRAGEDY

Before I bring you up to date on what's been happening to me, I'd like briefly to interrupt the narrative to look at one particular issue.

Many people outside my sphere of work ask me about the Princess Diana tragedy. Why did it happen? How could it have happened? When I tell them my thoughts on the matter they seem surprised that my opinion is as simple as it is. Like a lot of other people, they want to believe in the sinister side of the theories that are still flying about.

In fact, my considered opinion is not what they want to hear. Such people are full of all the crazy theories — mainly thrown up by the media, who should know better — such as:

Diana was killed by the Security Services because she was speaking out, abusing her privileged position by giving her views on politics and international affairs such as the mines issue. That's ludicrous. My experience working with MI5 or MI6 and other security agencies tells me that they would never have picked the tunnel as a place in which to take her out. Even I could have selected a better 'killing ground' than that! It's even more ridiculous to think that she would be taken out by our Security Services because she was seeing, and going to marry, Dodi Al Fayed, an Arab, which would have caused great embarrassment to our nation.

Another ludicrous belief is the planning of it by one shadowy top man in the Government, so that some cold-blooded killer comes out from some MOD arsenal in the Home Counties and does the job. To maintain that the execution of any operation like this can be achieved by one man alone is completely wrong. Others *have* to be involved, and, I reiterate, where secrets are concerned, the only secret that's truly a secret is the one you don't tell anyone else about. We human beings are very fallible when it comes to talking — especially when it comes to knowing something that nobody else knows.

So, what follows is my qualified theory on the entire Diana affair. Now, having worked in exactly the same position as her BG, for many different sorts of principals, I believe that what they all have in common is this: if they want to do something out of the arranged security brief, then they'll do it. I'm not saying that this is *exactly* what happened in this incident, but it appeared that there were some really serious cock-ups in the procedure of choosing the driver on this occasion. The principals pay the wages, and as a result dictate the state of play. So let's go with this scenario.

Dodi comes down from his room with Diana on his arm after a great evening with the woman of his dreams, then sees the world's press sticking its nose in all over the place — well, this would get any man's back up. Then bear in mind the word 'love' and all those inner emotions that go with it, detaching the mind from everyday realities; with that *and* their high profile, emotions were bound to be running high. So in order to get out of the situation he and Diana had put themselves in, Dodi probably grabbed the nearest employee, and told him to get in a car and to get them away from the situation.

The BG would really have little or indeed nothing to say about this: it's not his place to stand up and debate the issue with his boss in front of the world's press. He would be far too professional to do that. Within seconds the driver would have been told to get away from the hotel ASAP. Minutes later, there's a tragic road traffic accident where three people end up dead. I know it's simple, but I can't read anything more sinister into it than that: a statistic of high-speed driving.

It wouldn't be the first time the principal has done a runner in great haste. Many a time I've been in a similar situation, and I'm sure a great many other BGs can tell you the same. Once I was forced to take a black London cab because my principal didn't want to wait five seconds for our bullet-proof limo to pull up — yes, *five seconds*! I've been in circumstances where I've suddenly been told by my principal to ride in the back-up vehicle because he wants to ride in his vehicle alone. It's totally unprofessional and well risky — but what can you do?

And what happened next in this instance? When we arrived at a set of traffic lights on red, some chancer on the pavement, seeing £200,000 worth of motor with only two up, decided to make a beeline for it and gets into it on the principal's side. Of course, myself and the rest of team were out of the back-up vehicle like a shot. Immediately I took in that, although the principal was obviously shaken, no real damage had been done and the chancer was politely pushed to one side. So we carried on, this time with me firmly in the principal's vehicle. (The driver of the vehicle wasn't trained in the art of defensive driving but I'd known this and had given him a thorough brief before the job started. However, he obviously hadn't listened, otherwise he would have had all the vehicle's doors locked and the windows up.)

My point is, why have BGs if you don't use them, or at least take on board their advice? Security problems will always occur if you don't keep to the basics of security. After all, the basis of any security plan is just plain common sense — prevention is always better than the cure. The problem is, principals can always be difficult. Many principals believe a driver is just a driver and a BG is just a BG — wrong! The driver should also be trained in defensive driving techniques and in BG skills. Once mobile, the driver is the main player of the BG team and common sense dictates that he should be cross-trained in *all* security skills. Certainly he shouldn't just be an ex-cabbie — you're really asking for trouble if that's the case.

Now I don't want to get into a slagging match over people's personalities, but this is how some principals operate. An old friend of mine, BB, once told me the following story. He worked for the Al Fayed family as Dodi's personal BG, and one time when he was working on board one of their yachts in the South of France, he had a run in with Dodi. Dodi was soaking up the sun with a slack handful of bikini-clad beauties, when he ordered BB over.

'Come here, you big fat donkey, come over here.'

Now BB wasn't a small man. He was very skilled and liked to work out and never took shit from anyone. So he walked over to Dodi and his friends, who were all giggling like little schoolgirls do, and said, 'Don't you *ever* call me a big fat donkey again, shit for brains, and, oh, by the way, you can poke your job up your fucking arse.'

He packed up his kit, took one of the speedboats and went ashore. Then he phoned me up (I was back in London at the time) and asked if I could send him over some cash to get home. The point is, I don't speak ill of the dead but that episode underlines what I've just said: principals can be difficult. And the BG circuit is full of such true anecdotes.

EPILOGUE

For years I had tried unsuccessfully to get out of the security business. In some ways I craved a normal way of earning a living, a nice steady job with long-term prospects and being in a stable loving relationship. When I got close to securing this, something always came up — a long-term job overseas — and snuffed out any planned holidays, and even those things you might have arranged with your woman went tits-up in the pursuit of the buzz and the money that the business gave: the relationship with the woman whom you love had to take a back seat. It was no different from being back in the SAS, and that's the reason why a lot of men from my background don't manage to hold down a long-term relationship. I only wished I could be part of that very small percentage who make it work.

Then unexpectedly, fate intervened.

It was at the book launch of some famous cricketer in ex-Arsenal and Northern Ireland manager Terry Neill's celebrated London Sports Bar at the back end of 1995, chilling out over a few beers, that I first thought about writing my military autobiography. I'd just finished a three-week surveillance task, trailing the wife of some foreign industrialist all around the City and the Home Counties, in anticipation that the client might lay his worst fears to rest through me and my team's efforts in not recording any extra-curricular activity of a sexual nature by said wifey. As the beer began to flow, I was encouraged by a group of journalists to put pen to paper. Fourteen months later the result was my bestseller, *Terminal Velocity*, published in 1997.

Shortly after, my good friend Billy Budd, who had left the Royal Marines to pursue a career in the film industry, finished working on the James Bond movie, *Goldeneye*. He'd struck up a friendship with the actors Pierce Brosnan and Sean Bean (he presented them both with Royal Marine berets) and suggested I send Pierce a copy of *Terminal Velocity* via his production company. I did just that, not really expecting a reply, thinking that the book might get waylaid before it to got him. At best, I'd just receive a 'thank-you' letter from one of his secretaries. So I forgot all about it, then, about a couple of weeks later, I got a call on my mobile phone from someone who I thought was Billy taking the piss. Alison took the initial call.

'Steve, it's for you.'

'Who is it, darlin'?' I shouted from upstairs.

'Excuse me, who's calling?' asked Alison.

'It's Pierce Brosnan.'

'*Who?*'

'It's Pierce Brosnan, Steve sent me a copy of his book and ...'

'Oh, I'm sorry, Mr Brosnan, I'll just get him.'

Alison handed me the phone turning her face up, indicating that she wasn't sure who the caller really was.

'Hello, who's calling please?'

'Ah, Steve, it's Pierce Brosnan ...'

The caller, making out that he was Pierce, carried on talking about how much he was enjoying reading my book. I must say that it did sound like Pierce but knowing how good Billy is at impersonating famous film stars I let the voice go on for a bit before I interrupted and said, 'Listen, Billy, wind your neck in, will yer, you don't sound frig all like James Bond, what's your point?'

'No seriously, Steve, it's me, Pierce Brosnan.'

'Fuck off, Billy, you twat.'

'No, no. Well done on your book, I really like it. I'm reading it now, on the set of *Tomorrow Never Dies* and I've got a few minutes so I thought I'd give you a call to thank you ...'

It was then I realised that it really *was* Pierce Brosnan on the phone. We spoke at length for about 30 minutes but every so often he would get a call, probably from the director of the film, and he would say he would have to go, then just as quickly he would say, 'Oh that's alright, they don't want me now,' and would carrying on talking.

'Yeah, I've still got that Green Beret Billy gave me. I think the kids use it as a duster!' he concluded jokingly.

'I know what you mean — they're not as coveted as the maroon one. Green ones are two a penny,' I replied. I struck up a good banter with Pierce.

He was particularly interested in my description of 'fitting up' for a HALO jump, which he said he was going to re-enact in a few days' time. He reckoned that I should seriously consider writing a film script about the battle for Goose Green and that if I didn't mind, he would put me in contact with a friend of his who was a very good screenwriter to help me along. Did I mind!

I gave what Pierce Brosnan had said to me a lot of thought. After all, he knew his business and knew what might or might not be a good story to be made into a film. So I took his advice and began to put pen to paper once more, all along knowing that the famous bloody British victory at Goose Green had never been made into a movie. I could only wonder why, but if someone as famous as Pierce Brosnan said, 'Go for it,' then why not!

So Billy and I started to work on a screenplay. That was a year ago and since then life has gone at an extraordinary pace. In the summer of 1997 Billy was working on Steven Spielberg's blockbuster movie *Saving Private Ryan* as stand-in for Tom Sizemore, who was playing Sergeant Horvath. This was a stroke of luck as far as I was concerned. I'd never been on the set of a big film before, especially a war movie, and this gave me a much-needed insight into just how a movie gets made. I met with all sorts of behind-the-scenes technical people, actor Tom Hanks's make-up artist, the assistant directors, the renowned Captain Dale Dye, the film's military adviser, through to the security and catering people.

You could say I had a two-day crash course on movie-making and to top it all I had the greatest honour one could imagine, and that was to meet with Steven Spielberg and most of the film's cast: Tom Hanks, Tom Sizemore, Matt Damon and Jeremy Davies. This experience definitely made it far easier to understand what it takes to write a screenplay.

Needless to say, all those actors got a copy of *Terminal Velocity* and it was really encouraging to see Matt Damon in the mock-up of a Normandy village, dressed up in his US Rangers uniform and reading *my* book in between his scenes! I felt very humble that an actor of his stature was reading about my military experience. When he later said to Billy he found it fascinating that here he was playing the part of a soldier in combat and reading a true account of what it was like to be in a war situation, it was very gratifying, to say the least.

Finally, after the few weeks of filming in the grounds of the old British Aerospace factory in Hatfield, just outside London, all the crew packed up and moved back to Hollywood. During this time Billy and I had got to grips with the basic gameplan of our screenplay and were going full steam ahead with it, effectively spurred on by Tom Sizemore even though he, too, later flew back to Hollywood.

A couple of weeks after Tom left we got a call from him, asking how we were progressing with the script and inviting us both over to LA to finish writing it in his Hollywood apartment. He said he was off filming another movie and we could both have the run of his place without being disturbed. What could we say? We both jumped at this opportunity, and within a week boarded a Virgin flight for Los Angeles International Airport, each with an open return ticket in our pocket. I mean, you've gotta take these once-in-a-lifetime opportunities when they present themselves, haven't you?!

When we arrived in Hollywood, Tom and his actress wife Maeve Quinlan gave us the complete tour of the town. We were treated like their special guests — really, they couldn't do enough for us. Both Tom and Maeve are great hosts, and wanted to help us to succeed with our screenplay by introducing us to as many of their showbiz friends and getting us into as many doors in the film industry as they possibly could before they shot off.

Some weeks before, I had booked a well-earned holiday with Alison to the Caribbean, and as most travellers do for a long flight, we grabbed a load of reading material. I picked up the usual *Newsweek* and *Time* magazines and Alison bought a load of glossies and, completely by chance, one, that particular week's *Hello* magazine, had a five-page spread on Tom and Maeve, all shot in their fabulously decked out apartment overlooking LA in West Hollywood. Had anyone said that just a little later Billy and I would be spending six weeks in that same apartment, I would have thought them slightly on the mad side, to say the least!

I don't think I'm a natural writer, I find I really have to concentrate when I hit the keyboard, but when I do the hours just fly by. I can look at my watch and it might read midday, and the next time it'll be five or six in the evening before I get up and get some scoff or have a brew. It's only then, when my concentration is broken, that I feel mentally drained. I don't have to work in a totally silent environment, I can quite easily do it in a crowded restaurant or with the radio on, but the noise has to be constant. If, for example, the phone rings then I lose all concentration. Luckily, Billy works very much in the same way, so we complemented each other.

Perhaps this has something to do with our combat experience, being able to perform under a shower of bullets maybe! This was the first obstacle any team of writers has to address: compatibility with each other. The other one, of course, was that writing a screenplay is a totally different discipline from writing a book; the layout is completely different too. It took us a couple of days to get our heads around that, but after a crash course on screen writing (reading the many screenplays that were lying about Tom's apartment) we reckoned we had the basics of this new art.

Sometimes (but not all the time) I would start work during the day and sleep at night whilst Billy took the night stag and slept during the day; but more often than not, when I had had my fill of writing, Billy would be there standing over me waiting for me to vacate the seat. We worked in unison, just as the Number 1 and Number 2 on a machine gun would, feeding the machine gun with bullets — only this time it was feeding a lap-top with words. For the first few days we were so engrossed in what we were trying to achieve that we only went outside and across the road for a re-sup of fresh scoff. By the end of the first week we were so mentally bollocked, we had forgotten that we were living smack bang in the centre of Hollywood and hadn't even seen 'the lights' yet.

On the second Saturday, we decided to sample the delights of Sunset Strip. We did a lot of bars that night out and finally ended up in an Irish bar called Dublin's. Now Billy and I had both been to the US many times before and understood that the Yanks aren't that big drinkers — but that didn't stop us, we were going for it. A couple of hours and several bottles of Bud later, Billy and I noticed a really smart waitress dressed in a tight white blouse and long black boots and sporting a cowboy hat, walking round the place with a tray full of colourful-looking chasers. She and her sexy smile came smooching over to us.

'Hi guys, I'm Suzy. You ready to try something from my tray now?'

'Nice one, Suzy, I'll have a green one. What one you havin', Devs?' said Billy.

'Gotta be that pinky maroon one, hasn't it?'

At three bucks a shot we necked them down in less than a second. I got the feeling that this was going to be the start of a Para/Marine drinking contest. I was right.

As Suzy turned round to talk with a friend, she put her tray of coloured chasers on our table. Billy then picked up another one and knocked it back in one. I followed suit until the tray was empty. When I downed one, Billy would go one better. A second tray of 20 arrived and we did the same to that too — totally demolished it in a matter of a couple of minutes. By now we had an audience, people were laughing and clapping us on, and I guess that Suzy had never had it so good, two punters doing two trays all at once. But it didn't stop there. Billy, not one to give up or get beaten by an ex-SAS man, ordered yet another tray. This time we agreed that blue was a neutral colour to us both, so we ordered a tray of the blue jobbies. Then we gave that tray the same treatment as the previous two. Billy and I were keeping a childish but very drunk eye on each other, checking the other didn't spill a drop as we continued to drink one-for-one. I remember thinking as I was getting more pissed, this Marine is no way gonna beat me, fuckin' cabbage hat! Billy was probably thinking the same about me: Fuckin' Para twat!

I couldn't remember leaving Dublin's Bar — all I remember was waking up the following morning, still fully dressed, covered in this slimy blue-green puke — to the sound of the security phone ringing. Billy just about made it to the phone, only to find that Jeremy Davies, the actor from *Private Ryan*, had come up to visit us. Billy had to tell him, sorry but there was no way just yet; we were both wasted for the day at least.

Some weeks later, after we got the bottle to return to Dublin's, we were just about to join the entrance queue when one of the doormen spotted us and called us forward. He held the door open for us. Billy and I just looked at each other in amazement. Why were we being treated like this? What had we said or done the other week? Was there an outstanding bar tab to square away or what? We had no idea.

'Hey you guys. How ya doin' tonight?'

'Great, fine just fine,' I beamed.

'Toppers mate, toppers,' added Billy.

Once inside, we tried to look for Suzy, since she was the one who could tell us what the hell had happened that night. It turned out to be her night off, but we did find out that we had broken the bar record for chasers on our first visit. Shit, I thought. We had certainly done something more than just have a few too many! We were treated like real regulars from that day on.

Back on the writing front, things were going great. Tom's phone is quite busy and our concentration was always being broken, which I suppose was a small price to pay when people like Robert de Niro — one of Tom's closest mates — used to ring up to pass on messages for Tom. The first time de Niro called, Billy spoke with him.

'Hello, Tom Sizemore's residence, who's calling please?'

'Hi, it's Bob, I'm calling from Europe, is Tom there?'

Excuse me sir, Bob who?' Billy was rummaging around on a

table looking for something to write a message on.

'Oh, it's Bob de Niro, who's that?'

'Oh, OK Bob, I'm Billy. I'm looking after Tom's place while he's away.'

After the call Billy told me that he'd wanted to quote that famous line from the classic film *Taxi Driver*, where de Niro was talking to himself in a mirror saying, 'Are you talkin' to me? Are you talkin' to me?' but he had to stop himself, first impressions and all that said. I'm glad he didn't, because I don't think de Niro would have phoned up again for fear of Billy taking the piss out of him again.

There were many interesting calls during our stay but a classic one (and a bit of an omen) was when Billy's girlfriend phoned us up from the UK saying that Tom Hanks's PA had been in touch with her — Tom wanted to know where Billy was because he wanted to talk with him, reference the Falklands. The long and short of it was that Tom Hanks had recently had dinner with his actor friend, Johnathon Schaech, who had played alongside Tom in the film *That Thing You Do!*, and who was shortly flying out to the UK to play the part of a British Army soldier, from South London, suffering from post-traumatic stress brought about by the Falklands War. He wanted to know if we could do him a favour and give Johnathon a rundown on what it was really like in the Falklands War. We were both honoured, while Billy was both amazed and very pleased that Tom Hanks had remembered him from the *Ryan* set.

We met with Johnathon in Snake Pit Bar on Melrose. He was a really nice guy and he too gave us a lot of advice and encouragement. It was Johnathon who mentioned a new software called 'Final Draft' which was basically an idiot's layout guide to screen writing, which we eventually purchased. We spent the next three days briefing him up on the score, and when he flew out to the UK, we managed to get hold of another mate of ours, Smiler (who was also an ex-Royal Marine, living in South London), to take him around the pubs to get his accent up to scratch. Smiler also managed to get him down on the Royal Marine Commando Training Centre at Lympstone in the West Country for two days for a 'beasting' session on the assault course, which I think Johnathon was thankful for — in the long run! Well, I can't think of anything more realistic for an actor who wants to play the role of a soldier than a good couple of days getting booted and screamed at in the pouring rain; it's all good 'character-building' stuff!

We were living the Hollywood dream — well, the first part of it anyway — and it gave us so much inspiration. Here we were, in the middle of Hollywood with the sun shining every day, being hosted by one of the world's most admired actors and driving around in his cherished classic Chevrolet convertible, meeting all these other actors and film producers! We both felt very indebted to Tom and Maeve for all their support and hospitality, during and even after our stay. Most mornings were spent up on the apartment's roof garden, overlooking LA, writing and gazing across at all those other possible screenwriters sitting in their well-maintained offices with their ideas, hopes and dreams. The same as us really, but all we had was the basics: a lap-top, a sackful of war stories and a shedful of inspiration. In the afternoons we would take a walk down to Barney's Beanery for something to eat, the same bar where the late Janis Joplin ate her final supper, and where

Quentin Tarantino has his breakfast on Sundays.

We managed to finish the screenplay, *The Stowaway*, and had it read by all the contacts we had made. Of course, it seemed that every man and his dog in Hollywood had a script to sell and was trying to get an agent to represent them — and now we are at that same stage as this book goes to print, talking to those film agents. We've done a couple of re-writes and as everyone who's read the screenplay says it's a great story, we're very optimistic about the future. But it was Captain Dale Dye, *Ryan's* military adviser, who gave us a 'reality check' (as he liked to call it) when he said, 'Right, now you guys, you've done the easy bit and that's writing the damn thing in the first place. Trying to convince these "weenies" [his term for people in the industry] to turn it into a film is another. You know it took eight years or so to get the first camera rolling on the movie *Platoon* but, hopefully, you guys won't have to wait that long. If you guys believe in it, you've gotta give it your best shot.'

From one meeting that happened when we were pursuing our goal in getting *The Stowaway* into production, another canny encounter resulted. Billy got a copy of the screenplay to a friend, the actor Sean Bean, so he could give it a quick read and offer us some advice. So shortly after we got back to the UK, Billy rang him up from my place. Sean said that he'd only had time to read half the script since he'd only recently returned from working on a film with Robert de Niro in Europe.

'Hey, is that right?' Billy said.

'Yeah, I didn't get a chance to meet with de Niro, I was only filming for a short time. I wish I had, though.'

'Well, Steve and I wrote *The Stowaway* in Tom Sizemore's

apartment and Bob used to call us up quite frequently,' said Billy.

'First-name terms, Bob now, is it?' said Sean, jokingly.

In summer 1998, *Saving Private Ryan* was being premièred in London's Empire in Leicester Square. Billy by now was working full time for Tom as his PA and security manager. Tom invited Alison and myself to the occasion; he was concerned about security and asked me to BG him, along with Billy. We spent three great days being wined and dined at the Dorchester Hotel, courtesy of Tom and Maeve Sizemore. We were certainly given the celebrity treatment, but this was not the first time Billy and I had trod the 'red carpet', because when we were in Hollywood we went to the world première of *The Jackal* staring Bruce Willis, another one of Tom's pals.

I was getting to like all this 'arty farty' way of life and was thinking, Maybe this is my ticket to get out of the security industry — but on the other hand, pigs might fly. At the end of *Ryan* I felt physically shaken and really couldn't think straight for about an hour after. For me, the film was amazing visually, a brilliant piece of work. Coming down the stairs of the cinema with Tom to meet the world's press for a second time, Tom said:

'Hey, Steve, what did you think of it?'

'I tell you what, Tom, I'm still friggin' shaking, I don't know what to think just yet.'

My comment obviously moved Tom, because he grabbed my arm and said, 'Well, Steve, you've experienced this shit for real and I'm only an actor. It's good for me that you feel this way, because if it has shaken you then I know the film is right.'

He was correct, although there is no way one can compare my combat experience with that of the guys who ran up

Omaha Beach and saw the horrors of mass mutilation that day back in 1944. Individual 'one on ones' with the enemy are, by their very nature, a personal battle of survival and just as unnerving for both parties involved. I didn't think any war film could shake me up but this one certainly did.

At the time of writing, *The Stowaway* has yet to reach what they call in the film industry 'Development Hell'. But I'm the eternal optimist — I have to be because I really believe in the script. So, until the first camera starts to roll, I'll still be stagging on!